THAT FIRST SEASON

BOOKS BY JOHN EISENBERG

The Longest Shot: Lil E. Tee and the Kentucky Derby

*Cotton Bowl Days: Growing Up with Dallas
and the Cowboys in the 1960s*

*From 33rd Street to Camden Yards:
An Oral History of the Baltimore Orioles*

Native Dancer: Hero of a Golden Age

*The Great Match Race: When North Met South
in America's First Sports Spectacle*

*My Guy Barbaro: A Jockey's Journey Through
Love, Triumph, and Heartbreak with America's
Favorite Horse (with Edgar Prado)*

*That First Season: How Vince Lombardi Took the
Worst Team in the NFL and Set It on the Path to Glory*

THAT FIRST SEASON

★ ★ ★

*How Vince Lombardi Took
the Worst Team in the NFL and
Set It on the Path to Glory*

★ ★ ★

JOHN EISENBERG

HOUGHTON MIFFLIN HARCOURT
BOSTON · NEW YORK
2009

www.hmhbooks.com

Library of Congress Cataloging-in-Publication Data
Eisenberg, John, date.
That first season : how Vince Lombardi took the worst team in the NFL
and set it on the path to glory / John Eisenberg.
p. cm.
Includes bibliographical references and index.
ISBN 978-0-618-90499-0 (alk. paper)
1. Lombardi, Vince. 2. Football coaches—United States—Biography.
3. Green Bay Packers (Football team)—History. I. Title.
GV939.L6E37   2009
796.332092—dc22 [B]   2009028269

Book Design by Brian Moore

Printed in the United States of America

DOC 10 9 8 7 6 5 4 3 2 1

To my mother,
JEAN EISENBERG,

and in memory of my father,
SEYMOUR EISENBERG

AUTHOR'S NOTE

Material previously published in newspapers, magazines, and books greatly informed this narrative, but the primary source was new interviews with almost three dozen people who either witnessed or participated in the 1959 season: players and coaches, some of their family members, journalists, fans, and Packer board members. I sought to depict all thoughts, attitudes, and conversations precisely as they were relayed to me, using italics where supposition was required or memories conflicted. If any errors of fact, intention, or tone exist, they're mine.

INTRODUCTION

PEOPLE STARTED gathering at Austin-Straubel Field shortly after sundown. It was a cold, wet Monday night in December 1959, and the Green Bay Packers had just completed their first winning season since Harry Truman's early years in the White House. Now they were flying home after beating the San Francisco 49ers in California, and the fans were coming out to the airport to welcome them. By 8 P.M., when the team's charter flight was scheduled to arrive, the crowd had swollen to a rollicking eight thousand, filling a field by the terminal. Cars were backed up for a mile on the airport road.

Although the Packers had gotten themselves together too late to challenge for the National Football League's Western Division title, they had ended the season with a flourish, scoring a series of one-sided wins over opponents that had dominated them for the past decade. It was something of a miracle: just one year after embarrassing themselves with the worst season in their forty-year history, they appeared ready to challenge for a place among pro football's elite.

The Association of Commerce, a businessmen's group, had hastily planned an airport welcome, and typical of Green Bay, the littlest town in the big leagues, everyone pitched in. The local newspaper, the *Green Bay Press-Gazette,* publicized the event. A transportation company contributed flatbed trucks and a wagon to support the stage. The manager of the Brown County Veterans Memorial Arena brought a platform, lights, and a public-address system. The Civil

Defense Auxiliary Police were mustered to oversee traffic and parking. The ceremony would include a speech by Green Bay mayor Roman Denissen and music by the St. Norbert College band.

Only the weather — thirty degrees and rain — failed to cooperate, but when it was announced that the plane would be an hour late, people just smiled, turned up their collars, and huddled closer under their umbrellas. After suffering through years of atrocious football, Packer fans didn't mind enduring a little more to show their support for a winner. *Hey, it could be worse. We could have snow up to our knees.*

The Packers were like every high school football team in a small town, if on a somewhat larger scale, eliciting widespread but soft-spoken grousing when they lost and a giddy unanimity when they won. Fans had come to the airport with hand-painted signs that read, "Our Team Is Red Hot!" and "We Love Our Pack!" The lead editorial in that morning's *Press-Gazette* had congratulated the team for finishing the season so impressively.

While the fans waited in the rain for the Packers' homecoming, the band rolled through its halftime fare, drawing hearty applause after each tune. A cheer went up at 8:30 when the emcee, anchor Les Sturmer of WBAY-TV, announced that the airport tower had been in contact with the plane and the Packers would arrive in half an hour.

On board the returning flight, Don "Bud" Smith, pilot of the United Airlines DC-6 charter, leaned back from his conversation with the tower and told Packers coach Vince Lombardi that a crowd had gathered to greet them. *Thousands of people, they're telling me.*

Lombardi, a short, stout New Yorker in his first year with the Packers, got out of his seat and walked down the aisle with a smile, delivering the news to the players in his thick Brooklyn tongue. *How about that? The fans are out to greet us. They're standing in the rain. Thousands of Pack-ah fans! Heh! How about that?*

Lombardi had been a brutal boss throughout the season, continually subjecting players to volcanic outbursts of criticism, pushing them to the brink of their physical and mental limits, accepting nothing less than perfection. But he was as unpredictable as he was tough, and could turn chummy, almost paternal, without warning.

One of his favorite players, Max McGee, a wry receiver, shook his head in amazement when Lombardi told him about the crowd at the airport.

"What would they do if we actually won something?" McGee asked.

Heh! Good one, Max. Who knows?

The players were ready to be home. They had been in California for two weeks, playing games in Los Angeles and San Francisco, and now they had been crammed into a plane for eight hours. They were gratified to hear about the warm welcome. The year before, when they had been laughingstocks, they stopped going to restaurants around town because they grew weary of being ridiculed and asked what was wrong.

But incredibly, it turned out that the pieces of a winning team had been in place that season, just utilized incorrectly or, in some cases, not at all. Bart Starr, Paul Hornung, and Jim Taylor had spent most of the season on the bench, but now they comprised the starting offensive backfield. The whole team had been undisciplined, unorganized, and in poor physical condition, but now the Packers played with the crisp confidence of a military unit on marching maneuvers. Lombardi, formerly an assistant coach with the New York Giants, had engineered a remarkable transformation.

As the plane approached Green Bay, Bud Smith warned that the foul weather might prevent a landing, in which case he would "fly to Milwaukee, refuel, and head for Bermuda." Lombardi and his assistant coaches and players laughed hard; that sounded pretty good. But then Smith brought the plane through the clouds and down.

The fans cheered the sight of the aircraft chugging in for a landing. There was a flurry of activity as the DC-6 taxied toward the crowd. Someone turned on the spotlights. The mayor fingered a key to the city, which he would hand to Lombardi. Sturmer, the emcee, cleared his throat. Men from the Association of Commerce brought up a stack of green-and-gold Packer blankets to give to the players. The fans started clapping rhythmically as the plane stopped in front of them, engines still running. The band swung into a blaring version of "There'll Be a Hot Time in the Old Town Tonight."

Watching from on board, the players were stunned. No one spoke until Jesse Whittenton, a veteran cornerback, finally sputtered the question McGee had asked minutes earlier: "I mean, what would they do if we won something?"

McGee, sitting nearby, drawled, "They'd probably give us the whole town."

Players and fans alike sensed a new era dawning. Though a season had just ended, the Packers seemed at a beginning. The promise of a better future had drawn this crowd out to the airport on a cold, wet night.

Smith killed the engines. The players stood up, stretched, and headed for the exit as an airport crew rolled a portable stairway up to the door. The first player to emerge into the drizzle was Forrest Gregg, a burly offensive tackle. Fans chanted his name as he smiled and waved from the top of the stairway. One by one, his teammates followed him through the door and down the stairs as the crowd cheered and the band played.

Finally, there was one man left on the plane other than the pilot. He shrugged into his tan overcoat, adjusted his fedora, and ducked through the doorway. The fans, seeing him emerge, sent out their loudest roar. Lombardi took it all in, smiled the gap-toothed grin the whole world would soon know, and waved his right arm above his head.

Just one year in, and Green Bay was his town now.

PART I

PART I

★ 1 ★

I T WAS A GAME they would never forget, their worst defeat, a day so miserable some players just shrugged and gave up before the final gun.

On November 2, 1958, the Green Bay Packers were in Baltimore playing the undefeated Colts. They did little right on offense or defense as rain fell and fifty-two thousand fired-up fans screamed for their heads, and by early in the second half, they trailed by six touchdowns. A few players decided that since they had no chance of winning — and they sure as hell didn't — they could ease up and go through the motions for the last twenty minutes. Why not? Their coach, Ray "Scooter" McLean, wouldn't mind, as long as they didn't make it obvious. Scooter was a swell guy. Everyone liked him.

Not every Packer quit. Jim Ringo, an All-Pro center, quietly continued to knock down defenders as others stampeded past. Tom Bettis, a veteran middle linebacker, screamed for better effort in the huddle as the rout spiraled out of control.

A few Packers, in frazzled frustration, dreamed of stealing a sideline policeman's gun and shooting that damn white horse, the Colts' team mascot, which took a celebratory gallop across the field whenever Baltimore scored.

But more than a few Packer players just gave in, their minds drifting from this pitiful scene toward more pleasant thoughts, such as the steak dinner they would enjoy on the plane ride home that evening, or the paycheck they would receive later in the week — the paycheck they pocketed win or lose, thank goodness.

The Packers were fixtures on the bottom of the NFL pile, chronic losers who until recently had played their home games in a former high school stadium. They didn't practice hard, didn't mind losing, and hadn't produced a winning season since 1947. They were just happy to get to spend the fall playing football instead of selling tires or insurance, as many did during the rest of the year.

Their franchise's past was as glittery as its present was miserable: the Packers had reigned during the NFL's rough and rowdy early years, attracting loyal fans and accumulating six championships as charismatic legends Johnny Blood and Don Hutson led them to glory. But those heady days were just hazy memories now. The Packers' losing habit had swallowed up three head coaches in the past decade, and Scooter, just halfway into his first year on the job, was already seeing his dreams disintegrate.

A wiry bantam with a narrow face and squinty eyes, Scooter had been a quick-footed halfback for the Chicago Bears in the 1940s, and he resembled a mob machine-gunner now as he paced the sideline in a crisp dark suit and fedora. But in reality, he had a genial and forgiving nature and was grossly miscast as a boss. He had been a Packers assistant coach for the past seven years and still saw himself as one of the boys. He played poker with the players on the road, didn't enforce curfews, and failed to scold veterans who repeated mistakes. When he called for wind sprints at his laughably easy practices, he shouted the squad through a few until Billy Howton, a veteran receiver, groaned, "Come on, Scooter, we need to save our legs for Sunday." Scooter would smile, blow his whistle, and end practice.

The Packers had come to Baltimore for this midseason game with a record of one win, three losses, and a tie, and the Colts, winners of five straight, were favored by nineteen points. But the Packers, incredibly, in hindsight, believed they could win. They had almost upset the Colts earlier in the season in Wisconsin — as Western Division rivals, they played a pair of games every year on a home-and-home basis — and they thought they could finish the job this time.

Their optimism wasn't entirely unwarranted. They had capable veterans such as Ringo, Bettis, Howton, linebacker Bill Forester, and Bobby Dillon, a superb defensive back despite being blind in one eye. And Scooter, for all his shortcomings, knew offensive football. His system traced to the strategies of Clark Shaughnessy, a legendary guru who had reworked the T-formation in the 1930s to improve the passing game. Chicago Bears coach George Halas had picked up the offense and won four NFL titles in the 1940s, and Scooter, after playing on those teams, had added his own wrinkles — a lot of them. His playbook was a four-inch-thick maze of diagrams, so complicated that Jim Taylor, the Packers' rookie fullback, couldn't get a handle on it and had to sit on the bench. But the Packers could move the ball, or at least, had so far in 1958. Even though their quarterbacks, Bart Starr and Babe Parilli, had proved to be just modest talents, receivers Howton, Max McGee, and Gary Knafelc could get open, and the Packers were averaging more than twenty points per game.

Earlier in the season they had beaten the Philadelphia Eagles and tied the Detroit Lions, the defending NFL champions. But they had almost blown a twenty-four-point lead against the Eagles, needing a recovered onside kick by rookie linebacker Ray Nitschke in the final minute to survive; Scooter had looked ashen after that one, wondering what had gone wrong. And to say they were lucky to tie the Lions was an understatement. The Lions were in position to kick a game-winning field goal in the final minutes, but Lions quarterback Bobby Layne imperiously waved off the kicker and threw an incompletion on fourth down, preserving the tie. Layne, the hard-drinking leader of a Lions team that had won three NFL titles in the 1950s, was traded to Pittsburgh two days later.

Encouraged by such performances, the Packers didn't see an epic defeat brewing in Baltimore. But their bad habits were bound to catch up with them and finally did, turning the rematch with the Colts into the game that exposed them for what they were, a team destined to be recalled as one of the worst in NFL history.

On the night before the game, they stayed at the Washingtonian Motel in Gaithersburg, Maryland, nearer Washington, D.C., than Baltimore. It was out of the way, but the Packers had stayed there when they came to the area to play the Washington Redskins a few weeks earlier, and the motel cut the team a deal for agreeing to stay twice. That was how the Packers traveled, always looking to save pennies.

As the players checked in and headed for their rooms, Scooter hollered, "Practice in half an hour!" The bare-bones Washingtonian had a football field on its grounds (the Redskins used it during their preseason training camp) and the brief practice that ensued was typically light: a short run, some calisthenics, a run-through of a few plays. Scooter was "saving the legs" for the next day.

That evening, some players and coaches went to a movie while Scooter, Howton, McGee, second-year back Paul Hornung, and a few others played poker. They played religiously, on trips, during training camp, after practice during the season — often enough that they almost passed for a card club that dabbled in football. They talked animatedly about memorable poker hands more than memorable football games, and recorded their wins and losses on the backs of their playbooks, settling up at the end of the year. McGee, a lanky Texan who found the humor in most situations, was an intuitive card shark who had fleeced his teammates for hundreds of dollars over the years. Scooter regularly lost.

Some players didn't go to the movie or play poker. Before the Redskins game a few weeks earlier, Bettis, Knafelc, and Starr had headed out just to stretch their legs. They were married, by-the-rules guys. When they passed by the poker room, Scooter leaned back and said, "Hey, where you going?" When Bettis shrugged, Scooter said, "Well, make sure you're back by ten thirty." Bettis walked away cursing their poker-playing coach for believing he had any right to dictate how they should prepare to play.

On this Saturday night, before the Baltimore contest, the card game broke up a little after Scooter's curfew, but what the hell, Scooter said, at least the guys were in. The next morning, some players attended early church and then everyone ate breakfast and boarded a bus for the forty-five-minute drive to Baltimore. The players quietly stared out the window during the ride, contemplating what lay ahead. Despite the closeness of their earlier game, they

6

knew the Colts were capable of pounding them. Led by Johnny Unitas, a brilliant, hunch-shouldered young quarterback, the Colt offense had already scored fifty-one points against the Bears and forty against the Lions this season.

Hornung was disconsolate as the bus rolled through the Maryland countryside toward Baltimore. He knew he wouldn't get off the bench in this game except to kick field goals and extra points. Eyeing his reflection in a window, he glumly told himself, Your career is going nowhere, buddy.

Less than two years earlier, the Packers had made Hornung the first overall pick in the 1957 draft, thinking he would become their biggest star. During his college career at Notre Dame, he had been a triple threat on offense, running, catching, and passing the ball (as well as kicking it) and had won the Heisman Trophy as a senior. The Packers had been so excited about his potential as a quarterback that they traded Tobin Rote, their longtime starter, who had passed for more than eleven thousand yards, and signed Hornung to a three-year contract that included a $2,500 signing bonus and a $17,500 annual salary, more than many veterans earned.

But once Hornung was in uniform, the Packers realized he didn't have a strong enough passing arm to be an NFL quarterback, and also lacked the speed to be a running back or receiver. He was a player without a position.

Blond and handsome, he had been nicknamed the Golden Boy at Notre Dame because he seemed to have everything going for him. He played football with swashbuckling style and a nose for the end zone. Hollywood producers liked his looks and gave him cameo roles. He knew more beautiful women than any one man deserved to know; his female fan mail piled so high he paid a classmate to handle it.

But the Golden Boy had become tarnished. Lisle Blackbourn, the Packers' coach before Scooter, had tried him at quarterback and fullback without success. It was believed that Hornung cared more about what he did off the field. When the Packers played the Rams in Los Angeles in 1957, an attractive young woman approached him on the bench and asked to have her picture taken with him

— during the game! Her request was audacious, but Hornung stood and posed with her, a move some teammates and fans interpreted as clear evidence of his priorities.

Most of his teammates liked him in spite of it all. Although they derisively called him Heisman or Golden Dome or, worst of all, Goat, because he resembled one, being thick and strong from the waist down but narrow up top, they knew Hornung could take a joke. He was a man's man, hard not to like as he flaunted rules with a wisecrack and twinkling eyes. His best friend, McGee, was a kindred spirit; they shared an apartment, girls, and booze, and were regulars at bars and clubs all over Green Bay, where they were widely known as good-time guys who weren't too serious about football.

In truth, Hornung desperately wanted to play — he was embarrassed to stand on the sideline. But Scooter, like Blackbourn, didn't know what to do with him.

Discouraged, Hornung had started to contemplate giving up football. With his looks and personality, he could go to Hollywood and star in movies, or sell real estate back home in Louisville, Kentucky, where he would always be a hero. He craved more excitement. The guys playing for the Browns, Giants, and Lions had it so much better; they won games, played for championships, and still had a good time. In Green Bay, playing for the Packers, Hornung had a good time, but the team was unorganized, the environment unprofessional, the experience disappointing.

Feeling bored leading up to this rematch with the Colts, he mentioned to Howton and McGee one day that they should take the nineteen points that bookies were offering for a bet on the Packers. Having grown up in a city where horse racing was popular and the Kentucky Derby was held every year, Hornung enjoyed gambling and followed the football betting lines coming out of Las Vegas. Nineteen points? The game was bound to be closer than that, right?

The NFL strictly forbade players from betting on games, fearing a point-shaving scandal, but Hornung, knowing he wouldn't be playing in the matchup against the Colts, figured he could make his

Sunday afternoon more exciting if he had money on the line. He told Howton and McGee he could get a bet down. They agreed to take part in the wager.

But Hornung tried without luck to contact his bookmaker connection as the Packers completed the week's practice and flew to Baltimore. By Sunday morning, it was too late. Hornung shook his head as the team bus rolled toward Baltimore, depressed about not playing and disappointed about the easy money he believed he had lost.

A chilly rain fell as the bus approached Memorial Stadium. The streets around it were filled two hours before kickoff, the fans seemingly unconcerned about the weather. The throng was so thick that policemen, arms waving and whistles blowing, had to clear a path for the bus to reach the players' entrance.

Baltimore, a working-class city that had been without major-league sports until recently, was jazzed up about its winning team. The Colts' offense shredded opposing defenses with playmakers such as Unitas, receiver Raymond Berry, halfback Lenny Moore, and fullback Alan Ameche, and the Colt defensive included All-Pros such as end Gino Marchetti and tackle Art Donovan. And their home crowd was intimidating. The stadium would be packed with raucous fans and a white pony named Dixie that had become a celebrity for crossing the field after Colt touchdowns. A sportswriter would soon call Baltimore's crowd "the world's largest outdoor insane asylum."

The Packers found their cramped locker room, put on white jerseys, gold pants, and gold helmets, and jogged out for warm-ups, eliciting boos. The wet afternoon was so dank the stadium lights were on, setting an eerie tone. Parilli, who would start at quarterback, zipped passes to Howton. Ringo and the other linemen got down in their three-point stances and burst forward, working their muscles. Hornung practiced field goals. The Colts soon joined them, coming onto the field as the Baltimore Colts Marching Band played, and the fans stood and cheered for the opening kick, which sailed into the mist and lights and through the back of the end zone — first down Packers, at their 20-yard line.

The Packers' offensive starters jogged onto the field and formed a huddle. Other than Ringo and Howton, it was a nondescript group. Parilli, a former first-round draft pick, had accomplished little in the NFL. Young linemen Jerry Kramer and Forrest Gregg were raw unknowns. Of the veteran regulars — tackle Oliver Spencer, guard Hank Bullough, halfback Don McIlhenny, and fullback Howie Ferguson — only Ferguson had made it to the Pro Bowl, the NFL's end-of-year all-star game.

As those players formed a huddle, Bart Starr, Jim Taylor, and Hornung watched from the sideline, relegated to the second team.

Parilli called the first play, a run by Ferguson off right tackle. The Packers broke their huddle and trotted to the line of scrimmage, where the Colt defense waited. The crowd roared in anticipation. Pro football, since its inception just after World War I, had always been among the roughest of sports, an organized brawl between rugged athletes who relished violence, many having experienced real combat in World War II or Korea. They kicked, scratched, and clubbed each other, gouged eyes, knocked out teeth, and tackled around the neck.

But the game had evolved far beyond its simplistic roots, with offenses and defenses now employing sophisticated strategies and multiple alignments. Toughness remained the quality a player needed most, but speed was almost as important. The Los Angeles Rams were so desperate for it that after this season they would trade nine players for Ollie Matson, a big-play back with the speed to win games by himself.

The Packers had their share of tough guys but little speed. Ferguson picked up three yards on first down, and then McIlhenny, running left, gained one. On third down, Scooter put in veteran Al Carmichael to run a deep pass route. Carmichael broke open twenty yards upfield and Parilli hit him with a perfect toss, but Carmichael dropped the ball. McGee, who doubled as the punter, booted the ball away on fourth down.

The Packers' defensive starters met in a huddle and shouted at each other to play hard. The core of the group — Bettis and Forrester, linemen Dave Hanner and Nate Borden, and backs Dillon,

Hank Gremminger, and John Symank — had played together for several years with mixed results. The right side of the line was porous (crusty end Len Ford had played a decade, mostly in Cleveland, and was ready to retire) and the secondary was struggling. The Packers had yielded an average of thirty points a game so far in 1958. Deep down, the players knew this could be a long afternoon.

They started well, making stops on the Colts' first two possessions. But Parilli, looking lost, threw two interceptions, and the Colts turned the second opportunity into a score. When Baltimore's Lenny Moore crossed the goal line with the game's first touchdown, the fans cheered, a cannon situated behind the end zone boomed, and Dixie, the white horse, sprinted across the field, ridden by a smiling teenage girl wearing a frilly cowboy outfit and a white hat, tied under her chin by a string.

Bettis recovered a fumble at midfield early in the second quarter, but Parilli, with Marchetti and Donovan harrying him, missed receivers on first and second downs before finally registering his first completion, a six-yard pass to McIlhenny. Scooter sent in Hornung for a fifty-yard field goal attempt. The kick fell short.

Then the Colts began to roll. Unitas hit Moore with a pass in the left flat, and Moore, exhibiting the speed the Packers lacked, darted between defenders and raced down the sideline for sixty-three yards to the Green Bay 6. Ameche scored on the next play, and Dixie set off across the field once again as the cannon boomed. Following the kickoff, Parilli threw deep but was intercepted, and after two Packer penalties moved the ball near the goal line, Unitas hit a wide-open Ameche in the end zone. Again, the band played, the fans cheered, and Dixie ran. The Colts led, 21–0.

Standing on the sideline, Hornung shook his head sadly — not about the game so much as how badly he had misjudged it. Those nineteen points from Las Vegas were already gone! Jiminy! It looked like the Colts would cover the spread with ease. Hornung lamented the loss of his golden touch. He had thought the Packer defense would be able to keep the game close, but it was getting picked apart.

And I can't even get on the field in a ridiculous game like this.

11

With rain dripping off his fedora, Scooter looked even more confused than Hornung on the sideline. His offense was having just a
terrible time. Parilli had completed one pass to a teammate and
three to the Colts, and Kramer, the rookie guard, was no match for
Donovan, a veteran tackle with an assortment of tricks. Instead of
bulling past Kramer when the ball was snapped, Donovan stood,
wiggled his square body, and waited for Kramer to come at him,
then blew by the lunging, bewildered youngster. He was in the
Packer backfield on every play.

Scooter, who liked to alternate quarterbacks, put in Starr, an ear-
nest third-year pro with a lamentable record. Since making the
team in 1956 as a seventeenth-round draft pick, he had started a lot
of losing games and drifted in and out of the lineup, keeping his job
because he spent hours studying film and was always prepared to
play, ideal traits for a backup. Starr moved the offense better, but a
fourth-down pass in Colt territory fell incomplete.

Unitas returned to the field and drove the Colts toward another
touchdown just before halftime. He passed to Berry on the right
sideline for ten yards, and after Moore danced off left tackle for
eight, hit Berry for thirteen. The Colt offense knifed through Green
Bay's defense, every turn crisp. At the Green Bay 19, Unitas dropped
back, saw no one open, and dashed up the middle, his high-top
black cleats churning. Symank, a small but tough cornerback,
knocked him down and kneed him in the ribs. Unitas stayed down,
and the crowd protested what it thought was a cheap shot. (No flag
fell.) Unitas slowly rose and was helped off the field. His backup,
George Shaw, finished the drive by throwing a touchdown pass, and
the crowd booed the Packers as they left the field for halftime, trailing 28–0.

Scooter walked around the locker room but didn't know what to
say. What a horrendous showing. His receivers couldn't get open
and his linemen were being tossed around. Kramer had to come
out; the youngster couldn't block Donovan. The Packers seemed
overmatched everywhere, on both sides of the ball.

Hornung just sat quietly, staring at his cleats.

The Colts, meanwhile, were furious about Unitas's injury. The quarterback had gone to the hospital to have his ribs x-rayed, and his teammates vowed to pour it on. The Colts took the second-half kickoff, moved right down the field, and scored on a Shaw touchdown pass that sent Dixie off to the races. Then Starr's first pass of the second half was intercepted. Ameche dragged a pile of defenders twenty yards, finally going down with a splash just short of the end zone. When Shaw scored from the 1, Dixie, still breathing hard from the last sprint, took off again.

As the colt tired, the Colts taunted Symank.

You little bastard, John can't hit you back so we're doing it for him.

Symank, a spunky Texan who had made the Packers as a twenty-third-round draft pick, virtually spat back at his tormentors.

Fuck all of you. I'm just playing ball.

Between the band, crowd, rain, cannon, and Dixie, the Packers were living a nightmare. There were still twenty-five minutes to play. At this rate, the Colts would score eighty points. But rather than fight, some players eased up so obviously that *Green Bay Press-Gazette* sports editor Art Daley, watching from the press box, was outraged. Normally supportive of the team, he would write in Monday's paper of "an almost complete lack of effort" in the second half, and call the performance "the biggest 'quit' in Packer history."

For a franchise that had experienced many highs through the years but only lows recently, the players' capitulation during a game was the true depth of despair.

Colts coach Weeb Ewbank pulled his starters to keep the score down, but Shaw continued to puncture the Packer defense with his throwing and running, and Dixie circled the field for the seventh and eighth times in the fourth quarter. Meanwhile, Starr kept misfiring; he would complete just three of fourteen pass attempts, his misses splashing and skipping wildly across the turf like stones flung onto a pond by a boy.

Looking for someone, anyone, to make a positive play, Scooter gave eight Packers a chance to run the ball, including Taylor, the young fullback, and Jim Shanley, a free agent from Oregon who seldom played. But Hornung, the supposed star, never left the sideline. *Looks like I'm on the end of the bench now—the last man on the worst team in the league.*

With the score 56–0 and time running out, Carmichael returned a kickoff sixty-one yards to put the Packers in scoring position. A final drama played out. All but a few of the soaked fans were still in their seats, relishing the mismatch. They exhorted their defense to play tough. The Colts had never shut out an opponent.

Scooter replaced Starr with Joe Francis, a rookie from Oregon State who could run but had little passing skill. Francis gained twenty-one yards on scrambles as the Packers moved inside the 10. There was time for one more play. The Colt defense dug in, determined to keep the Packers out of the end zone. Francis ran again, put his head down, and tried to bull into the end zone, but three Colts threw him down a yard short. The fans cheered so hard, the final gun was barely audible.

Back in the locker room, the Packers slowly pulled off their muddy uniforms after the worst defeat in the long history of their franchise. The players sat at their lockers, stunned and embarrassed. Jerry Kramer stared dully at the floor; he had thought he was hot stuff starting as a rookie, but Donovan had schooled him. He spoke to Gregg, who had been similarly manhandled by Gino Marchetti.

Jesus, Forrest.

I know.

Scooter let reporters into the locker room but was uncharacteristically terse. "There just isn't anything I can say," he said. As the players showered and dressed, a few visitors tiptoed in. One was Ron Kramer, a young Packer tight end sitting out the season while he fulfilled a military-service commitment. Posted for a year at an Air Force base in nearby Washington, he had come to support his teammates and watched the massacre from the bench. He spoke to Hornung.

Holy shit, Paul.

We don't look too good, huh?

What is going on?

Hell if I know.

Don McIlhenny's older brother, Jim, a shoe-company executive in New York City, had come down on the train to see his brother play. He visited the locker room before the Packers' bus left for the airport. A canny businessman, Jim shook his head ruefully. Normally, he said, it takes a few years of observation to know whether a business is succeeding or failing. But in this one day, he told Don, he could tell the Packers were the football version of a failing business.

Don shook his head slowly from side to side; there was no disputing his brother's assessment.

2

G ALLOWS HUMOR PREVAILED as the Packers' charter flight from Baltimore landed in Green Bay late Sunday night, hours after the 56–0 loss. McGee, ever the comedian, wondered if their wives and girlfriends would be at the airport to pick them up or just ignore their existence and stay home.

I might need a ride, guys.

Some players normally spent Monday, their day off, at the Piccadilly, the Candlestick, and other bars and clubs around town, but they agreed not to venture out after such a pitiful game, figuring they should just lay low. As Monday dawned, a low-flying blanket of dark clouds spit sleet, and Green Bay's mood was as grim as the weather. People shrugged into heavy coats, pulled wool caps low over their eyes, dropped the kids at school, and drove to work with their headlights on and windshield wipers thumping, listening to radio newsmen discuss Sunday's debacle. At the paper mills, cheese factories, rail yards, hospitals, and department stores where they worked, they shook their heads and commiserated with coworkers.

Did you see that?

Yeah.

Good gracious.

Yeah.

A mill town situated at the mouth of the Fox River in northeast Wisconsin, Green Bay was, in the late 1950s, predominately white, Catholic, conservatively Democratic, and, with sixty-two thousand residents, vastly smaller than America's urban centers. But the Packers' hometown had a lot going for it — four paper mills, three rail hubs, good schools, tidy parks, and a traffic-clogged downtown lined with restaurants, clubs, and department stores.

People worked at thriving local businesses such as Schreiber Cheese, Larsen Canning, Green Bay Packaging, and Schneider Transport & Storage, or at the rail yards serving the Chicago and North Western, Milwaukee Road, and Green Bay and Western lines, which brought clattering trains through town all day and night. The Fort Howard Paper Company employed three thousand people at its mill. The National Cheese Exchange set prices for buyers and sellers across the country out of an office on the east side of town.

But what Green Bay had going for it above all — what made it different from the many other American cities of its modest size — were the Packers.

Pro football teams had sprouted in many such towns during the sport's pioneer days after World War I, but the others, all of them, had long ago been elbowed out of business by big-city teams such as the New York Giants and Chicago Bears. The Packers had survived, primarily because of their community's support. They were the local secular religion, affording Green Bay the right to call itself major league in at least one respect.

The bond between the team and town was especially intense. The Packers weren't owned by some wealthy entrepreneur or old-money scion, as many other pro sports teams were, but by the very fans cursing them on this dank Monday. In an arrangement unlike any other in sports, Green Bay Packers Inc., a nonprofit corporation with more than sixteen hundred stockholders, owned the team and oversaw its operations. The stockholders ranged from mill owners to mill workers owning anywhere from three hundred shares to just one, but no matter their stake, they had a say in the Packers' fortunes. They elected from their ranks a forty-five-member board of directors which, in turn, selected from its ranks a thirteen-person executive committee that ran the team, making all decisions, from hiring a coach to choosing the ad campaign.

The thirteen executive-committee slots were filled by Green Bay's business and political leaders, people trusted to run important institutions. In 1958 Dominic Olejniczak, a realtor who had recently served five terms as mayor, headed the committee with the title of team president. Dick Bourguignon, also a realtor, was vice president. John Torinus, publisher of the *Press-Gazette*, was secretary. The treasurer was a lawyer, Fred Trowbridge. Other committee members included Jerry Atkinson, chairman of the H. C. Prange department store; Tony Canadeo, a popular former star halfback for the Packers; Fred Leicht, head of a transportation company; and Bernard "Boob" Darling, a lineman on the Packers' Depression-era championship teams.

Prosperous and controlling, these men were heavily involved in the Packers' day-to-day business. It wasn't unusual to see them watching practice or traveling with the team to road games. In 1957, as the Packers' season fell apart, some met privately with players to hear gripes, undermining Coach Lisle Blackbourn.

After Blackbourn, tired of the meddling, resigned at the end of the season, the committee searched for a replacement in January 1958. Then-president Russell Bogda was dying of cancer and Olejniczak had agreed to fill in temporarily. (He took the job permanently months later.) Amid the uncertainty, the committee elected not to chase boldly after a big-name college coach, not that any seemed to want to take on the lowly Packers. Scooter McLean eventually was hired over Lou Rymkus, another assistant under Blackbourn.

Scooter was initially excited, telling reporters during training camp that he thought the Packers would have a winning season. But now, months later, his optimism was in tatters. On the day after the 56–0 loss, he and his assistants were at work by 8 A.M., reviewing films of the debacle on the second floor of the Downtowner Motel on Washington Street, where the Packers had their business offices. The films were a horror show; sitting in a dark room as the projector whirred, Scooter saw that, as he suspected, some players had simply quit.

At noon Scooter hunched into his heavy coat and walked over to the Northland Hotel for his weekly Monday lunch with the executive committee, which always met with the head coach on the day after a game. To a man, the committee members liked Scooter and had played golf with him, but they came down hard on him now, second-guessing his play calls and personnel moves. Like everyone else in town, they wondered what in the hell was going on.

Scooter was tired of sticking up for his friends in uniform. He wasn't getting the same loyalty in return. Pressed by the committee, he admitted some veterans were going through the motions and just picking up paychecks. Such criticism normally stayed private, but Scooter also told newsman Art Daley as much later that day. Lackadaisical veterans were "bad roots," and "they're getting to be a problem because they're starting to affect the rest of the team." When Daley asked if changes were coming, Scooter replied, "I'm not cutting anybody right now but we'll be watching things real close before and after Sunday's game in Chicago."

After those comments appeared in Tuesday's *Press-Gazette* under the headline "Defeatist Veterans Must Go, Coach Says," fifty fans showed up to watch practice, thinking they might see a veteran get cut. (Packer practices were open to the public.) But the day contained no fireworks. Olejniczak came over from his real estate office and addressed the players, reminding them of the Packers' winning past. The speech had no impact.

Some coaches would have balked at having to deal with such involved owners, who in most cases had never played football. But after almost a decade in Green Bay, Scooter understood that dealing with the executive committee was part of his job. The Packers' ownership arrangement was unusual but immutable, dating to the franchise's origins in 1919. Local business leaders had always run the Packers, so it was best, Scooter believed, just to acknowledge that they were in charge.

The franchise traced to, of all things, a young man from Green Bay coming down with an ill-timed sore throat. Earl Lambeau, a handsome fullback nicknamed Curly for the shock of dark curls that flounced above his forehead, starred at East High School and then went to Notre Dame and played as a freshman in 1918 under a new Irish coach named Knute Rockne. But Lambeau came home that Christmas with a severe sore throat his doctors diagnosed as tonsillitis. The tonsils couldn't be removed until a lingering virus dissipated, so Lambeau stayed in Green Bay instead of returning to school for the spring semester. He took a $250-a-month job as a shipping clerk at the Indian Packing Company.

He liked getting a paycheck so much that he gave up on college, but he sorely missed playing football. Walking downtown one day, he ran into George Calhoun, sports editor of the *Press-Gazette*, who had covered his high school exploits. Lambeau expressed how much he missed the game, and Calhoun suggested he put a team together. Lambeau talked the Indian Packing Company into donating money for jerseys and letting the team practice on its grounds, which had a playing field — hence the team name Packers. In August 1919 a group of potential players met in the *Press-Gazette* newsroom, answering an ad. Some really wanted to play football and others were just looking to brawl, but the cornerstone of a team formed.

College football was enormously popular in the aftermath of the Great War, its games drawing vast crowds and dominating newspaper headlines despite the opposition of many school presidents, aghast at its violent nature. In the Midwest, Illinois, Ohio State, Notre Dame, Wisconsin, and Minnesota fielded top teams and played before crowds of seventy-five thousand or more.

Against that backdrop, the Green Bay Packers lurched to life in the fall of 1919, playing athletic clubs, American Legion squads, and other ragtag outfits at Hagemeister Park on the east side of town. The Packers won ten games and lost one before sparse crowds. The game was called pro football and a hat was passed to collect money for the players. It was a meager enterprise.

In 1921 Lambeau's team joined the American Professional Football Association, a forerunner of the NFL, which featured, among many short-lived organizations, the Dayton (Ohio) Triangles, Canton (Ohio) Bulldogs, and Rock Island (Illinois) Independents. The Packers were promptly kicked out for using college players under assumed names. They had to pay twenty-five hundred dollars to rejoin, and Lambeau didn't have the money. But the people of Green Bay liked having a team and stepped in to help. One fan sold his car and gave the proceeds to the Packers in exchange for one minute of playing time.

Seeing how popular the team was, Andrew Turnbull, publisher of the *Press-Gazette,* conceived of the idea of turning it into a nonprofit entity. Four hundred people attended a start-up meeting at an Elks Club lodge and combined to purchase one thousand shares of stock at five dollars apiece. The Packers were saved.

The early NFL was a loose coalition of small-town teams such as the Packers, Triangles, Frankford (Pennsylvania) Yellow Jackets, and Pottsville (Pennsylvania) Maroons, with a few big-city teams such as the Bears and Giants mixed in. Seldom passing, the squads brawled in front of boozed-up fans and occasionally scored touchdowns. Gambling pervaded the stands and locker rooms.

Franchises came and went, but the fast-talking Lambeau put together a winning squad that Green Bay fans enjoyed. In 1925 the Packers moved into City Stadium, a wooden structure with slatted bleachers at East High School. By the late 1920s games against the Bears were drawing crowds of seven thousand spectators. Sports fans elsewhere believed pro football was a circus act more than a legitimate sport; the game itself was so closely associated with the college experience that playing it for money was deemed unseemly. But Green Bay didn't have a major college team and liked its hometown boys.

The Packers' star player was Johnny McNally, a handsome runner who drank, gambled, and womanized. The Hornung of his day, he had been kicked out of Notre Dame for playing semipro ball, and now played for the Packers under an assumed name, Johnny Blood. His blockers included "Iron Mike" Michalske, a rugged two-way player, and Cal Hubbard, a gentle giant who demanded a trade from the New York Giants because he preferred the small-town environment.

With Lambeau now strictly in the role of coach, the Packers went unbeaten in 1929, allowing just twenty-two points in thirteen games. After clinching their first NFL title with a win over the Bears in Chicago, they were met at the Green Bay train station by ten thousand screaming fans. The city's bars never closed that night as people toasted their team. The next year, the forward-thinking

Lambeau, who loved passing the ball, stumbled onto a star thrower when he gave a tryout to one of the team's towel boys, a Green Bay native named Arnie Herber. The Packers won two more titles in 1930 and 1931 with Herber heaving passes downfield to open receivers.

When fourteen thousand fans crammed into City Stadium to watch the Packers beat the Bears in 1931, the team seemed on solid financial ground. But then a fan fell out of the stands, sued, and won, forcing another stock sale that raised fifteen thousand dollars, just enough to keep the Packers from suffering the same sad fate as the NFL's other small-town teams, which folded as the Depression squeezed their wallets and they faced the grim reality of trying to beat better-funded teams from New York and Chicago.

The Packers' fortunes improved dramatically when Lambeau signed Don Hutson, a lanky receiver from the University of Alabama who would become the franchise's greatest player. The NFL was deemed so second-rate in the South, where college football ruled, that Hutson believed his playing career was over after he scored two touchdowns in the 1935 Rose Bowl. But a bidding war for his services erupted between Lambeau and the Brooklyn Dodgers. Hutson signed with both teams, but Lambeau's contract reached the league offices an hour earlier, making Hutson a Packer.

Arriving shortly after several rules were changed to encourage passing, Hutson, known as the Alabama Antelope, was a devastating weapon, running nifty routes and catching tosses from Herber and his successor, Cecil Isbell. The Packers won titles in 1936 and 1939, and in 1941 Hutson became the first receiver to catch fifty passes in a season. The Packers were in their heyday. The U-shaped bleachers that surrounded the City Stadium field on three sides were filled on Sundays. A glassed-in press box was considered the best in the business. Packer games were the high point of Green Bay's social life. Friends held Sunday-morning parties and went to the stadium together, the men wearing suits, the women dressed in hats, high heels, and furs. They promenaded before kickoff and dined at supper clubs after the game.

Truthfully, City Stadium was still minor league in many respects. Kids snuck through the turnstiles and sat behind the end zone. The

Packers dressed in a dark, cramped locker room under the stands, and since there was no visiting locker room, players on opposing teams got ready for games in their rooms at the Northland Hotel. Fathers and sons gathered in the hotel lobby on Sunday mornings to watch the massive players step off the elevators in their shimmering uniforms, cleats and helmets in hand.

Fans rooted desperately for victories, and even when the Packers lost, the invasion of teams from Chicago and New York made everyone's shoulders feel broad. But after carrying the Packers for eleven seasons and leading them to yet another title in 1944, Hutson retired in 1945, and the team immediately declined. Pro football, though still not as popular as the college game, was strictly a big-city enterprise now, and a rival league, the All-America Football Conference, started up, creating a free-for-all talent market that led to higher player salaries. The Packers lost players to better-funded big-city teams, posted a 3-9 record in 1948, and went 2-10 in 1949. Suddenly, they were an anachronism, the last link to the NFL's romantic early years. Their opponents played in Yankee Stadium and the Los Angeles Coliseum, and they played at East High School. It became a struggle for them just to stay competitive. In 1949 they staged a Thanksgiving Day doubleheader featuring an intra-squad game and an old-timers' game just to raise enough money to pay their bills.

Fans tired of Lambeau, who, twice divorced and still handsome, spent the off-season in California frolicking with movie stars. His relationship with the Packer board of directors soured as the losses mounted. The board took away some of his power, putting new committees in charge of negotiating contracts and other important tasks. Few tears were shed in 1949 when Lambeau resigned from the team he had started three decades earlier to coach the Chicago Cardinals.

The executive committee became more involved with Lambeau gone, adding more committees and holding another stock sale that raised $118,000 in 1950. Fans still felt a tug for the team despite its recent struggles. One woman came to the team's offices with $25 in quarters and bought a single share of stock.

To replace Lambeau, the executive committee hired Gene Ronzani, a burly former Bears fullback, as both general manager and head coach. He won just fourteen of forty-six games before resigning in 1953. The committee then divided up his job, hiring the scholarly Blackbourn as head coach (he had been a winning high school and college coach in Milwaukee) and Verne Lewellen, a lawyer who had played halfback for the Packers in the 1920s and 1930s, as GM. A brief revival ensued. With quarterback Tobin Rote throwing touchdowns to the speedy Howton, the team went .500 in 1955, splitting twelve games.

But Blackbourn couldn't sustain the improvement and the Packers fell back again, losing seventeen of twenty-four games in Blackbourn's last two seasons. They were at a dangerous crossroads. Television, its popularity and influence growing exponentially, was now broadcasting NFL games into millions of homes across the country. Fans were becoming hooked on the skill, drama, and violence they saw on Sundays. Attendance was skyrocketing. After decades on the fringes of the sports scene, pro football was taking off. But it was doing so without the Packers, who played before seventy-five thousand fans in Los Angeles, fifty-nine thousand in San Francisco, and fifty-four thousand in Detroit, but barely drew ten thousand paying customers to games at City Stadium.

Their reputation was so dismal that other teams dealt with unhappy players by threatening to trade them to Green Bay, the "Siberia of the NFL." The Packers were a cheap, second-rate outfit. They held training camp in remote Stevens Point, Wisconsin, on a high school field with dim lights; punts disappeared into the sky during evening scrimmages. Other teams stayed at first-class hotels and gave players a per diem when they traveled, but the Packers frequented out-of-the-way bargain motels and ate sandwiches that management handed out. Other teams flew on newer planes, but the Packers crammed into a pair of DC-3 turboprops, with half of the team's quarterbacks, runners, blockers, linebackers, and safeties on one plane and half on the other, a precaution taken so the starting lineup wouldn't be entirely wiped out if one of the rickety planes went down.

When receiver Gary Knafelc joined the Packers in 1954, he was shocked to find facilities not up to the standards he had known at the University of Colorado or, for that matter, at his high school in Pueblo, Colorado, shortly after World War II. Packer players weighed themselves on a meat scale and soaked their aches in a whirlpool that was little more than a bathtub with a hose. Their shoulder pads were stored under the City Stadium stands in an open-air enclosure with a dirt floor and chicken-wire walls. Knafelc took one look at the worn pads, called his father, and asked for the pads he had worn in a college all-star game.

The cost cutting reached a nadir in 1955 when the Packers took a train instead of flying to California to play the Rams and 49ers. Blackbourn tried to keep the players fresh by having them run through plays during a stopover at the Great Salt Lake, but after three days of nonstop eating, drinking, and playing cards, they were stale when they arrived and lost badly.

Playing for a small-town team had a few advantages. During his rookie season in 1952, Bobby Dillon lived at the YMCA for eight dollars a week. But players who yearned for more nightlife bemoaned their fate. Green Bay had few available women, and between that and the cold, snow, darkness, and losing, a young man could get depressed. When lineman John Sandusky was traded to the Packers from the powerful Cleveland Browns in 1956, he looked around on his drive in from the airport and sighed, "Ah, Green Bay, end of the earth." The wife of Packers tackle Norm Masters, a Detroit native, wept when he told her their hometown Lions had traded him to Green Bay.

Making matters worse, the players lived among many glory-years Packers who had married local girls and settled down in Green Bay. The police chief had played on the 1919 team. The fire chief had played with Johnny Blood. Two dozen former players lived nearby and attended games. Reminders of better times were everywhere.

The situation was so bad by the mid-1950s, it was whispered the league might move the Packers to Milwaukee, a larger city experiencing a sports boom. It had a new stadium that seated fifty-four thousand and had attracted a major-league baseball franchise, the Braves, who had moved from Boston in 1953 and set attendance records, won two National League pennants, and captured a World Series. The Packers played two "home" games a year in Milwaukee, hoping to build a second-city audience, and while they didn't draw nearly as well as the Braves, they might if they moved permanently, focused on selling themselves to the larger market, and started winning again.

The NFL's other owners wouldn't object to the move. They didn't see the romance of having a team in "little Green Bay." With road teams earning 40 percent of the gate at games, the Packers filled their pockets playing before big crowds on the road, but failed to reciprocate at home. The other owners complained about them not holding up their end of the business arrangement.

The chances of the Packers leaving Green Bay were slim, though. After realizing, a bit belatedly, that City Stadium was absurdly outdated, the city built the team a new stadium on forty-eight acres of west-side farmland. When the funding was floated as a bond referendum in April 1956, the Bears' George Halas drove up from Chicago and stumped for the Packers, his bitter rivals but also his partners in the football business. The referendum easily passed, and the new City Stadium opened in September 1957 with a capacity of 32,500. A sellout crowd, which included Vice President Richard Nixon and NFL commissioner Bert Bell, attended the inaugural game as the Packers upset the Bears, 21–17. But the Packers didn't win another home game all season.

Green Bay also had Bell's enduring support. When the commissioner had experienced his own money problems as owner of the Philadelphia Eagles in the 1930s, the Packers helped him out. He never forgot and, upon taking charge of the entire league in 1946, pledged unfailing support. "There'll always be pro football in Green Bay as long as I'm commissioner," he told the *Press-Gazette*'s Art Daley.

But what kind of pro football? Packer fans had no idea as they watched their team's 1958 season going from bad to worse. They loved rooting for a team that took on rivals from America's urban centers — it made their lives more exciting and put their little city on the map. And the Packers had measured up to the challenge for years, piling up wins and titles. What fun that had been!

Now, though, it seemed they would never win again.

$\star$ **3** $\star$

T HREE DAYS AFTER the 56–0 loss, the *Milwaukee Journal's* Oliver Kuechle wrote a scathing column suggesting the Packers' biggest problem wasn't the players or coaches, but the executive committee.

"Green Bay's performance in Baltimore was an insult to all Packer followers and to a million television viewers," Kuechle wrote. "There can be no excuse for such a show of ineptness by men who accept money to play the game. [But] the trouble lies first with the executive committee [and] the jealous zeal of some of its dominating old-timers to be a part of the picture. Actual meddling on the field? Oh, no. That's always the pious 'out' when the committee changes coaches: 'We give our coaches a free hand.' But [there is] meddling nonetheless. There are the weekly reports the executive committee demands at its Monday luncheons, including the 'whys' and 'wherefores' of this and that. There are the friendly 'hints' that Parilli, not Starr, should start. There are the meetings with players, without coaches present, that Lisle Blackbourn experienced. Isn't that a fine way to engender morale? There is the procedure that the GM must discuss important things first with the committee, or a subcommittee.

"The Packers are in the big leagues, but in a lot of ways, don't show it. They invite a lot of their ills themselves. The day the committee clipped Curly Lambeau of absolute authority in the midforties and substituted administration by soviet — that's the day the team's troubles began. There hasn't been a winning season since. An executive committee of new blood, a new framework of administration, is almost a must. That must come first."

Kuechle was a Lambeau loyalist who had become a steadfast naysayer, as Art Daley pointed out in a rebuttal column — and defense of the executive committee — that ran in the *Press-Gazette* the next day. Daley, whose publisher was secretary of the executive committee, dismissed Kuechle as a "knife-ist" and wrote: "Why hack the executive committee? They weren't even in Baltimore." Daley suggested Scooter McLean "wouldn't take any guff" from the committee, and printed the names of the thirty-five Packers who played in Baltimore. "They're all guilty," Daley wrote.

But while it was true the committee hadn't played in the epic loss, many Packer fans agreed with Kuechle — poor playing and coaching obviously were problems, but mismanagement was the biggest issue. After watching the Packers lose for a decade, the fans believed the committee knew less about football than it did about business or politics. Its Monday grillings of the head coach were demeaning, and its hands-on management style was counterproductive. Like many businesses run by committee, it couldn't navigate through a crisis.

Dominic Olejniczak, known as Ole, took the brunt of the criticism. Fans sent him caustic letters, complained about him on the radio, and fired off angry missives to the *Press-Gazette*. Short and round, the butt of Polish jokes whispered around town, Ole was an easy target.

His career in politics had prepared him to handle criticism, but on his worst day as mayor he hadn't been subjected to the kind of savagery directed at him now, as president of the executive committee. By the end of the 1958 season he would see himself hung in effigy from a light pole outside the Packer offices.

But Ole was not without canny leadership skills, and as he watched the Packers stumble through the 1958 season, he found himself agreeing with his critics. There were too many committees and too much bureaucracy. The executive committee was too involved. A for-profit company would never operate with so many bosses.

In typical Packer fashion, he convened a subcommittee to study the situation and suggest a management overhaul. The subcommittee included executive committee stalwarts Dick Bourguignon and Jerry Atkinson, but Ole was most interested to hear from Tony Canadeo, the former Packer halfback and newest executive-committee member, who sold steel for a living now. He had forgotten more football than most of the other committee members knew.

The press didn't report that a reorganization of the front office was in the works; Ole kept it quiet, not wanting to give his critics another reason to crucify him as he groped for a solution to the team's woes. He wished the rest of the 1958 season also could take place privately. A week after the Baltimore game, the Packers lost to the Bears in Chicago, 24–10, dropping their record to 1-5-1. They played better than in the dismal matchup with the Colts, scoring first, trailing by just four points at halftime, and opening up several scoring chances that could have made the game close if they hadn't blown them. But the offense faltered, Parilli and Starr combining to complete just eleven of twenty-five passes. Hornung got off the bench when starting fullback Howie Ferguson was injured, but the Golden Boy gained just eleven yards on six carries. Jim Taylor also got into the game late and scored the Packers' touchdown, their first in eight quarters.

After the game, Scooter kept reporters out of the locker room until the players had showered and left. "I wanted to let the guys relax," he said. "There were thirty-five boys out there trying. I was satisfied with their effort."

The next week the Packers failed to sell out new City Stadium for the first time, and a crowd of 28,051 grumbled as the Rams won, 20–7, on a chilly, misty afternoon. Parilli threw four interceptions, Hornung missed two field goal attempts, and Scooter lamented, "We just can't come up with the big play, can we?" Normally the players dined out after home games, but now that meant confronting fans who had lost patience. On this Sunday, the wives brought food into the locker room and set up a buffet. The players arranged chairs around portable tables and ate with the only people in town who wouldn't give them a hard time — each other.

The season became a blur. A 33–12 loss to the 49ers, in front of just 19,786 fans in Milwaukee, was followed by a 24–14 loss in Detroit on Thanksgiving. The players became fatalistic, expecting the team to make the mistakes that lost games. Art Daley came down harder and harder in the *Press-Gazette*, pointing out poor efforts and gently chiding Scooter for the lack of discipline. (The players were taking advantage of a good guy, Daley wrote.) He continued to exclude Olejniczak and the executive committee from the calculus of failure.

Meanwhile, Ole's subcommittee on management restructuring quietly proposed a plan, much of it suggested by Canadeo. The executive committee would shrink from thirteen people to seven. A real GM — a football expert, not a bean counter — would take over the on-field operation. The position of chairman of the board would be eliminated. The executive committee would no longer grill the coach on Mondays during the season.

Ole presented the plan to the forty-five-member board, expecting to encounter resistance, but it passed easily; something obviously needed to be done. Ole would announce it after the season. He also met with Scooter before the team's season-ending trip to California and told him that a new coach would be hired. As a thank-you for eight years of service, Scooter was offered the chance to finish the season and resign, as opposed to being fired. Good soldier that he was, McLean took the deal and left for California.

The Packers always concluded their schedule with road games against the 49ers and Rams; they played at home earlier in the fall, when the weather in Wisconsin was milder, and traveled to the warmer climate once winter arrived in December. The players always enjoyed the trip, treating it as a season-ending party with a little football attached. They had won just one of sixteen games in California since 1950.

They flew to San Francisco but, in typical Packer fashion, saved money by staying in Palo Alto, outside the city. They practiced at Stanford during the day, had evening team meetings, and either went out or played poker at night. Scooter didn't enforce curfew. Ray Nitschke, the rookie linebacker, had a few too many drinks one night and, while flirting with a young woman, bumped the pinball table she was playing at so hard the tilt switch engaged, shutting down the game. As she complained, Tom Bettis hustled the young player out of the bar.

It was not a harmonious week. The locker room was splitting down the middle as the losing season neared an end. The defense blamed the offense, which had ground to a halt, scoring just forty-three points in the past five games. But the offense didn't believe the defense should be absolved of blame. Their dispute went public when several players complained to Art Daley, who wrote about it in the *Press-Gazette*. The defense was especially upset with receivers Howton and McGee, Daley wrote.

Scooter heard about the article from a board member back home. At a team meeting that night, McGee raised his hand as the coach was discussing a formation.

"Wait, I've got a problem," McGee said.

Scooter looked hard at the receiver and said, "Max, you're just going to have to handle that problem yourself. Scooter has enough problems of his own."

That was readily apparent on Sunday at Kezar Stadium in San Francisco. The Packers played their worst game since the Baltimore fiasco. Starr's first two passes were intercepted, and the 49ers turned both mistakes into touchdowns. Scooter subbed in Parilli, whose first pass also was intercepted. The score was 27–0 after a quarter, 34–7 at halftime, and 48–7 early in the third quarter. As the 49ers eased up, Joe Francis led the Packer offense to two late scores that made the final score almost respectable at 48–21.

Amid the wreckage, there was one bright spot: Jim Taylor. Finally given a chance to run the ball, he hammered away between the tackles, bowled over defenders, and gained 137 yards on twenty-two carries — by far the best performance of the season by a Packer runner. The five-feet-eleven, 205-pound youngster was all smiles after the game, saying he knew all along he could do that if given a chance. "He could be a great one, no doubt. He's as strong as an ox," Parilli commented.

The next morning, the Packers flew to Los Angeles for a week of practice before their season finale against the Rams. They checked into the Green Hotel in Pasadena, where they always stayed. Opened in the 1880s as an exclusive resort, it had fallen on hard times and now housed retirees as full-time residents. It would be condemned a few years later.

The Packers trained at a nearby public park and went out at night. Scooter's departure hadn't been announced, but given the team's dismal season and the fact that he had signed a one-year contract, rumors about his demise swirled. A board member spoke to Curly Lambeau, who lived in California but still had many friends in Green Bay, and that led to a rumor that Lambeau would return as GM and hire a big-name college coach. Lambeau, with typical drama, denied it at first but then told Daley he might be interested.

One evening a group of Packers including Jerry Kramer, Hornung, Taylor, and McGee ran into Lambeau while dining at the Ram's Horn, a restaurant owned by a retired Rams defensive back. Lambeau came and sat at their table, told stories from the glory days, and said he wanted to come back and revive the Packers. The awestruck players came away thinking the charismatic legend was the obvious choice to replace Scooter. They were excited.

Meanwhile, some veterans sent a telegram to Ole, accepting blame for the season and absolving their coach. "A lot of us feel real bad about Scooter," Dave Hanner told Daley. "Some guys just let him down."

Scooter, still on the job, surprisingly suspended defensive end Len Ford for Sunday's game after Ford stayed out too late one night. Scooter's belated attempt at discipline was laughable; he had ignored such offenses all season. But he was angry at Ford, who was at the end of an eleven-year career (that would result in a Hall of Fame selection) and, in Scooter's opinion, among those simply going through the motions.

On Sunday, Scooter started Francis at quarterback and Taylor at halfback; they had given the offense some life. Francis, scrambling madly, ran for 87 yards and threw for 84 even though he wasn't entirely sure what he was doing. Taylor hammered up the middle and gained 106 yards on twenty-two carries. The Packers took an early lead on a Francis touchdown before 51,684 spectators at the Coliseum, and after a defensive collapse, still trailed by just seven late in the third quarter. They wound up losing, 34–20. Their final record of one win, ten defeats, and a tie was the worst in Packer history.

The team flew back to Green Bay on Monday, and Scooter resigned the next day. Before the week was over, he had a job as an assistant with the Detroit Lions. He made plans to move in January, but before he left, his friends gave him a hearty farewell. The West Side Social Club held a party for him at the Riviera Club. There was a gathering at the Spot, a popular nightclub. At 3 A.M. on New Year's Eve, Scooter was in Art Daley's kitchen, cooking eggs for friends and toasting his time in Green Bay. No one had given Lambeau, Ronzani, and Blackbourn parties when they left, but Scooter was such a nice guy.

★ **4** ★

THE PACKERS' SEARCH for a new coach did not travel in a straight line directly to Scooter McLean's successor. It meandered through twists and turns, tantalizing fans with possibilities through December and January. Would Curly Lambeau really come back? Would Forest Evashevski, the hottest coach in the Big Ten, really take on the Packers? Those questions dominated speculation in the media and among fans.

No one outside the team's Washington Street offices had any idea that a little-known assistant coach with the New York Giants was also a candidate.

The search actually began earlier, after team president Dominic Olejniczak gave Scooter the bad news in late November. Ole then asked the executive committee to give him a list of possible successors, and requested that Jack Vainisi, the Packers' personnel director, check on any current NFL coaches who might be suitable.

Vainisi was an invaluable member of the front office. Just thirty-one years old, he was a keen football observer who had led the Packers' scouting efforts and overseen their college draft selections since 1951. Most NFL teams cared little about scouting; some just consulted *Street & Smith's College Football* guide before making picks. But Vainisi was consumed by the process, to the Packers' benefit.

Rotund and outgoing, Vainisi had grown up in Chicago in the shadow of the Bears; players shopped at his father's deli and occasionally ate at his house. Vainisi earned a football scholarship to Notre Dame, but a stint in the Army and a serious heart ailment ended his playing career. He found another niche in the sport after graduation when Ronzani, one of the Bears who had patronized the deli, hired him as a Green Bay scout. It was immediately apparent he was a natural. Ceaselessly working the phones, he built a nationwide network of insiders who scoured their areas for potential players. He traveled extensively, even carving out time on his honeymoon to check out prospects. His hard work paid off; as inept as the Packers were on the field, they were known as shrewd drafters, having scored with Howton, Dillon, Hanner, Forester, Bettis, and Ron Kramer — all players other teams would take.

When Ole asked him to suggest candidates, Vainisi went to work. You had to dig around to find out about NFL assistants, who were unknown commodities, receiving little publicity or acclaim. Vainisi tapped his many contacts in the league, speaking to Bert Bell, George Halas, and Cleveland's Paul Brown, among others. One name kept coming up — Vince Lombardi, the Giants' top offensive assistant. Everyone spoke highly of his character, organizational abilities, football knowledge, and forceful personality. His offense was one of the NFL's best.

The Giants' top defensive assistant, Tom Landry, was also a prospect. A young, forward-thinking former cornerback, he had pioneered a popular new alignment. Most defenses had previously featured five or six linemen and two or three linebackers, but Landry invented the "4-3," built around a "middle" linebacker who roamed the field making plays as the two tackles in front of him occupied blockers and four defensive backs protected against the pass. Led by Sam Huff, a tough and agile middle linebacker, the Giants had a formidable defense.

The Giants had won an NFL title in 1956 and consistently contended for the Eastern Division title with Landry and Lombardi in charge of their units. The head coach, Jim Lee Howell, joked that with such sharp assistants, "All I have to do around here is pump up the balls."

Landry, just thirty-four years old, was clearly a head coach in the making, while Lombardi, forty-five, was at a point where some NFL teams might think he was too old to be a first-time head coach; it had taken him longer to rise through the ranks, and he had been passed over a few times. But Bell, Brown, and Halas all endorsed Lombardi as the one the Packers should hire.

A short, square-shouldered bulldog of a man, Lombardi was an indelible character with an array of extreme qualities, an intense Italian American incapable of not leaving a strong impression. He had light-olive skin, close-cropped dark hair, and a prominent, triangular nose. When he smiled, gaps showed between his upper front teeth and a rectangle of deep creases formed around his mouth. His expensive clothes and round frame glasses gave him a scholarly air, as did his abilities as a blackboard instructor; he could take up the chalk and make complex offensive tactics and philosophies easy for players and other coaches to understand. But his buttoned-down appearance masked his temperamental, loud, demanding personality, which was legendary among those who knew him. Impatient with players who fell short of perfection, he bristled and snapped like an exposed electrical wire during practices and games, uncorking sprays of sarcastic profanities that could reduce hulking linemen to tears.

A lifelong resident of the New York area, Lombardi had grown up in Brooklyn's Sheepshead Bay neighborhood, the eldest son of immigrant parents. His father, Harry, a meat wholesaler and devout Catholic, attended mass every day, and now Vince, after attending Catholic schools, was also a daily communicant. Harry had been a stern but affectionate father and Lombardi exuded similar qualities as a coach. If he knocked a player down with criticism, he picked him up later with a pat on the rear.

He had played college football in the 1930s, his strength and innate fierceness enabling him to survive as a five-feet-ten, 175-pound guard on a Fordham University offensive line known as the Seven Blocks of Granite. Too small for the NFL, he considered entering the priesthood after college but instead worked for an insurance company, played semipro football, attended law school for a year, and married the only woman he had seriously dated, a stockbroker's daughter named Marie. They had two children, a son, Vincent Jr., and a daughter, Susan.

In the late 1930s he took a job as the offensive line coach at St. Cecilia's, a Catholic prep school in Englewood, New Jersey, where he also coached basketball and baseball and taught physics, chemistry, algebra, and Latin, all for seventeen hundred dollars a year. After a promotion to head coach, he won six state titles in eight years, shouting, demanding, praising, pushing — never allowing his players to give less than their best.

Setting his sights on becoming a major college coach, he left St. Cecelia's in 1947 to join the staff at Fordham. Two years later, Army coach Earl "Red" Blaik, one of the nation's preeminent football men, called him about a job. Blaik had won two national titles, fashioned a thirty-two-game winning streak, and always fielded strong teams. His approach was devastatingly simple. His players were well conditioned and mentally tough. The team's playbook was slim but allowed for few mistakes. Army beat you not with offensive wizardry but with ferocious blocking and tackling.

Many of Blaik's assistants became head coaches elsewhere, and after Sid Gillman left for the University of Cincinnati, Blaik heard from many coaches wanting to work for him. None excited him. His friend Tim Cohane, the sports editor of *Look* magazine, suggested he call Lombardi; Cohane had been the sports publicist at Fordham when Lombardi played there. Blaik interviewed Lombardi, and although Lombardi had neither played nor coached at a major college, "I knew he was ready. I saw the sparkle in his eyes," Blaik said later. "I could tell he had a good knowledge of the game, much more than just an ordinary mentality, and an unusual amount of imagination. Right then, as a young fellow, he had that special quality of being able to electrify a room."

Blaik hired Lombardi and mentored him in all aspects of the coaching craft. Lombardi learned how to organize a short, useful practice, analyze game film, prepare for a big game, and motivate players. After watching Lombardi explode angrily on the practice field, Blaik lectured him on managing his temper. "At first he didn't have control of his emotions. He was explosive," Blaik said later. "But while he was immature, he could overcome it because he had such a dynamic personality."

Lombardi adopted Blaik's straightforward philosophy. Football didn't need to be complicated. The best players were fit, disciplined, and tough, willing to inflict and endure pain. They could win by

37

mastering a small set of basic formations and plays, executing so crisply it didn't matter if the other team knew what was coming.

Lombardi also favored discipline, routine, and hard work. His workday began at 8 A.M. and often didn't end until midnight. His focus and drive bordered on maniacal. Obsessing over a new offensive wrinkle one day, he forgot to put on his pants after practice and left the locker room wearing just his underwear; a security guard told him to go back and finish dressing. After driving to work with Marie and a male friend one morning, he absently leaned over and gave the friend a "bye, honey" kiss. His mind was always on football. Forever diagramming plays and debating their merits, "he was in another world when he was playing around with X's and O's," Blaik recalled.

Thinking all along that his future lay in college ball, Lombardi paid little attention to the NFL. But then the Giants tried to hire Blaik to replace their longtime head coach, Steve Owen, after the 1953 season. Blaik turned the Giants down but suggested they hire Lombardi to run their offense under Jim Lee Howell. Lombardi took the job after Blaik endorsed the move. Blaik wasn't going anywhere, and if Lombardi, now forty, was ever going to become a head coach, he needed to move on.

Lombardi got off to a rough start with the Giants. Some veterans didn't care for his sarcastic, critical style, and the offensive linemen practically revolted when he showed them his blocking system. They previously made blocks according to the defensive alignment, but now their assignments would be dictated by the offensive play-call. And instead of blocking a specific man, they were assigned a space and told to block any defender who entered it. Lombardi later recalled that when he unveiled the concept, "I could tell from the way they looked at each other and from their air of resignation that they were skeptical of this 'college stuff.' They thought I was crazy."

But Lombardi won over a new generation of Giant blockers who mastered his system and played with the jaw-rattling toughness he demanded. They became the heart of his offense. Eschewing the pass-happy schemes that had become popular, Lombardi designed a simple power attack built around a strong running game, with a sprinkling of surprises mixed in. Like Army, the Giants ran few plays, but ran them flawlessly. In the 1956 championship game they rolled to a 47–7 victory over the Bears on an icy field at Yankee Stadium.

The key for Lombardi was finding a use for Frank Gifford, a former Southern Cal star floundering as a pro. Owen had put him at defensive back, but Gifford was a nimble runner, effective receiver, and could throw. Lombardi put him at left halfback in a four-man backfield and designed plays that utilized his varied skills, such as the halfback option, which looked like an end sweep until Gifford stopped and threw downfield. In 1956 Gifford totaled more than fourteen hundred rushing and receiving yards, leading the league.

After the 1957 season, in which the Giants finished second in the Eastern Division, Lombardi was approached by the Philadelphia Eagles about becoming their head coach. They offered a short-term contract with the possibility of an extension if the team won. Lombardi had dreamed about the chance to run his own team, but Giants owner Wellington Mara talked him out of going. The Eagles had meddling owners who would interfere, Mara warned. Lombardi turned down the offer and received a raise from Mara.

Now, a year later, the Packers were interested. Vainisi mentioned Lombardi to Ole in mid-December 1958. Ole already knew the name, having seen Lombardi at a coaching clinic in Ohio that fall. Tony Canadeo had suggested they attend the clinic to check out other coaches. Lombardi had commanded the classroom, exuding self-confidence.

At Vainisi's suggestion, Ole called Bell, Halas, and Paul Brown. They repeated their praise. Lombardi, they said, was an innovative strategist and dynamic leader who believed in discipline. Bell, who desperately wanted the Packers to improve, said he was "a great believer in desire and proper conduct; you'll like him." Halas said, "I shouldn't tell you this because you're liable to kick the crap out of us, but he'll be a good one." Paul Brown told Ole the Packers might not be able to pry Lombardi away from the Giants because he was a lifelong New Yorker liked by the Mara family. If he stayed put, Brown said, he probably would succeed Howell as the Giants' head coach.

Ole phoned Mara and asked for permission to speak to Lombardi. Mara denied the request and suggested Ole consider Landry. But Ole persisted and, after several conversations, finally obtained Mara's permission.

Reached at his home in Fair Haven, New Jersey, Lombardi told Ole he was interested. Lombardi and his wife had a heated discussion later. A tall, blue-eyed blond with an attention-getting figure, Marie Lombardi had never lived anywhere other than in and around New York. She and Vince had many friends, led an active social life, dined out, went to sophisticated nightclubs. No less strong-willed than her husband (she barked back when he snapped at her in the harsh tone that caused players to crumble), she hadn't minded the idea of Vince coaching the Eagles, just down the road in Philadelphia; maybe she and the kids wouldn't even move. But Green Bay was the middle of nowhere.

Green Bay?! Green Bay?!

Look, Marie, I don't know where this will lead. But I'm going to listen to what they have to say.

Deep down, she knew they would go, had to go, if the job was right. Her blustery, football-obsessed husband had frustrations and insecurities like everyone else, and his involved getting older without having been a pro or college head coach. Howell, his boss, was two years younger, and like most NFL head coaches had been hired before turning forty. Lombardi, forty-five, wasn't out of time yet, but as the years passed, he felt increasingly restless, pent-up, and anxious; it frustrated him to be full of ideas about how to run a team, yet unable to execute them.

Starting at his age meant he might get just one shot to run a team, which was partly why he had turned down the Eagles — he didn't want to waste his shot on a situation so rife with problems. This Packer job might fall into the same category, he feared. But his only other choice, at least as of now, was to wait for Howell to retire and then take the Giants' job, a scenario that might not play out for years.

Before considering the Packer job, Lombardi had to finish coaching the Giants in 1958. They beat Cleveland on the final Sunday of the regular season to force a one-game playoff for the Eastern Division title, and then shut out the Browns to win the playoff. On the last Sunday of 1958, a national television audience of 40 million watched them play the Baltimore Colts for the championship. The Giants were favored to win their second title in three years, but the Colts jumped ahead, 14–3. The Giants rallied to take a 17–14 lead in the fourth quarter and had the ball in the final minutes, but Gifford fell inches short on a third down and the Giants punted. Johnny Unitas led a drive that produced a field goal forcing overtime, and then drove the Colts to the winning touchdown.

Disappointed to lose what *Sports Illustrated* called "the greatest football game ever played," Lombardi started his off-season job at a bank a few days later. Coaching pro football wasn't a full-time job for assistants, many of whom worked outside the game in the off-season to augment their meager salaries. Lombardi experienced a profound change as he went from the shattering noise of a championship football game to the quiet purr of a bank, but he needed the money to maintain his family's standard of living, and he enjoyed the professional environment. Hired by the bank's sales office, he checked out other jobs in the building and wondered if he might like such work if his coaching career fizzled. A dapper dresser and quick learner, he felt he fit right in.

His phone rang again in early January when Blaik resigned at Army after eighteen seasons. There was a flurry of talk about Lombardi replacing him — he was ever a logical candidate — but Army eventually stuck to its tradition of hiring only West Point men to coach its football team. Yet another opportunity had eluded Lombardi. It made him more frustrated. He knew he was a good football coach, and knew exactly what he wanted to do if he was ever fortunate enough to take over a team. He was confident enough to assume an opportunity would come, but whenever a dark mood struck, he wondered if it was possible he would end up working at a bank.

Ole was under pressure to make a splashy hire. The members of an American Legion post that owned a substantial amount of Packer stock had demanded the resignations of the entire executive committee; the post commander said they had "not demonstrated they were capable of gaining and retaining the confidence of the

41

community." A popular retired Packer, Charley Brock, had agreed in a public appearance that the entire committee should resign, saying the team should "start over from scratch." Ole's forthcoming management restructuring, which he had announced, hadn't assuaged the critics. They still believed the committee could do no right.

A big-name hire would calm the situation at least temporarily, and the opportunity presented itself when Curly Lambeau campaigned hard to return as GM and be put in charge of hiring the new coach. The idea stirred excitement and headlines, but Lambeau had made enemies during his bitter departure a decade earlier, and Ole resisted making the easy, crowd-pleasing play.

The committee focused on hiring a coach rather than a GM, thinking the new person might end up with both jobs. Cleveland's Paul Brown had always run the Browns on and off the field, and so did Lambeau for much of his tenure. Gene Ronzani hadn't been able to handle both jobs by himself, but maybe an estimable football man could. The committee contacted University of Kentucky coach Blanton Collier; University of Iowa coach Forest Evashevski; Otto Graham, the Cleveland Browns' former All-Pro quarterback; and Jim Trimble, coach of the Hamilton Tiger-Cats of the Canadian Football League and formerly coach of the NFL's Eagles.

Collier and Graham were disciples of Paul Brown, who had won three NFL titles and seven Eastern Division titles in Cleveland since 1950 (and four straight All-American Football Conference league titles before that). Collier, fifty-two, had been Brown's assistant for seven years before going to Kentucky as Bear Bryant's replacement in 1953; he had a winning record but wasn't an exciting choice. Graham, who had just retired, wasn't interested in coming to Green Bay, saying he preferred to start his coaching career at the Coast Guard Academy. "I don't want to tackle that Green Bay situation with anything less than a two-year contract," Graham said.

In early January, Evashevski, a square-jawed former star quarterback at the University of Michigan, emerged as the Packers' top candidate. Iowa hadn't won a Big Ten title in three decades when he took over in 1952, but he had remade the Hawkeyes into a power, winning Big Ten titles in 1956 and 1958. At age forty, he was just the kind of coach Ole wanted. Much of the committee supported going after him.

Evashevski expressed interest when Ole contacted him shortly after the Hawkeyes pounded California in the Rose Bowl. Ole, Vainisi, and Canadeo interviewed him at the National Collegiate Athletic Association convention in mid-January and then quietly brought him to Green Bay for a second interview. But Evashevski abruptly took himself out of the running after that. He didn't plan on coaching much longer (1960 would be his last year on a sideline) and the rebuilding of the Packers figured to take years.

That left Lombardi as Ole's top choice. They arranged to meet at the Warwick Hotel in Philadelphia, site of the NFL draft and league meetings on January 20. The Packer delegation that traveled to the event included Ole, Vainisi, Canadeo, Lewellen, executive committee members Fred Trowbridge and Boob Darling, and the team's publicity director, a lanky former player named Tom Miller. Lombardi sat just yards away from them during the draft, as part of the Giants delegation.

The sad state of the Packers was a hot topic among reporters covering the event. Some wrote columns suggesting the franchise was in disarray. One chased Ole into an elevator at the Warwick while making the point that the Packers had become a charity case, living off their gate intake from road games. "All is not lost," Ole insisted.

That night Ole, Canadeo, and Vainisi interviewed Lombardi for forty-five minutes in Ole's suite. The restless head-coach-in-waiting was asked how he would run a team and what he would expect of players on and off the field.

I like a power offense built around the running game.

I like the 4-3 defense, just like the one the Giants have used.

The players will be in shape and they'll listen to what I say. If they don't, they'll be gone.

His interviewers found it slightly unsettling that he had never been a college or pro head coach, and Lombardi insisted that he would only come to Green Bay as a dual coach/GM, with full control of the team. He had turned down the Eagles because Mara said

43

the owners would interfere, and he knew that could also happen in Green Bay unless he had the authority to ignore the executive committee.

If this is my only shot, he thought, I'm going to do things my way.

With the winning influences of Earl Blaik and the Giants pumping through his veins, he came across as an intelligent, ambitious coach with high expectations and strong convictions. Canadeo, whose opinion Ole valued, told Ole to go get him.

Lombardi went back to work at the bank, thinking the interview had gone well. His phone rang within days. Could he come to Green Bay and meet the rest of the executive committee, the people he would work for? Ole had settled on him as the choice, ignoring a last, desperate attempt by Lambeau to wriggle in the door. It didn't matter that Lombardi had never been a head coach. He was impressive.

Lombardi said he would be happy to come to Green Bay, and Ole arranged for a private plane to bring him to town on January 26. Before he went, Lombardi asked Mara for advice. What should he do if they offered him the job? Mara told him to use the good judgment he had developed during his Jesuit college days at Fordham.

Canadeo and Dick Bourguignon met the plane at the Green Bay airport and drove Lombardi downtown to meet the rest of the committee. Incredibly, Lombardi's name still hadn't appeared in the *Press-Gazette* or the Milwaukee papers.

During the ride, Bourguignon asked Lombardi if he could envision leaving the Giants. Lombardi repeated what Mara had told him about using the good judgment he developed at Fordham. Canadeo and Bourguignon responded that they were Jesuit-educated also, Dick having gone to Marquette and Tony to Gonzaga.

Lombardi smiled and said, "You know, between us three Jesuits here, we could kick the shit out of these non-Catholics."

Meeting the rest of the committee, Lombardi repeated that he would only take the job at Green Bay as a head coach/GM with full authority over the team. During the past decade, when the committee had exerted suffocating control, it never would have ceded so much power. But now it was willing to let a football man take charge.

Ole offered Lombardi a five-year contract, an extraordinarily long deal. Lombardi asked for an annual salary of thirty-six thousand dollars, much more than he had ever made, and Ole quickly gave it to him. Lombardi had no doubts now. He agreed to take the job.

The deal wasn't immediately announced because the forty-five-member Packer board of directors still had to approve it, and Lombardi wanted to be the one to break the news back home. Mara endorsed his decision, saying the offer was too good to turn down. Marie swallowed hard but knew he had to take the job. Her husband had waited so long for this. And the money was good.

On January 28, the Packer board convened in the Northland Hotel's Italian Room, a fitting setting. The response wasn't entirely positive when Ole said the executive committee wanted to hire Lombardi. Some directors wondered why the choice wasn't Evashevski, a bigger name. Some wanted Lambeau. One board member, John Torinus, spoke for many in the room when he asked, "Who in the hell is Vince Lombardi?"

Down the hall, newspaper and radio reporters filled a pressroom with cigarette smoke and wisecracks. At 2:15 P.M., three board members walked in and said Ole would have an announcement in forty-five minutes. Some directors had been unable to attend the hastily arranged meeting and were being polled by phone. In the end, twenty-six of forty-five members gave Lombardi the thumbs-up. One said no. Eighteen didn't vote.

As the vote dragged on behind closed doors, the phones at the *Press-Gazette* offices rang almost nonstop, as did those at Green Bay's radio and TV stations, which had broadcast bulletins about the board's going into a meeting. *Who is the new coach? When will we know?* Finally, Ole entered the pressroom at 3 P.M., cleared his throat, and announced Lombardi as the new coach and GM.

As he began to take questions, the room phone rang. Ole picked it up. "We're in the middle of a meeting. Listen to the radio," he said.

45

The caller persisted. Ole continued haltingly: "A half hour. I know. I can't. I'm sorry. Just listen to the radio."

He hung up, read a brief biography of Lombardi, and apologized for leaving reporters in the dark during the search. But he said he thought he had done the job right. The reporters scattered to find phones, and word of the hiring spread across town. The public's reaction varied from shrugs to bafflement to anger.

The Packers hired . . . who?

What happened to Evashevski?

Did Curly turn them down?

To the fans, Lombardi seemed an odd choice. Since Lambeau's departure, the Packers had been coached by taciturn, Midwestern football guys (Scooter was from New England but had been around so long he seemed like a local), so in background and manner alone, Lombardi represented a change. Plus, he seemed awfully old to be getting his first chance to run a team. Oliver Kuechle would point that out in a column the next day, wondering what it said about Lombardi.

Most of the Packer players had never heard of him. Their reaction was the same as the public's — *who?* The young players who had shared a dinner with Lambeau in Los Angeles near the end of the 1958 season were angry. They had thought it was obvious the team should bring Lambeau back. The board had really blown it, they felt. They could have hired a legend, a guy who knew how to win in Green Bay, but instead they were bringing in some no-name, a guy who had never been a head coach!

Most of the players literally knew nothing about Lombardi. Jerry Kramer expressed outrage when he spoke by phone to several teammates shortly after the hiring. *What a bunch of jerks. How can they do this when Curly wanted to come back? That board of directors has to be the dumbest bunch of idiots ever. This is so disappointing!*

Art Daley knew about Lombardi because Daley's father was a longtime *New York Times* sports columnist who had written about the Giants. Lombardi was a smart guy with a strong personality, Daley's father said. Daley arranged to speak to Lombardi, who had taken a suite at the Manhattan Hotel in New York to wait out the vote. Several reporters were with him, and an Associated Press photographer snapped a shot of him smiling as he looked in a mirror and adjusted his tie.

When Daley got Lombardi on the phone, he heard a rumbling Brooklyn accent and knew pro football's small-town team had been handed over to a big-city guy.

"Good aftah-noon," the Packers' new head coach thundered.

★ 5 ★

S TEPPING OUT of a North Central Airlines plane into slanting midday sunshine, Lombardi was grateful for every fiber of his camelhair overcoat. The early February weather was brutal, the temperature near zero, a west wind whipping snow that had dropped the night before.

Lombardi had come back to Green Bay to sign his contract, speak to reporters, meet the board of directors, and get started on the enormous job of rebuilding the Packers. Marie was with him, anxious to find a place to live. Olejniczak and several directors waited on the tarmac, shivering and smiling. Few had seen Lombardi in person. They showed no sign of nervous anticipation as he walked down the portable stairway. Lombardi wasn't a legend. Grown men didn't gape when he walked by. He was just a football coach, a career assistant until now.

He stepped off the stairway and introduced Marie to Ole and the others. They shook hands and hustled inside to escape the cold. Stealing curious glances at the newcomer as they walked, the directors thought Lombardi was awfully small for a former offensive guard and that, despite his thick chest and square shoulders, he looked almost bookish with his glasses and Wall Street clothes. He was a rarity in vanilla Green Bay, a swarthy son of Old Europe. When he spoke, teeth gleaming and voice thundering, he seemed as formidable and self-assured as his hometown.

Reporters were waiting inside the terminal, hoping to speak to him. A newsman from a small radio station asked for a one-on-one interview. Ole tried to usher Lombardi away, saying this wasn't the time, wait for the press conference tomorrow. "This way," Ole said, gripping Lombardi by the shoulders to maneuver him. Scooter would have shrugged and gone along with the team president, but Lombardi put his foot down.

"No, no, this way," he replied, tugging free of Ole. "This man called me when I was in New York, and I promised him an interview as soon as I got here. He's going to get it."

Mara had warned Lombardi to beware of meddlers, know-it-alls who hovered around, hoarding power and intimidating coaches. Lombardi wasn't about to put up with them. He wouldn't tolerate meddling any more than he would tolerate a softhearted player who didn't care about doing a job well.

Wanting it known, immediately and indisputably, that this lousy team was his now, he turned and spoke to the radio man for several minutes while Ole and the directors waited silently.

It was, indeed, a new day in Packerland.

The delegation proceeded in an informal motorcade to the Northland, where Lombardi and Marie checked in. (A state trooper stopped all the cars at one point and warned the drivers to come to a full stop at stop signs.) Then it was on to the Packers' Washington Street offices. Lombardi had already met Jack Vainisi, Tom Miller, and Verne Lewellen during the team's search for a coach, but he was introduced to the rest of the staff, including Ruth McCloskey, his secretary. They went to work immediately, spending the rest of the day making final changes to his contract before he signed it.

The next day, he met the entire board at a luncheon. Introduced by Ole, he stood up and outlined his no-nonsense philosophy for the players—be in shape, be on time, don't screw up. He emphasized that, unlike the Packer coaches before him, he wouldn't tolerate interference.

"I want it understood: I'm in complete command here," he stated, pausing to let his words sink in. "I expect full cooperation from you. You will get full cooperation from me in return. I've never been associated with a loser and I don't expect to be now. You have my confidence. I want yours. I'm not against anything that will help the Packers."

Trying not to sound too confrontational, he said Ronzani had written him a note wishing him luck and calling Green Bay "a wonderful place with wonderful people." The directors smiled; they liked Gene even though he had flopped miserably.

"The Packers are steeped in tradition, and I expect, with plenty of hard work, to bring them back to the position they once held," Lombardi concluded.

As applause sounded, Ole, standing against a wall in the back, couldn't suppress a smile.

Later, Lombardi held his introductory press conference. More than a dozen newspaper and radio reporters from around the state (but only one of Milwaukee's two major papers) asked questions for an hour. Would he be a hands-off coach like Jim Lee Howell, or more involved? What did he think of the players on the team? What kind of offense would he run? How different would it be coaching in little Green Bay after having coached in New York?

Lombardi had answers. As the executive committee had learned, he was resolute in his football beliefs, knew what plays he wanted to run, how to prepare players, what would be emphasized.

On his involvement as a head coach: "I expect to take a more active part in coaching than Jim [Lee Howell]. I'll have a coach in charge of the offense and a coach in charge of the defense, but I'll work with them more than Jim did."

On the offense: "We won't be using the [Clark Shaughnessy] slot system as you have been using here. Our emphasis will be on power plays."

On the talent: "There's a good nucleus of veterans with the likes of Jim Ringo and Tom Bettis, but I'm going to refrain from making judgments until I have looked at the [game] movies of last season. I'm going to spend time doing that first, and then I'll have a better understanding of what we have."

On practices: "I hope to hold workouts down to an hour and a half, an hour and fifteen minutes if possible. The players will know exactly what they're supposed to do at every minute."

On coaching in a smaller city: "I have given considerable thought to my adjustment on this matter. I know it will be different here where most everybody knows the players personally. The coaches and players have a different set of problems here than in a big city where they can get lost."

After the press conference, Lombardi retreated to his room at the Northland; he was tired, having gone nonstop since he landed the day before. But Bud Lea, the beat reporter for the *Milwaukee Sentinel,* phoned the room and asked to come up and ask more questions. Lombardi said that was fine.

When Lea, a Green Bay native, knocked on the door and entered, he found Lombardi and Marie relaxing in chairs. They smiled, introduced themselves, and peppered Lea with questions when they found out he had grown up in Green Bay. *Where should we live? What are the good schools? Where are the best places to eat?* They spoke for a half hour, and then Lea got his quotes and left. As he walked away he thought, Seems like a nice guy. Years later, Lea would recall that as one of the last pleasant conversations he had with Lombardi.

Lombardi and Marie decided to build a one-story brick house on Sunset Drive in Allouez, a Green Bay suburb. They would rent a house a few blocks away in the meantime.

Having made that decision, they went back to New Jersey, collected the kids, and moved. Vince Jr., known as Vincent, was a high school junior. Susan was five years younger. Lombardi piled them into the family station wagon and drove to Green Bay. The 1,050-mile trip took several days, and the back seat got quiet when Lombardi reached Chicago and turned north toward Wisconsin. Snow was piled so high by the side of the highway that Vincent and Susan couldn't see the countryside beyond it.

What kind of a place is this?

Susan shed tears, and Vincent, a reflective and athletic teenager, was apprehensive. But they felt better after finding that Allouez was a pleasant neighborhood. Vincent started at Premontre High School, a Catholic institution. He missed his friends, but the negatives were outweighed by the positive of his father becoming an NFL head coach, especially in a town so small. Vincent was a bigger deal in Green Bay than he had ever been in New Jersey, not that he wanted or needed attention. He spent many evenings at home, watching pro basketball on television. His parents were busy. The rental house was cold.

Lombardi and Marie jumped right into a busy social life, accepting numerous invitations to meet people and dine out. They discovered they could get a good steak at Wally's Spot, a downtown supper club, and first-rate Italian food at Jimmy Manci's. The busy nights made Marie's first Wisconsin winter easier to take, as did the fact that the Packer coach received a membership to the Oneida Golf and Riding Club, an exclusive country club on the west side of town. In the mornings Lombardi ate breakfast with the kids before school and stopped for mass at St. Willebrords Church on his way to the office. He was instantly at ease in a city with so many Catholics.

At work, his first task was to hire assistant coaches and organize the front office. Vainisi, he decided, would be his second in command, with the title of business manager, while continuing to scout and run the draft. "Everyone knows what a great job Jack does," Lombardi said. Although he promoted Vainisi over Verne Lewellen, he kept Lewellen as a special assistant in charge of paperwork and finances.

For his on-field staff Lombardi wanted four assistants, one of whom would run the defense, allowing him to focus on the offense. He quickly made that hire: Phil Bengston, the 49ers' chief defensive assistant for the past eight years. A soft-spoken, analytical Minnesota native, Bengston had just been passed over by the 49ers, who had hired another assistant, Red Hickey, to replace fired coach Frankie Albert. Disappointed, Bengston had called the Packers about their head-coaching vacancy, and also called several other teams. When the Packers hired Lombardi, Bengston called him about a job. They related well. Both were forty-five, Catholic, and longtime assistants. Bengston liked the 4-3 defense that Lombardi wanted to use. Plus, despite his low-key personality, Bengston coached an attacking defense featuring unpredictable red-dog blitzes by linebackers, and Lombardi always wanted to play aggressively.

Lombardi then announced that John "Red" Cochran would coach

the offensive backs, as he had for the Detroit Lions for the past three seasons. A fiery southerner who had played halfback for the Chicago Cardinals under Lambeau a decade earlier, Cochran, ironically, needed a job because the Lions had just hired Scooter McLean to take his place. (Scooter and Lions head coach George Wilson were close friends who had pledged to always take care of each other.) Cochran heard on the radio that he had lost his job, contacted Lombardi, interviewed at the Detroit airport one day when Lombardi was laying over between flights, and was thrilled to get the job, which paid eighty-five hundred dollars a year. He had two young children and his wife was pregnant.

Cochran and Bengston came to town to start working and rented rooms at the downtown YMCA while they waited for their families to join them in Green Bay. Walking to work one day as a howling wind blew snow in their faces, Cochran, a native of Alabama, looked at Bengston and said, "Phil, what in the hell are we doing in this place?"

Cochran's pregnant wife, Pat, soon arrived with their two children, but the truck bringing their furniture was delayed by a snowstorm. The house they had rented was empty when Lombardi and Marie dropped by to welcome them. Worried about Pat, the Lombardis invited the couple over that evening, fed them ribs and sauerkraut for dinner, and welcomed them to town.

In the next few weeks Lombardi filled out his staff with first-time NFL assistants. Bill Austin, recently retired from the Giants, would coach the offensive line. Just twenty-nine, Austin had made the Pro Bowl under Lombardi, and Lombardi thought he would be an effective mentor. Norb Hecker, thirty-two, would coach the defensive backs; he was a six-year NFL veteran who had played in Canada in 1958. Combined with Bengston and Cochran, the young assistants gave the staff a mix of generations and personalities.

"I'm a perfectionist," Lombardi warned his new staff. "I'm going to demand your best. There's absolutely no excuse for anything other than that."

The coaches found it intimidating to hear him mention perfection — this was a game of broken tackles, fumbles, incompletions, and penalties. Hard-boiled college coaches such as Bear Bryant could get away with demanding that impressionable youngsters not make mistakes, but pro players were older, wilder, and harder to manage — frankly, not paid enough to put up with such high-minded bull from their coaches. Lombardi might have a fight on his hands, the assistants feared.

But Lombardi had watched Earl Blaik demand perfection and receive it at Army because athlete-soldiers were trained not to tolerate making mistakes. They had the requisite discipline — and so did pro football players, Lombardi figured. Just because they weren't in the military didn't mean they couldn't learn to eliminate mistakes. It was all in their minds, Lombardi said, and he simply wouldn't accept anything less.

We are going to do things right until everyone is doing them right.

We are going to run plays over and over and over until everyone is running them right.

I mean everyone!

Paul Brown had pioneered the use of film in the NFL a decade earlier. Now every team used it to review player performances and study opponents. Lombardi found it invaluable. Blaik had been a huge proponent, even filming Army practices to see who was hustling — or not hustling. Lombardi had watched film for a decade, and while there obviously was no substitute for seeing a player in person, he could learn a lot about the Packers while just sitting in a dark room. How hard did they hit? What kind of shape were they in? Had they mastered the fundamentals of their positions?

Throughout his first month on the job — a cold, snowy February — he and his assistants watched the Packers' entire 1958 season on film, from the opening kickoff in September to the final gun in California. They watched the Packers give up fifty-six points to the Colts and forty-eight to the 49ers. They watched Scooter's complex offense continually misfire. They watched the Packers score twenty-two touchdowns while their opponents scored forty-eight.

It was, for Lombardi, an up-and-down time emotionally. As he watched the losing players he had cast his lot with after waiting so long for the chance to run a team, he sometimes wondered what he had gotten himself into; he called Blaik, incredulous at the ineptitude. After one especially depressing day, he emerged from his office and asked Ruth McCloskey to pray for him. *I knew they were bad, but they're even worse than I thought.* But then there were days when he saw surprising potential in the crevices of the Packers' worst season. Near the end of one embarrassing defeat, he noticed Paul Hornung playing halfback, a position the Golden Boy had seldom manned because of his lack of speed. Running an end sweep, Hornung ran parallel to the line, made a sharp cut behind a blocker, and darted through the line for an eight-yard gain. Lombardi bolted upright. *What a cut! Frank Gifford couldn't have done it better.*

Lombardi wondered if Hornung, who had bombed at quarterback and fullback, might fare better as a halfback. Paying close attention as he watched the rest of the season on film, Lombardi noticed Hornung's soft hands, lower-body strength (for blocking), and knack for cutting. Hornung wasn't unlike the versatile Gifford, whom Lombardi had turned into a star. Hornung wasn't as fast, but he was a strong-legged runner, potentially dangerous receiver, and could throw, making him ideal for the option pass. He certainly wasn't a lost cause, Lombardi felt. An offense could be built around him, just as the Giants' attack had been built around Gifford.

Lombardi called Hornung, who was spending the off-season in Louisville wondering if he was going to have an NFL career.

"I've been looking at the films. You're not going to play quarterback anymore," Lombardi said. "You're my left halfback. You're either going to play left halfback, or you're not going to play at all."

Hornung said that was fine with him. "I'm tired of being moved around and tired of sitting on the bench. Put me on the field and give me a role and I will play good football for you, Coach," he said.

Liking what he heard, Lombardi brought up the rumors about Hornung's penchant for staying out late, chasing women, and drinking — rumors that routinely circulated in Green Bay. When Lombardi and Marie went out with friends at night, the conversation inevitably turned to Hornung, every Packer fan's number one target.

Listening to the stories and talking to others around town, Lombardi, fresh from the big city, didn't think Hornung sounded as outlandish as advertised.

"I know your reputation here. I've investigated you," Lombardi told him. "You've done some things you shouldn't have done, but I don't think you've done as many things as people say. I trust you.

"But don't let me down or it'll be your ass."

Hornung smiled on the other end of the line. "Coach, I will be ready to go on Sundays. You won't have to worry about me," he said. He hung up with renewed enthusiasm for football. Maybe he wouldn't go to Hollywood after all.

Lombardi also noticed another player on film, a fullback who could be an important part of the power offense he planned to install. Jim Taylor had rushed for almost 250 yards in the last two games of the 1958 season, often knocking over defenders and dragging them. Howie Ferguson had been the Packers' fullback since 1954, but Taylor might be ready to take over, Lombardi thought.

What about the quarterbacks? Many fans believed that position was the Packers' biggest problem, and it was hard to suggest otherwise after the 1958 season, in which Parilli, Starr, and Francis combined to throw twenty-seven interceptions and just fifteen touchdowns. But Lombardi developed a different perspective while viewing the films. It was unfair to judge the quarterbacks, he felt, because they were hounded all season by opposing rushers. The Packers' offensive line had offered little protection. Ringo was a first-rate center, but the guards and tackles had barely blocked anyone at times.

Defensively, just about everything was a problem, Lombardi felt. The unit was susceptible to both the run and pass, and only got worse as the season progressed. There were a few saving graces, the ball-hawking Dillon, the relentless Bettis and Forester, but overall, the defense was short on talent, late to recognize keys, forever a step slow. By the end of his film marathon, Lombardi knew he had to upgrade his defensive personnel or the Packers would never improve.

As he learned about his new team throughout February, Lombardi slowly got around town and met players. They would always remember their first encounters with him, just as they would remember their weddings or the births of their children.

One night Lombardi, Marie, and Lewellen went to a Green Bay Bobcats ice hockey game at the Brown County Veterans Memorial Arena. Gary Knafelc, the Packers' veteran wide receiver, was sitting nearby; a year-round Green Bay resident, he sold insurance during the off-season. Lewellen motioned for Knafelc to come over and meet the new coach. Lombardi and Knafelc shook hands. "Doesn't he remind you of Frank?" Marie said, comparing Knafelc to Gifford, a handsome magazine cover boy. Knafelc said he hoped he could play as well as Gifford for Lombardi.

The conversation turned to the Packers. Lombardi outlined his plans. There would be tougher practices and new rules; no more running amok on Scooter's loose ship. The offense would be built around a power running game. Knafelc nodded, saying little. This guy scared him.

"Gary, I'd like to see you in my office at nine o'clock tomorrow morning," Lombardi finally said.

Knafelc barely slept that night. He had been with the Packers since 1954 and owned a house in town. He had put down roots. What did this Lombardi guy want to say to him? It couldn't be good, he figured.

He was waiting outside Lombardi's office a half-hour early the next morning. Ushered in, he found himself across a desk from a coach no longer interested in pleasantries.

"How much do you weigh?" Lombardi barked.

"Two twenty-five," Knafelc croaked.

"Well, you're going to play tight end for me," Lombardi said.

Knafelc was stunned. He had always been a wide receiver, catching passes downfield. A tight end had to block.

"Coach, I haven't blocked anyone in five years in this league," he sputtered.

"You want to play for another team?" Lombardi snapped.

Knafelc shook his head. No, he was a Packer. And now, it seemed, he was a Packer tight end.

Bob Skoronski, a young offensive tackle, also met Lombardi shortly after the coach arrived. He had signed with the Packers as a fifth-round draft pick in 1956, turning down a better offer from a Canadian team when Vainisi sold him on Green Bay as a place where a bottle of milk cost a nickel — not true, it turned out. After his rookie season, Skoronski went into the Air Force and had spent the past two years there. Now, he was out, back in Green Bay, and hopeful of resuming his career. He also was short on cash until the season started. The Packers were helping, paying him to make public appearances. That brought him into the team's offices now and then, and one day, he met Lombardi. "Oh, yeah, nice to meet you," the coach said matter-of-factly as they shook hands. Before another word was spoken, Lombardi snapped, "You look like you're putting on weight. Are you working out?"

One by one, the players discovered a new era had dawned. Bart Starr, living in Alabama that off-season, realized it from a distance when he saw the photo that ran alongside the newspaper article about Lombardi being hired. He studied Lombardi's face, wondering, Where have I seen this guy? Then he remembered: In an exhibition game against the Giants a few years earlier, Starr had been trotting off the field after leading the Packers to a touchdown when he heard a commotion on the New York bench. Glancing over, he saw Lombardi ferociously berating the defense, almost like a dog that couldn't stop barking. And the defense wasn't even his responsibility! Wow, Starr thought, this would be interesting.

Forrest Gregg, another young lineman, had a similar epiphany shortly after Lombardi's hiring. He had been out shopping in Dallas, Texas, his off-season home, and ran into Tiny Goss, a fellow former Southern Methodist University star who had played for the Cleveland Browns and later spent time with the Giants, and Lombardi, during a training camp.

"Hey Forrest, ya'll got a new coach," Goss said.

"Yeah, Vince Lombardi," Gregg replied.

"Ya'll know anything about him?" Goss asked.

"Nope. Do you?" Gregg replied.

"Yeah," Goss said, grinning. "He's a real bastard."

★ 6 ★

L OMBARDI'S OFFICE SHADES were pulled, blocking his view of the relentless white winter. He was watching film again with his assistants, the room mostly dark and silent except for the whir of the projector. Outside the door, Lombardi heard Ruth McCloskey grinding through another workday.

Sometimes Lombardi could barely believe what he saw. In the last games of the 1958 season the Packers almost seemed to quit, especially when they fell behind.

Lombardi fingered buttons on the projector, stopping and rewinding to show a dismal play from the San Francisco game, in which the Packers gave up forty-eight points in the first thirty-five minutes.

Look at that, Phil. It's almost as if the right side of the line isn't there.

You're right. There's no fight at all.

Then he stopped to take another look at an offensive play. Parilli threw over the middle for Howton, but the ball sailed well ahead of the receiver and hit the ground.

No blocking, half-assed pass, terrible route.

You're right, Vince.

They look completely beaten down.

They do.

Lombardi grimaced and twisted in his chair; seeing the team give in so easily almost made him physically ill. He was used to

59

coaching players who were in shape, worked hard, knew their stuff, gave their all, played with aggressiveness and discipline, and expected to win. The Packers, conversely, didn't seem to work hard and clearly had a debilitating case of what Lombardi called defeatism. Beaten down by failure, they expected the worst and palpably sagged when things didn't go their way.

They had, Lombardi felt, accepted their lot as a losing team.

We have to change their attitude before we change anything, Phil. This is terrible.

No doubt about it.

He had told the Packer board of directors he'd never been associated with a loser and had no intention of starting now. Having seen the game films, he believed he might have the physical material to make good on that pledge — the team had more talent than people thought. But he needed to start from scratch mentally. He had to teach the players not to think like losers.

His old team, the Giants, had exuded confidence, partly because they were a winning team and had faith in their talent, and also, he believed, because they behaved like winners. Wellington Mara believed if they were going to compete with baseball's preeminent Yankees for the hearts and minds of New York sports fans, they had to be as classy as the Yankees. They wore ties and jackets on road trips and traveled in a winning style, staying at first-class hotels. That didn't help them block or tackle, but it helped them feel like champions.

Lombardi's new players had stayed at cheap motels, eaten pasty sandwiches on bumpy flights, and dressed sloppily on the road. They felt like a junior college team, not the Yankees. Their opponents almost felt sorry for them, being stuck in Siberia as they were.

Lombardi vowed to change the culture. If the Packers were ever going to rise above their second-class status, they had to start acting like major leaguers who expected to win. He asked team president Olejniczak for the financial backing, and Ole said yes. Closely following the Giants' model, the Packers would start flying on better planes, staying in better hotels, eating better food. They would adhere to a dress code on road trips, wearing ties and shiny new green Packer blazers that Lombardi pledged to buy with his own money to show his commitment. Their home and road uniforms, which Lombardi found drab, would be updated. Back home, the team's depressing offices would be redecorated more brightly.

If we're going to become winners, Ole, we have to start looking, acting, and feeling like winners.

Of course, new drapes and sports jackets alone wouldn't erase the losing attitude that hung in the Packer locker room like the smell of dirty socks. Lombardi would have to do a lot more to get the players thinking positively, especially after such a horrid season. He would start by enforcing curfews and conducting harder practices with far more conditioning work, holding the players to a higher standard of professionalism. Although they would be pushed, they would hopefully start to develop some self-respect. That and a few victories would help matters.

Some guys would balk, naturally. The league was full of players who felt they weren't being paid enough to go all out. The Packers had their share.

That vestige of the losing culture had to be purged, Lombardi said.

As he started getting to know players, he gauged which would likely continue to wear the Packer uniform. Who had the right mentality? Who was amenable to a new order? Who had to go? He knew Hornung was with him, and he had confidence in hardened veterans such as Bettis and Don McIlhenny. He wasn't as sure about players who, at least on film, seemed to be going through the motions.

He sent 1959 contract offers to veterans, prompting a handful of visits and phone calls. Max McGee, the carefree receiver, stopped by the team's offices while in Green Bay on business and asked Lombardi for an advance on his salary. McGee had a high forehead, dancing blue eyes, and a crinkly smile that suggested he knew jokes about you but wasn't going to tell them. A free spirit with a sardonic wit, he would rather laugh than work hard, which had tested the patience of his coaches. Yet they couldn't help liking him.

A native of East Texas, McGee had been an elusive, high-stepping running back at Tulane. He led the nation in kick returns and Vainisi took him in the fifth round of the 1954 draft. Blackbourn made him a receiver and, at six feet two and 200 pounds, McGee had proved to be a handful for smaller defensive backs, catching thirty-six passes as a rookie. After spending two years in the Air Force, he returned to Green Bay in 1957, got back in shape, and was one of the few Packers who had played well for Scooter McLean in 1958, catching a team-high thirty-seven passes.

Twenty-six years old now, he needed cash to make it through the off-season; he liked to stay out late, play cards, and eat well. Before the 1958 season he had asked Lewellen for an advance, and Lewellen had helped him out. Lombardi wasn't such an easy mark. He knew McGee and Hornung had never been to a party they couldn't take over. Lombardi conducted his life differently, yet he appreciated the players' high spirits. Maybe, some would suggest later, he was even slightly jealous.

Lombardi was amused by McGee's request, but he wanted players who gave their all and Max quite possibly didn't.

"Max," Lombardi said, "I'd love to help you but how do I know you're going to make the team this year?"

McGee stared at him, the light in his eyes suddenly dulled.

"If I give you money now, I could end up on the hook for it if I have to cut you," he said.

Shocked, McGee left the offices realizing that, at the very least, he couldn't take his roster spot for granted.

Lombardi smiled to himself. The chances of McGee not making the team were slim. Lombardi couldn't juggle his personnel much. Player movement was severely restricted in the years before free agency — once a player signed with a team, he was its property until it let him go. As much as Lombardi wanted to overhaul the roster, he knew it would be comprised mostly of the players who had lost under Scooter.

Still, he hoped to add a trickle of new blood, players who could help on the field and also contribute to creating a new, positive environment. He would have to draft such players, trade for them, or sign them off the scrapheap, and initially, he had figured to start the process with the team's top draft pick, Randy Duncan, a quarterback who had led Forest Evashevski's Iowa Hawkeyes to the Big Ten title and a Rose Bowl victory in 1958. Vainisi had made him the top overall pick in the 1959 draft, envisioning a solution to the Packers' quarterback dilemma.

But was Duncan, in fact, an NFL star in waiting? He was an above-average passer at best, and not especially nimble. Lombardi tried to sign him but also told Duncan not to expect to play much as a rookie. When a Canadian team, the British Columbia Lions, offered a similar contract and the chance to start, Duncan signed with them. "Randy wants to play immediately," Duncan's father told reporters. "In the NFL he would have had to wait a few years before he played regularly."

It was never a positive step when a team lost its number one draft pick, but Lombardi wasn't devastated. "Evidently, he didn't have the confidence to play in our league," he said. (Duncan played two seasons in Canada, one in the AFL, retired, and later ran a successful law practice.) Lombardi was more upset about losing Hank Bullough, an offensive guard who abruptly retired in February to become an assistant coach at Michigan State, his alma mater. Bullough, whose hulking frame cast shadows in the interior, had played as well as any Packer lineman other than Ringo in 1958. "Losing him is a blow," Lombardi said.

Vainisi had drafted more than two dozen other players, including Alex Hawkins, a South Carolina running back, in the second round, and Boyd Dowler, a tall back/receiver from Colorado, in the third round. Between the draft horde and slew of fringe players Lombardi had signed off the scrapheap, "they're going to be coming and going like trains at a station," Lombardi told newsman Art Daley with a grin, referring to training camp in July. Maybe a couple would make the team as new blood, he hoped.

But Lombardi knew rookies and fringe players couldn't really help him eliminate the team's defeatist attitude — he needed to make a major trade to take that on, change his personnel with a bold stroke. The idea percolated in his head as winter eased and he made the rounds of local civic clubs that wanted him to appear at their functions. Lombardi had put them all off until he completed his film study and could speak with authority about the team.

At the Traffic Club's annual Truckers' Night Dinner, he addressed an audience of four hundred. "I have always followed the words of General MacArthur," he said, "who once told us at West Point, 'Gentlemen, there is no substitute for victory.' That will be applied here. We as coaches, an organization, and the team shall play every game to the hilt with every ounce of fiber we have in our bodies. Whatever personnel we have available, we realize football is a violent game and that's the way we'll play it."

The crowd gave him a rousing ovation, and the event's toastmaster, a judge, stood and said, "There can be no doubt in any of our minds that the Packers are going to go in a different direction. Mr. Lombardi breeds confidence that we will not follow the losing pattern of the past."

Lombardi also elicited a roar at the team's annual stockholders meeting, where Ole's plan for restructuring the front office was officially approved. More than 150 stockholders attended the meeting at the downtown courthouse. After a debate that lasted past 11 P.M., they approved bylaw changes reducing the size of the executive committee from thirteen members to seven and eliminating the position of chairman of the board. The changes represented a seismic shift in how the Packers operated, but they were overshadowed by Lombardi's fiery speech:

"A good football team is my number one job and I am keeping that in mind at all times. I can't make any predictions, but I guarantee this: You will be proud of the team because I will be proud of the team. The Packers have many weak points but they also have lots of good points and it's around those good points that we'll build. We have finished grading every player in each of the twelve games from last season, and we discovered that some players who saw little action had high marks while others who we expected to get high marks actually got lower ratings. My coaches and I are now discussing every phase, step by step, of our offense, and the kinds of defenses we can use. I am hopeful we will win some games next fall, somehow, in some way."

Some stockholders crowded around Lombardi after his speech, extending outstretched hands and best wishes.

While on his public tour, Lombardi continued to meet more players, sometimes over the phone, sometimes in person. Jim Ringo surprised him by demanding a trade. The veteran center, who had overcome his lack of size to become a superb blocker, said he was tired of losing.

"But we're going to win here," Lombardi replied.

Ringo had barely weighed two hundred pounds when Vainisi drafted him out of Syracuse in 1953. Ten days into his rookie training camp, he borrowed seventy dollars for a bus ticket and went home to Easton, Pennsylvania, tired of getting knocked around. Vainisi talked him into coming back. Smart and agile, he learned to cut down bigger defenders and had evolved into the centerpiece of the Packers' line.

Ringo told Lombardi that Blackbourn and Ronzani had also promised to win but failed miserably. That irritated Lombardi.

"If it costs you your job, we're going to win here," Lombardi barked.

Ringo eventually rescinded his trade demand.

In early March, Lombardi phoned Billy Howton and suggested the star receiver come to Green Bay for an in-person discussion of the Packers' future. Howton, who lived in Houston, Texas, readily agreed and flew up on a Saturday. Several days beforehand, he had called Knafelc and asked for a ride from the airport to the Packer offices. When Howton arrived, Knafelc was waiting for him.

"I'm glad Vince wants to talk like this," Howton said on the drive in from the airport.

"Billy, I wouldn't call him Vince," Knafelc replied. "Scooter is gone. Things aren't like they used to be."

Howton, a fearless pass catcher, shrugged off the advice. He was known for telling quarterbacks to ignore a called play and just throw the ball to him.

"Vince just wants to talk," Howton assured Knafelc.

It was widely believed around the NFL that Howton would play a central role if Lombardi ever succeeded in rebuilding the Packers. The Rice Redhead, as he was known (having graduated from Rice

University in Texas), had been to the Pro Bowl in four of his seven seasons. He had caught fifty-three passes, including thirteen for touchdowns, as a rookie, teaming effectively with six-feet-three, 220-pound quarterback Tobin Rote, who had also come to the Packers from Rice. Rote was a force, bowling over would-be tacklers, throwing bullet passes, and treating the huddle as his sovereignty, barking instructions and pledging to "win this damn game by myself" when others seemed hesitant.

The Rote-Howton partnership had peaked in 1956 when Howton caught fifty-five passes, averaging more than twenty-one yards per reception. But after the Packers traded Rote before the next season, Howton's production had plummeted. Lombardi saw on film that the receiver, while indisputably gifted, wasn't playing his best. Some of the defensive players had been displeased with his effort.

Knafelc dropped off Howton at the team offices and headed home; he had agreed to drive the receiver back out to the airport later in the day, and figured he had hours to kill. But Howton called almost as soon as Knafelc made it home.

"Come get me," he said tersely.

Knafelc got back in his car, drove downtown, and found Howton waiting on the sidewalk outside the offices, his face ashen.

"Billy, what happened?" Knafelc asked.

"Nothing," Howton mumbled.

They drove to the airport in silence.

A month later, while at a league meeting in Philadelphia, Lombardi huddled with Cleveland's Paul Brown, who liked Lombardi and, in a way, felt responsible for seeing that he succeeded, having recommended him repeatedly during the Packers' search for a coach. Brown gave Lombardi a list of Cleveland players who could be obtained because they wouldn't make Brown's starting lineup. Lombardi saw names that interested him, negotiated with Brown, and announced the major deal he had sought as a way of shaking up the Packers. Howton was going to the Browns in exchange for Bill Quinlan, a starting defensive end, and Lew Carpenter, a veteran halfback.

66

Packer players were stunned. Howton had never played any-where else, so it was hard to imagine him wearing another uniform. He had been the team's best player, a rare source of light amid the gloom of a losing decade. And Lombardi had traded him! Wow!

Lombardi believed Howton was a bit too comfortable with los-ing, a serious problem given his stature in the locker room. He also didn't block much and was leading a drive by players throughout the league to organize a union, annoying management everywhere, Lombardi included.

Fairly or not, Lombardi concluded he would have an easier time making over his team's attitude without the smart, strong-willed, independent-minded Howton.

In Quinlan, Lombardi had acquired some of the defensive help he desperately needed. Quinlan was big, fast, tough, and recklessly threw his 250-pound body around the field. He had been a starter in Cleveland, the most accomplished player on the list Brown gave Lombardi. Why was he even on the list? He was just as fast and tough off the field, a heavy drinker and off-season gambler who flaunted curfews and other rules. Brown was tired of policing him. Lombardi knew he also would have to police Quinlan, but guessed he could control the young man. The coach was gambling that Quinlan's Sunday performances would make him worth the trouble he generated during the rest of the week. He played the game just as Lombardi liked, looking to punish the man across the line. He instantly made the Packers' defense better.

"We had to do something about the defense," Lombardi told re-porters. "We think we got help where we needed it most. We know Howton is a fine ballplayer but we're trying like everything to build up the defense. Quinlan is a top-flight end. He's young, tough, and mean. You've got to be that way. He will put pressure on the passer. He will do a job for us."

Quinlan initially balked at coming to Green Bay, telling a re-porter in his hometown of Lawrence, Massachusetts, that he wasn't pleased to be going from a contender to a last-place team. He said he was considering taking a coaching job with the Hamilton Tiger-Cats, a Canadian team.

"Would you want to go from the Yankees to the [last-place] Athletics?" Quinlan asked.

Quinlan quickly apologized to Lombardi and Vainisi for that remark, explaining that he was upset about hearing of the trade from a sportswriter, not Paul Brown. He continued to insist he was still thinking about going to Canada until Lombardi sent him a contract that included a pay raise. Quinlan was soon signed and on board.

"I changed my mind," he told the Associated Press, "because of the [salary] increase and because they've convinced me Green Bay has cleaned house. There's a whole new regime there."

Indeed, a whole new regime and, under construction, a whole new attitude.

★ 7 ★

BART STARR WAS at his off-season home in Montgomery, Alabama, when he spoke to Lombardi for the first time. The coach called to tell him there would be a camp for the Packers' quarterbacks in Green Bay near the end of June.

"Yes, sir," Starr said.

Lombardi said he wanted to introduce his offense, which was different from Scooter McLean's.

"Yes, sir," Starr said.

Giving the quarterbacks a head start would enable them to grasp the new playbook by the start of training camp in July, Lombardi said, and that would speed up the installation of the offense.

"Yes, sir," Starr said. "I'll be there."

Later that day, Starr told his wife, Cherry, about the call.

"The guy really sounds organized," Starr said.

On the other end of the line, Lombardi hung up thinking he had never heard a more polite football player.

Starr was twenty-four years old and had been with the Packers for three losing seasons. At six feet one and 190 pounds, he had a solid frame and an oval face with slightly puffy cheeks and close-cropped dark hair. He spoke in the soft butterscotch voice of a southerner, and crinkles formed at the corners of his eyes when he smiled. Cherry had been his high school sweetheart. Now they had two young sons.

Starr looked forward to the camp, hoping Lombardi would provide what he and the Packers needed to get going in the right direction. To say that Starr had struggled was an understatement. Scooter and Blackbourn had given him plenty of chances since his rookie year in 1956, but the Packers had a 3-15-1 record in games he started, and Starr had never played all four quarters of a victory. He didn't have a strong arm, wasn't a nimble runner, and seemed almost cursed with a habit of making mistakes at critical moments. Though he was popular in the locker room, some Packers believed he was just not meant to lead the team. A kindly family man, he seldom raised his voice and never told anyone to get in line. His predecessor, Tobin Rote, had been an irascible but inspiring force in the huddle, barking instructions and screaming at teammates. A quarterback had to do that sometimes.

No Packer worked harder than Starr. While some of his teammates drank and chased girls at night, he sat at home with a projector, studying film until his eyes were bleary. Blessed with a quick mind, he easily memorized playbooks, mastered the nuances of different offensive systems, and was always ready to play. At times his zealousness paid off. In the Packers' first game against Baltimore in 1958, Starr threw for more than three hundred yards and the Packers jumped ahead early. But the Colts rallied and then scored the winning points late when, summing up Starr's career, a defender intercepted his pass and returned it for a touchdown. Even on his best days, something went wrong.

Starr was the first to admit he had not fared well. There was no debate. He had thrown almost twice as many interceptions (twenty-five) as touchdowns (thirteen) in three years. A humble, team-first guy, he would never blame anyone besides himself.

But gosh, he thought, it was awfully hard to win when your team lacked discipline, organization, and leadership, as the Packers did. Starr privately wondered if some of his teammates cared about winning. Things hadn't been so bad under Blackbourn, but with Scooter the team absolutely disintegrated.

Starr was frustrated by the undisciplined environment. The son of a U.S. Air Force master sergeant, he had been raised in a strict household, by a father who was as tough on him as any strong-jawed football coach. Starr learned to respect a chain of command

70

and to appreciate rules and order. His mother, a gracious southern lady, had softened his edges as he grew into a shy, deferential young man, and Starr's high school coach wondered if he was too quiet to play quarterback. But Starr wanted the job and, beneath his polite exterior, possessed the determination his father had drilled into him. He willed himself into a star player.

Recruited by schools across the prestigious Southeastern Conference, Starr chose to play at the University of Alabama. After completing seventeen passes in the Orange Bowl as a freshman reserve, he started as a sophomore; the Tide won five games, lost two, and tied three, earning a trip to the Cotton Bowl, where they lost to Rice. But instead of continuing to rise from there, Starr's star abruptly fell. He injured his back as a junior and barely played, and then sat on the bench as a senior when a new regime took over.

As his college career ended, pro scouts had little interest in him as a quarterback; he worked out as a defensive back at the Blue-Gray All-Star Game, and the Packers selected him in the seventeenth round of the 1956 draft almost as a favor to Johnny Dee, the basketball coach at Alabama, who knew Jack Vainisi, felt badly for Starr, and recommended him. When Starr told Cherry he had been taken by Green Bay, she said, "Where is that, honey?" She sighed when he showed her a map.

He prepared for his first training camp by throwing passes through a tire with Cherry as his receiver, but the Packers assigned him uniform number 42 when he reported, thinking his best chance of making the team was as a defensive back. His passes lacked zip. Rote told him to "stop throwing cream puffs."

But he wound up making the team, beating out several more-experienced quarterbacks to back up Rote. Thrilled, he earned seventy-five hundred dollars as a rookie, and he and Cherry lived in the upstairs apartment of a family home. Rote mentored him on and off the field. They roomed together on road trips, and Rote and his wife had Starr and Cherry over for dinner. But Starr barely played, and the Packers obviously didn't think much of him. Although they traded Rote before the 1957 season, they drafted Paul Hornung and traded for Babe Parilli to fill the vacancy.

Years earlier, when Starr was in high school, his coach had arranged for him to spend a week with Parilli, then a high-profile All-American at the University of Kentucky after having been a Pennsylvania high school superstar. Starr came away idolizing the older Parilli, a deft ball-handler and sharp passer who had led the Wildcats to an historic win in the 1951 Sugar Bowl, breaking Oklahoma's thirty-one-game winning streak.

Parilli left Kentucky as college football's career leader in touchdown passes, completions, and passing yards, and the Packers selected him with the first pick in the 1952 draft, envisioning him as the game's next great quarterback. He had started relatively well as a rookie, throwing thirteen touchdowns while splitting time with Rote. He continued to split time the next season but experienced a drastic falloff, throwing nineteen interceptions and just four touchdowns. Parilli then spent two years in the military and the Packers traded him to Cleveland when he was discharged in 1956. Browns coach Paul Brown, unimpressed, shipped him back to Green Bay a year later.

Starr felt strange competing for playing time with his idol, but Parilli was so horrendous for the Packers in 1957 — he threw four touchdowns, twelve interceptions, and completed just 38 percent of his passes — that Starr took most of the snaps. Parilli was better under Scooter in 1958, but Starr again took more snaps.

Packer fans argued about whether Starr or Parilli should start, but Vainisi doubted either was the permanent solution. Lombardi felt similarly after studying them on film. While it was true he felt they (and Joe Francis) weren't entirely to blame for their 1958 performances because they had played behind a faltering line, he had a hard time envisioning them as solid starters even with more time to throw. Parilli just made so many mistakes. Starr wasn't exceptional in any way. (Blackbourn and Scooter started him because they had no other options, Lombardi conjectured.) And while Francis was bigger, stronger, and faster than the other two, he hadn't developed as a passer in Oregon State's single-wing offense. He was raw.

Lombardi told reporters his quarterback situation was "a puzzle." When he was in New York, the Giants had utilized a pair of quarterbacks in an unusual way, letting Don Heinrich start and play the first quarter before giving way to Charlie Conerly for the rest of the game. Heinrich, a future coach, adroitly probed opposing defenses, giving Conerly ideas about what to call when he took over. The Giant players didn't care for the odd arrangement, and it was never clear whether the idea was Lombardi's or Jim Lee Howell's, but it worked. Now that he was in charge, Lombardi wondered if he would need to use a similar gimmick — not because he had two quarterbacks, but because he didn't have one who was good enough to excel every week.

Throughout April and May he talked to other teams, trying to find an available quarterback who could come in and play. George Shaw, who backed up Johnny Unitas, fit the description and was on the trading block, but Baltimore wanted a high draft pick for him and Lombardi didn't like him that much. Then Lombardi heard that Lamar McHan, the Chicago Cardinals' starter for the past five seasons, was available. That interested him. McHan was a strong-armed athlete who had stepped right into a starting role in the NFL after a stellar career as a single-wing tailback at the University of Arkansas. The second player picked in the 1954 draft, he had thrown for more than sixty-five hundred yards and rushed for almost a thousand yards in five years with Chicago.

Lombardi knew McHan because the Giants and Cardinals, as Eastern Division rivals, had played twice a year. The Giants usually won, but Lombardi was always impressed with McHan's toughness and natural ability. Life on a losing team wasn't easy. McHan had thrown fifty touchdowns and seventy-seven interceptions while winning just eighteen games in five seasons. He had been beaten up and humiliated, his leadership questioned. He had never put everything together. But he had natural talent, more experience than the Packers' quarterbacks, and several years of good football left.

Walter Wolfner, the Cardinals' owner and general manager, was rebuilding. He had just shipped running back Ollie Matson to the Rams for nine players, a stunning move. A year earlier, he had drafted another quarterback, Rice's King Hill, in the first round. He had decided McHan wasn't a quarterback around whom a winner could be built. McHan was amiable enough, Wolfner thought, but he sulked when criticized and complained about dropped passes. In a bizarre incident in 1956, he had ignored his coaches during a mid-season game after asking not to play because of nerves, and then walked off the practice field the next day. Wolfner levied a three-thousand-dollar fine, the largest in NFL history, and briefly booted McHan off the team, but revoked both penalties when McHan apologized.

When Lombardi proposed a deal for McHan, Wolfner asked for a high draft pick in return. Lombardi refused, knowing Wolfner would never trade the young man to another Eastern Division team, fearing losing to him twice a year, and therefore had few suitors. They haggled until Lombardi agreed to take McHan on a conditional basis. If McHan made the team and played, the Packers would give the Cardinals a third-round draft pick. If McHan didn't make the team, the Packers would just send him back, as if a deal had never been made.

News of the trade surprised some Packers but didn't disappoint them. McHan probably made their team better, they figured. Gary Knafelc, who had played with McHan in Chicago before coming to Green Bay, knew McHan could be cranky but had considerable physical gifts. He would beat out Starr and Parilli, Knafelc guessed.

Lombardi was pleased, believing he had found a number one quarterback. He knew McHan could be a pain but "he's the best athlete in the league," Lombardi said, "and we have nothing to lose. We're getting a free look at a good prospect."

Starr shrugged when he heard about the deal. He didn't expect Lombardi to hand him the starting job; he hadn't played well enough. And he was accustomed to the Packers doubting him. They had chosen quarterbacks with their first pick in two of the past three drafts. Starr didn't blink at having to compete for a job with players whom the Packers liked more. He figured he would be fine if he worked hard.

Lombardi was anxious to get started now that McHan was on board, but training camp didn't start for another two months. Finding ways to fill time, he played golf, spoke at several coaching clinics, and dispatched Red Cochran to Louisiana to help Jim Taylor learn the offense. Vainisi had told him about Taylor's struggles with Scooter's playbook, and Lombardi wanted to give the young fullback a head start. Lombardi's offense wasn't as complicated, but he wasn't leaving anything to chance.

Many of Lombardi's golf outings took place at the Oneida Golf and Riding Club. Golf's popularity had soared in the United States during the 1950s (President Dwight Eisenhower loved the game so much he was jokingly called Duffer in Chief), and Lombardi, like many men, played it with a passion. He quickly became part of a regular game with Jack Koeppler, an insurance man he met on the first tee at Oneida. Lombardi was a long driver and adept enough around the greens to shoot in the low eighties, a respectable level. But he was frustrated that he couldn't score better, and his temper gave him fits. He couldn't intimidate a golf course like he could a football player.

Many charities and clubs in Green Bay sponsored springtime golf events, and Packer players and coaches often participated. Jesse Whittenton, the defensive back, was a superb golfer. So was Parilli. At one event Parilli and Lombardi were paired together. They hadn't met, and when they smiled and shook hands on the first tee, they agreed to bet a dollar. Lombardi played his usual up-and-down game, became frustrated, and handed Parilli a bill at the end of the round.

Parilli would later wonder if he should have just let his new coach win.

Finally, in late June, it was time for the quarterback camp. Lombardi invited McHan, Starr, Parilli, Francis, and rookies Boyd Dowler and Bob Webb, the latter a low draft pick. Starr was excited as he traveled from Alabama to Green Bay. Lombardi had told him to prepare for a week of blackboard study. That was Starr's specialty. He loved the geometry of play design, the science of breaking down defenses, the varying philosophies of different systems — football's scholarly qualities.

The players reported to the Packers' Washington Street offices at 9 A.M. on the last Monday in June. They shook hands and made

75

small talk, and then posed for a *Press-Gazette* photographer before getting down to work. In the picture, Lombardi wears a wide grin and holds a ball aloft as the players watch. McHan and Starr are the only players smiling in the photograph. McHan stands by Lombardi in the forefront, assuming the prominent role he expected to play. Starr stands in the back with a broad smile.

After the photographer left, Lombardi led the players to a meeting room. A portable blackboard was wheeled in and the players sat down in chairs. Lombardi picked up a piece of chalk and began to speak.

"Gentlemen," he said, "we have a great deal of ground to cover. We're going to do things a lot differently than they've been done here before."

Starr glanced around the room. Six quarterbacks were in attendance, but only three would make the team. Starr recognized the challenge he faced. McHan had more experience than the rest of these quarterbacks combined. McHan and Francis were terrific athletes. Parilli might finally put things together. Starr pledged to study hard, work on fundamentals, and polish his technique. His career was on the line.

He stared, mesmerized, as Lombardi moved out from the blackboard to within a foot of the players. The coach could have reached out and touched Starr.

"Gentlemen," he said, "we're going to relentlessly chase perfection, knowing full well we will not catch it, because perfection is not attainable. But we are going to relentlessly chase it because, in the process, we will catch excellence."

He paused and stared, his eyes moving from player to player. The room was silent.

"I'm not remotely interested in being just good," he said with an intensity that startled them all.

When the group took a break after an hour, Starr raced downstairs, found a phone, and called Cherry in Alabama.

"Honey, we're going to start to win," he said breathlessly. *The guy talked about perfection!*

Lombardi paced the room for the rest of the morning, discussing his philosophy and detailing his offense. The change from Scooter's system would be subtle in some ways, profound in others. Under Scooter, every play call had included a number for the ball carrier, a number for the hole he was supposed to hit, and blocking calls for the linemen. An end sweep was "forty-nine oh grace pop" — four for the left halfback, nine for the right end of the line, and the subsequent sounds representing blocking assignments. Lombardi used the same numbers but didn't include the blocking calls. The end sweep was just "forty-nine." The linemen called their own blocks at the line.

Starr loved the simplicity. Passing play-calls were similarly culled of much of their wordiness and complexity.

"What we're doing," Lombardi explained, "is throwing out the garbage."

As for the offense itself, Lombardi's was built on a power running game rather than a heavy passing load. He wanted to establish the run, forcing defenses to fortify their fronts, and then mix in passes. He recognized the passing game's importance and quick-strike potential, he said, but when a coach was too enamored of it, the offense suffered.

"More than half the passes attempted in the league last year resulted in incompletions," he said. "That's too many plays on which the ball doesn't move forward. You can move it more consistently with the run, maintain possession longer, and keep the other offense off the field. A good running game has many positive effects and also stresses the importance of being physically superior on the field."

His playbook would be staggeringly simple, one-fourth the size of Scooter's, totaling around forty plays. And the plays were as basic as white bread — runs off tackle, up the middle, and around end, passes to receivers over the middle, toward the sideline, and out of the backfield. The alignment wouldn't change from play to play. The Packers would have five interior linemen, a tight end, and a backfield of two halfbacks and a fullback behind the quarterback, with one halfback lined up wide in the "slot" position. A split end would line up on the other side. There would be no "man in motion" before the snap (some teams were experimenting with that) and two receivers would never line up on the same side.

"If you block well, execute, and eliminate mistakes, this is all you need," Lombardi said. "It doesn't matter that the other team knows what is coming."

Later that day he explained his system for changing plays at the line. The Packers had seldom done that under Scooter, but in Lombardi's system these "audible" calls were easy to execute. Having set a "snap count" (the varying signal, such as "hut one," on which the center was supposed to hike the ball) in the huddle, the quarterback signaled that he was changing the play simply by barking out that snap count when he started to shout at the line. The next number he called would be the new play. For instance, if in the huddle he had called for the ball to be snapped on "hut one," he could change the play to a sweep at the line simply by shouting "one, forty-nine."

Again, Starr marveled at the simplicity. The quarterback had time to approach the line, study the defense, and make changes without the defense having any idea what was going on.

Lombardi spent the whole day lecturing. Starr loved every minute. Lombardi would demand much more of the players. They would be fit, smart, and disciplined from now on, or they wouldn't remain on the team.

The next day, Lombardi again lectured all morning but took the players to the practice field by City Stadium in the afternoon. He ordered Dowler to line up at receiver and catch passes from the others. Dowler shrugged; that was fine with him. He was six five, all arms and legs, an angular, speedy, all-around athlete who had played both ways at Colorado. Vainisi had drafted him not knowing what role he would play, but thinking he might be an effective receiver. Dowler dropped several balls during this first practice but Lombardi liked his rangy athleticism.

On Wednesday there was more lecturing in the morning and another afternoon practice. By the end of the camp, the players had the basics down. Starr was ready for the season to begin. He was more excited about football than at any time since his high school days. Alabama had gone 4-15-2 in his last two seasons, and Green

Bay had gone 10-25-1 since he arrived. Starr was weary of losing. He couldn't wait to memorize his playbook, study as much film as he could, throw passes until his arm was sore. When the Packers started to win, he wanted to be around. McHan's arrival meant he had to compete harder for a job, but Starr wasn't concerned about his chances. He was stirred by the challenge. And he wanted to play for Vince Lombardi.

★ 8 ★

AS TRAINING CAMP neared, Jack Vainisi received a surprising phone call.

"I'm not coming back. I'm through," Bobby Dillon said.

The announcement was surprising because Dillon was just twenty-nine and had plenty of good football left. A five-time Pro Bowl selection (out of seven years in the league), he had played safety with supreme confidence the year before, grabbing six interceptions and making first-team All-Pro while the rest of the Packers stumbled. He had signed a two-year, thirty-six-thousand-dollar contract before the 1958 season, and Lombardi had counted on him to bolster the pass defense.

But Dillon had gone home to central Texas after the 1958 season and taken a promising sales job with a start-up manufacturing company. He was ready to put the losing Packers behind him and get on with his life.

Not knowing Lombardi, he spoke to Vainisi and Verne Lewellen about his decision.

"We'll miss you but that's fine," Lewellen said.

Lombardi didn't try to talk Dillon out of quitting. He focused on finding a replacement. The Packers' defensive backfield had been sliced up during the 1958 season even with Dillon at safety; it would get absolutely humiliated now unless Lombardi found help.

He called the Giants about Emlen Tunnell, a mainstay of their secondary for the past decade. An African American, Tunnell played safety like a jazz trumpeter's song, gracefully darting here and there to steal passes. He had played in every Pro Bowl from 1951 to 1957, but his skills declined so noticeably in 1958 that the Giants believed he was done. Tunnell, thirty-four, had a hard time arguing. He had been one of Lombardi's favorite Giants, smart, resourceful, positive — a winner. He might not be good enough for them now, but he certainly could play in Green Bay, Lombardi thought. The Giants offered to trade him for a small amount of cash. Lombardi just had to talk Tunnell into moving from a winning team to a loser, and from the Big Apple to little Green Bay.

"Emlen, come on out here and help me get the Packers going," Lombardi said when they spoke by phone.

"I don't know, Coach," Tunnell replied.

Green Bay's population was almost entirely white, as opposed to New York's stew of ethnicities. And the Giants always seemed to suit up three or four black players, including All-Pros Tunnell and offensive tackle Roosevelt Brown, while the Packers' record with blacks was short. Bob Mann, a receiver, had been the first black Packer, catching passes for four seasons in the early 1950s. A quarterback, Charley Brackins, took a few snaps in 1955 before being cut for missing a curfew before a game. Nate Borden, the starting defensive end, had been the only black player on the team for the past few seasons.

Most NFL teams had stopped excluding blacks in the late 1940s, shortly after Jackie Robinson broke baseball's color barrier, and black stars such as Marion Motley, Lenny Moore, and Ollie Matson had become headliners. But black players still experienced difficulties. Some white players from the South didn't want them as teammates, making life uncomfortable at best. And many black players believed an unwritten quota existed — teams just wouldn't suit up too many blacks at once, fearful of offending fans. The Redskins, owned by George Preston Marshall, a virulent racist, had never suited up a black player. The Packers had moved cautiously.

Lombardi was determined to use more black players in Green Bay. Loyal to the league, he wouldn't overtly challenge any of its operational tenets, even unwritten quotas, but having been on the receiving end of his share of taunts and slights as an Italian American growing up in New York, he was disgusted by intolerance and in favor of increased integration. He also knew from his Giants experience what black players in general, and Tunnell in particular, could bring to his team.

Tunnell had been the first black man to play for the Giants. After starring in football, basketball, and baseball as a youngster living near Philadelphia, he joined the Coast Guard and saw action in the Pacific during World War II. (A broken neck suffered in a football game kept him out of the military.) After the war, he played football at the University of Iowa and semipro baseball during the summers. In 1948 he hitchhiked to New York and asked the still-segregated Giants if he could try out, thinking the door might open in the wake of Jackie Robinson's rookie season with the Brooklyn Dodgers. Tim Mara, Wellington's brother, gave him a tryout because he had the guts to ask. The first time Tunnell wore a Giants uniform, he intercepted four passes in an exhibition game against the Packers. Management worried about what southerners on the Giants would think, but he was embraced because of his sunny nature and because he was so good.

Now, a decade later, he could help the Packers, Lombardi felt, by mentoring younger black players, injecting his winning attitude into the locker room culture, and playing anywhere close to the level he did in New York. But Tunnell continued to express reservations about Lombardi's offer. There were no jazz clubs and few available black women in Green Bay, he said. And Borden, he knew, had experienced problems. The Packers had some southern players who didn't care for blacks. (Bart Starr, on the other hand, brought Borden home for meals and made sure he was included in team activities.) And Borden, a family man, had been unable to secure decent housing, ending up in what Tunnell later described as a rundown hovel on the outskirts of town that "you wouldn't keep your dog in."

Lombardi worked on convincing Tunnell to join the Packers, suggesting life would be better in Green Bay than he thought. He could find women and jazz in Chicago, which wasn't far away. And as for a place to live, Lombardi offered to put him up all season at the Northland Hotel, the nicest place in town. The Packers would pick up his entire tab, Lombardi said.

Tunnell finally agreed. He wanted to keep playing and hopefully end his career on a better note. And he was curious to see the intense Lombardi as a head coach. It would be good theater if nothing else, Tunnell thought.

"Three laps around the goalposts!"

Shouting those words on July 24, 1959, at 10 A.M., Lombardi opened training camp. Thirty-nine players dressed in gray shorts and white T-shirts started running across the Packers' practice field next to City Stadium. The morning was overcast and hot. Lombardi wore long khaki pants, a white T-shirt, and a dark green baseball cap. His mood was buoyant, his booming voice ricocheting across the field. After a decade under Earl Blaik and Jim Lee Howell, he finally had his own team.

During the 1950s the Packers had held camp in out-of-the-way places such as Grand Rapids, Minnesota, and Stevens Point, where rental prices for fields and dorms were cheap and players couldn't get into much trouble. (Some tried, climbing through windows after curfew to drink and chase girls.) Once City Stadium and its adjacent practice field opened, though, the front office saw no need to train elsewhere. That put the team in full view of its hometown fans, so everyone in Green Bay heard Scooter McLean predict the Packers would have a "terrific" season in 1958 — an ill-advised forecast that ultimately added to the perception that he didn't have a clue. But Lombardi liked the camp setup Scooter had arranged. The team would practice twice daily, in the mornings and afternoons, and the players would sleep, eat, and meet at St. Norbert College in De Pere, six miles south of town. With its dorms, cafeteria, classrooms, morning mass services, and leafy campus, St. Norbert had everything Lombardi wanted.

Most of the players at this first workout were rookies, ordered to report two days earlier than the veterans. (Boyd Dowler and three other first-year players were in Chicago, training with a college all-star team to play the Baltimore Colts in August; the exhibition season always started with a game between the reigning champs and a team of top rookies.) A few veterans also were on hand — quarterbacks McHan, Starr, Parilli, and Francis, and linemen Jim Ringo, Jerry Kramer, Dave Hanner, and Jerry Helluin.

Kramer and Francis had expected to be on a golf course, not the practice field. They had driven to camp together from out West (Francis lived in Oregon, Kramer in Idaho), planning to enjoy a few days of fun before they got down to work. Scooter McLean and Lisle Blackbourn had allowed the veterans to come in early and play golf, drink, sleep late, and eat for free while the rookies practiced.

But nothing had gone as Kramer and Francis planned. When they arrived at St. Norbert, they found the doors locked at Sensenbrenner Hall, the three-story L-shaped brick dorm where the players stayed. They drove to the team offices on Washington Street, found Jack Vainisi, and asked him to open the dorm or put them up in a hotel. "I shouldn't have to pay eight bucks a night," Kramer groused. Lombardi walked by and growled, "What's going on?" When Vainisi explained the situation, Lombardi snapped, "Just take care of it, Jack," and walked away. Vainisi let Kramer and Francis into the dorm when the rookies reported. The next morning, before this first practice, they awoke early, grabbed their golf clubs, and headed out. But Lombardi stopped them at the door.

"Where the hell do you think you're going?" he asked.

"We're going to play golf," Kramer said.

"Like hell you are," Lombardi said. "If you sleep in this dorm, you're in this camp for good, and you make all meetings, practices, and curfews, just like everyone else."

Kramer and Francis stared at him in disbelief.

"Go get ready for practice," he said.

Surprised to find themselves on the field, they were, with the rest of the players, even more surprised by the practice itself. A Scooter-like stroll it was not.

If watching films of the 1958 season had taught Lombardi anything, it was that the Packers needed to be in better shape. Their poor conditioning had been an embarrassment; they were outscored by a combined 192–86 in the second halves of their games.

Lombardi vowed to change that. Nothing irritated him more than players who weren't in shape. They were letting down themselves and their teammates. How could you win with corner-cutting loafers looking for the easy way out?

His first coaching commandment was that players had to be in shape. At clinics, he lectured that football was a series of brief, violent confrontations, and being in shape enabled players to hit harder for longer and win more of those battles. The Packers would have that edge from now on, he vowed, telling himself he would establish that if anything in this first season. Seeing the out-of-shape Hanner and Helluin at dinner the night before, he warned them, "Just telling you right now, if you don't lose twenty pounds, you're gone."

It wasn't unusual for players to come to camp needing to drop pounds. Few trained in the off-season. Conditioning wasn't emphasized. Many players smoked cigarettes, not knowing how harmful it was. Lifting weights was frowned upon, believed to add bulk and slow you down. Diets weren't sophisticated; a player just ate less if necessary. And running more than a few miles at a time was considered silly.

If they worked out at all in the off-season, players mostly just honed their skills, throwing or catching balls. They waited until camp to "play their way into shape" in scrimmages and workouts.

The easygoing Hanner had spent the off-season at home in West Memphis, Arkansas, working as a soil conservationist and occasionally running on a Mississippi River levee for exercise, but mostly just hunting and fishing. A stout run-stopper who plugged the middle of the defensive line, he had played in Green Bay since 1952 and made All-Pro in 1957, but he feared for his future now. Scooter and Blackbourn had always let him report overweight and play his way into shape, but Lombardi wasn't nearly as forgiving. Hanner, who had a pale complexion and weighed 270 pounds, tended to wilt in the heat. He was breathing hard after the first three laps around the goalposts.

Then Lombardi called for calisthenics. The players lined up in rows expecting to limber up casually before moving on to football work; Scooter had never asked for more than a few jumping jacks. Lombardi had other ideas. He pushed them through multiple sets of pushups, sit-ups, and jumping jacks, then had them run in place. As the players huffed, he walked up and down the rows making comments.

Come on, Hanner, you can do better!

Helluin, come on, this is just the first morning! It'll be hotter this afternoon!

Ringo felt his face redden. Hanner began to feel faint. Helluin, a 275-pound defensive lineman who had sat out the entire 1958 season after dislocating a shoulder during a training-camp scrimmage, feared he might get sick.

The last exercise was Lombardi's favorite. It was known as the grass drill. The players ran in place, lifting their knees high, until Lombardi hollered "Down!" and they flopped on their bellies. When Lombardi hollered "Up!" they scrambled to their feet and ran in place again until the next down command. They went through the cycle of up-downs for two, three, five minutes, sweat pouring off their chins. Lombardi finally blew his whistle, ending his "warm-ups."

The players knew what to do next, having studied the detailed practice schedule posted in the locker room. They separated into groups and worked with their position coaches for a half hour, the offensive backs with Red Cochran, the offensive linemen with Bill Austin, the linebackers and defensive linemen with Phil Bengston, and the defensive backs with Norb Hecker. Lombardi worked with the quarterbacks and receivers. Each group moved through drills focusing on fundamentals, running, throwing, catching, and blocking.

After twenty minutes Lombardi went to watch the offensive linemen, the foundation of his run-oriented offense. Seven were lined up in a row in front of an iron blocking sled. Lombardi jumped on the back of the sled, facing the linemen, and shouted for them to get into their stances and explode in unison into the padded dummies hanging from the sled. "Drive! Drive!" he cried as together the blockers hit the sled, pushing it across the grass in jerks. When they were finished, he shouted, "No, that didn't feel good. Do it again."

The blockers returned to their stances and hit the sled, moving it as Lombardi held on with both hands.

"Better, better. That felt good," he said.

Another seven blockers stepped in front of the sled and hit it.

"Damn! That's good!" Lombardi exclaimed.

After ten minutes on the sled, Lombardi blew his whistle. The offensive and defensive units gathered on opposite ends of the field and ran through plays. Lombardi ran the offense while Bengston focused on the defense. They called out different formations and plays and watched the players in "dummy" sequences, without opposition. After a half hour, Lombardi blew the whistle and the units came together and practiced against each other without making contact. Finally, Lombardi called for a series of forty-yard sprints and ended the workout.

The players were hollow-eyed as they trudged up the hill to the locker room and boarded two yellow buses for the ride back to St. Norbert. Scooter's workouts hadn't been nearly as crisp, organized, or demanding. Back at St. Norbert they spilled out of the buses, went to their rooms, and flopped on their beds, exhausted.

Soon, lunch was served at the cafeteria, located across a quadrangle from the dorm. The players would eat, return to their rooms to rest, and then reboard the buses and head back to Green Bay for another practice that afternoon. Lombardi planned to hold these "two-a-day" sessions for three weeks, until the team's slate of exhibition games began in mid-August. They would play six such games, one per week, as preparation for the regular season, which began on September 27.

During lunch, more veterans arrived expecting to enjoy a few days of fun. Norm Masters, the offensive tackle, received his room assignment and saw Bill Austin, his position coach, as he walked down the hall carrying his bags. "Good to see you, Norm," Austin said, extending a hand. They spoke for several minutes and then Austin said, "OK, the bus leaves for practice at three." Masters replied, "What do you mean 'the bus leaves at three'?" Austin explained that Lombardi expected any player in camp to attend all practices and meetings.

When Masters told him what had gone on before, Austin suggested Masters speak to Lombardi about it, knowing how that would go. Masters dropped off his bags, found Lombardi's room on the first floor, and knocked. The coach answered, shook hands, and quickly cut off the conversation. He was in charge now, he said, with new rules in place. And that was that. Masters trudged back upstairs to change before going over to eat lunch. He ran into Ringo, still recovering from the morning practice.

"Better get yourself ready, pal," Ringo said with a wan smile. "We've never had practices like this around here. This guy means business. The conditioning is brutal."

Masters soon found himself on a bus headed for practice, and a few minutes later, in the midst of his first grass drill, flopping up and down like a fish on a line. The Packers, he realized, would never be the same.

After lunch Hanner rested in his room, unsure whether he would survive the afternoon practice. He received a phone call from Forrest Gregg, who was in Milwaukee, one hundred miles from St. Norbert. Gregg had driven up from Texas and didn't have to report for another thirty hours.

"Hey, what's going on, Dave?" Gregg asked.

Hanner said, simply, "Wow."

"What?" Gregg asked.

"This guy is . . . working our asses off," Hanner said.

Gregg said he planned to wait until the veteran deadline to report.

"If I were you, Forrest, I would get your ass up here immediately," Hanner said.

Gregg drove up that afternoon and met Lombardi at breakfast the next morning.

"I'm glad you're here. Good move, son. You're smart to come in early," Lombardi said.

Gregg found Hanner and thanked him for the advice, but Hanner was preoccupied with his own situation. That morning he became lightheaded during the grass drill and vomited. All this running and jumping had pushed him to the brink of what he could handle so early in camp. There was no water on the field — its presence would soften players, the thinking went — but a trainer gave him a handful of the ice kept on hand to limit swelling on bruises and sprains. Hanner sucked on the ice but kept vomiting, his body temperature soaring. Lombardi told him to go sit under a tree. Hanner did but couldn't stop throwing up. Finally, he left practice with a trainer and was driven to St. Vincent Hospital, where he was given fluids in the emergency room. He stabilized during an overnight stay and was at practice the next afternoon.

Lombardi didn't back off. Hanner made a return visit to the emergency room a few days later, and was back again for a third time shortly after that, wondering if he might die before Lombardi got him in shape. His teammates started joking that he had two rooms in camp this year, one at St. Norbert and one at St. Vincent.

Max McGee and Howie Ferguson also arrived early thinking they didn't have to practice. They ate dinner with the team, disappeared, and came home drunk after curfew. The next morning Lombardi told them they would be practicing with the rookies that day. The carefree McGee didn't complain, but Ferguson blew up.

"I don't have to be on the field until tomorrow!" he shouted.

"As far as I'm concerned, mister, when you ate a meal here, you became part of this camp," Lombardi replied. "Therefore, you abide by all of my rules."

They argued until Ferguson huffed out, not knowing his role as the number one fullback was already tenuous because of what Jim Taylor had shown Lombardi on film.

Ferguson, who had been with the Packers for six seasons, grumbled but went to practice. Four days later, Lombardi traded him to Pittsburgh.

The NFL draft lasted thirty rounds, enabling each of the twelve teams to pick up far more players than they needed. Every summer, hordes of rookies descended on training camps, scurried around for a week, got cut, and went home to anonymity, dreams dashed.

The rookies at Lombardi's first camp included many soon to be forgotten — Jim Hurd, Sam Tuccio, Leroy Hardee, Ken Higginbotham, Jerry Epps, Ken Kerr, Tom Secules, Ben Lawyer, and more. Vainisi had seen enough in each of them to want to take a look at them, but Lombardi started making decisions after just a few days of camp.

Not good enough.

Too slow.

Bad hands.

Sorry, we have to let you go.

Tim Brown, a running back from Ball State, in Muncie, Indiana, didn't figure to last long. His small-time school had never produced an NFL player. He had been the 312th player selected overall out of 360 league-wide. He wasn't physically formidable at five feet eleven and 190 pounds.

When he arrived at St. Norbert, he picked up a *Press-Gazette* and read that he was one of many players who shouldn't even bother to unpack his bags.

That annoyed him.

Brown, an African American, had overcome enormous hardships to make it this far. His father, an Army cook, didn't believe in education and tried to pull him from school. His divorced parents lacked the money to raise him, so Brown entered the Indiana Soldiers' and Sailors' Children's Home, near Knightstown, Indiana, at age twelve. But he thrived in the strict environment, excelling in the classroom and starring on the football field as a darting, speedy ball carrier. Moving on to Ball State, he continued as a game-breaking runner while working six hours a day to pay for his tuition. He had graduated just before he came to Green Bay for camp, taking his first plane flight.

Brown didn't expect to last long in camp. He knew he could play football, but other guys could, too. If it didn't work out, he would just go on to something else, he figured. He wasn't a typical jock. He had a terrific singing voice, could take over a dance floor, and after years in mostly all-white settings, had developed a strong inner spirit. If he wasn't going to make it in pro football, he was at least going to fail with his head held high.

Shouldn't even unpack, huh?

The taunt echoed in his head as he checked into Sensenbrenner

Hall and went to meet Lombardi, who made him wait at the office door for fifteen minutes while he talked on the phone — a trick coaches used to make cowed youngsters more nervous.

Finally, Lombardi got off the phone and motioned for Brown to come in. They shook hands, and Lombardi slowly and silently looked him up and down.

"So, you're Brown," he finally said.

Brown wanted to say, "In more ways than one," but checked his tongue.

"Yes, sir," he said.

"You don't look like a football player," Lombardi commented.

"Well, I'm not sure what you think a football player looks like," Brown replied. "I'm not a big lineman. I'm a running back."

Lombardi eyed him. "So you're a smart guy, huh?" he asked.

"Well, sir, I did just graduate from college," he answered.

Lombardi waved a hand and said, "Go on, get out of here."

Brown turned to leave, but stopped at the door and looked back. "You know what I'm going to do, sir? I'm going to go unpack," he said.

He couldn't help himself and didn't regret saying it, but the remark put him squarely in Lombardi's crosshairs. Suddenly, he was no longer just another faceless low-round draft pick. He was Brown, the wiseass.

By the eve of the first full-squad practice, fifty-six players were in camp. They gathered in a meeting room after dinner, squeezed into tight rows of varnished oak classroom chairs. Lombardi paused briefly before entering, double-checking what he planned to say. In two months, by the Packers' first regular-season game in late September, he had to have his offense and Bengston's defense up and running, and starters selected at many positions, including quarterback. Most importantly, he had to have the players believing in his new, strict regimen.

Many of the players had either met Lombardi or heard about his brutal practices. They fell silent when he stepped in front of them and began to speak.

"Gentlemen, we're going to have a football team here," he said, "and we're going to win some games. Do you know why? You are going to have confidence in me and my system. By being alert, you are going to make fewer mistakes than your opponents. By working harder, you are going to out-execute, out-block, and out-tackle every team that comes your way."

He paused. The room was silent.

"I've never been a losing coach and don't intend to start here. There is no one big enough to think he's got the team made and can do what he wants. Trains and planes are coming in and leaving Green Bay every day, and he'll be on one of them. I won't. I'm going to find thirty-six men who have the pride to make any sacrifice to win. There are such men. If they're not here, I will get them. If you're not one, if you don't want to play, you might as well leave right now."

Starr, who had been so inspired by Lombardi's opening speech at quarterback camp a month earlier, could tell by looking around that many of his teammates were reacting similarly to their first brush with the new coach. It was stunning to imagine the languid Packers in the hands of such a clear-eyed, forceful leader.

Bill Forester, a veteran team captain who thought he had seen everything, felt sweat on his palms. Lombardi made him want to put on pads and hit someone.

Lombardi continued: "I've been up here all year, and I've learned a lot. I know how the townspeople are and what they think of you men. I know that in a small town you need definite rules and regulations. Anybody who breaks the rules will be taken care of in my way. You may not be a tackle. You may not be a guard. You may not be a back. But you will be a professional."

The players looked at each other. *Well. So much for the easy life.*

Lombardi laid out his rules, which, he said, would be vigorously enforced. The training camp curfew was 11 P.M., midnight on Saturdays, and that meant in bed with lights off. Players would be fined at least twenty-five dollars for missing curfew, and ten dollars for every minute they were late to meals, meetings, and practices.

"A man who is late for a meeting or the bus will be sloppy. He won't run pass routes right," Lombardi declared, adding that all fine money would be used to pay for a party at the end of the season.

On the subject of drinking, Lombardi acknowledged that players were adults who needed to relax; Lombardi himself liked going to supper clubs and having a cocktail or two. But players on the Packers had to be extra careful about where and how they drank, he said, because they lived in a small town where everyone gossiped and knew what they did.

Since coming to Green Bay, he said, he had met hundreds of fans claiming to have seen Packers having a good time — a little too good on occasion, he added, glancing at Hornung and McGee. That wasn't good for the team's reputation, he said. Some fans thought the players cared less about winning than having a good time.

As a result, several bars would now be off-limits, Lombardi said, including the Picadilly, Hornung's and McGee's favorite spot. And wherever they were, they had to sit at tables or booths. No standing at the bar and drinking.

"I won't stand for that," Lombardi said. "I don't care if the player is drinking ginger ale and talking to a friend, it just doesn't look good."

The fine for getting caught standing at a bar was $150, he said.

The players listened silently to these new rules, a fine for this, a fine for that. Some were annoyed, others terrified. When Lombardi finished and asked for questions, no hands went up. Lombardi dismissed them and, watching them leave the room, wondered if some might decide to quit the team.

As the players walked to their rooms, Jerry Kramer spoke to Jim Taylor.

"This guy is nuts," Kramer said softly.

Taylor smiled and shrugged.

Yeah, maybe a little. But you better get used to it.

Maybe he's just scaring us, just seeing who can take him being a hard-ass.

Maybe.

Maybe he'll ease up once he weeds out the guys he doesn't like.

93

Maybe.

But what if he doesn't ease up? What are we going to do then?

Before practice the next morning, Lombardi pulled McGee aside and asked how the speech had gone over. McGee was surprised to see him so nervous.

"It went great, Coach, just great," McGee said with a smile.

No player took a train or plane out of town. They practiced together for the first time under Lombardi that morning. In front of several hundred fans, they started with three laps around the goalposts and a set of calisthenics culminating with the grass drill, and then worked in groups for an hour before ending the workout with sprints.

What is this shit? Where did Scooter go?

Sharp-eyed and sarcastic, Lombardi pulled two lethargic rookies out of their groups and made them run more. *If you don't want to give me a hundred percent, go on up to the locker room and turn in your equipment!* When McGee trotted back to the huddle a little too casually after missing a pass, Lombardi ordered him to take two more laps. *If you don't feel like running hard today, just let me know!*

Watching McGee, the team's top receiver, run extra laps, the players knew Lombardi was serious about having everyone follow his rules.

Then the same point was driven home off the field when the first player to be fined for breaking curfew was Tunnell, one of Lombardi's favorites.

"That'll be fifty bucks, Em," the coach barked as Tunnell tried to sneak past his room one night shortly after 11 P.M.

A few days later, Lombardi went on a room check at 11 P.M. and found Jim Taylor sitting on the edge of his bed with his socks and shorts on.

"What time you got, Jimmy?" Lombardi asked.

"Eleven, sir," Taylor replied.

"You're supposed to be in bed at eleven, right, Jimmy?" Lombardi asked.

"Yes, sir."

"Jimmy, that'll cost you twenty-five dollars."

After a week of practices, Lombardi ratcheted up the intensity. "We may not have the best team in the league, but we're going to have the best legs," he told reporters with a smile.

The players put on pads and helmets and were introduced to the nutcracker drill, another of Lombardi's favorites. A quarterback lined up behind a blocker, in front of a running back and opposite a single defender, took a snap, and handed the ball to the back. The blocker's job was to keep the defender off the runner. The defender's job was to get to the runner.

Lombardi loved the bare setting, players going one-on-one, nowhere to hide. He ran the drill in front of the whole squad, criticizing and complimenting as he saw who relished contact and who just endured it. "Fire out!" he yelled at the linemen. "Bark those signals!" he shouted at the quarterbacks. When he liked a block, he clapped his hands and shouted "Hot dog!" When he saw a mistake, he jabbed a finger at the player's chin. *What the hell are you doing? You call yourself a pro football player?*

Some players quickly learned to dread the drill, preferring not to hit anyone. As they waited in opposing lines until it was their turn, they counted to see who they would be matched up against. McGee shuffled back and forth in line to avoid having to face Tom Bettis, the hard-hitting linebacker.

Always pushing harder, Lombardi added a punishing twist to a basic drill in which the offensive and defensive units lined up, ran through plays without opposition, and sprinted forty yards downfield to complete the assignment. If they didn't come off the ball in perfect unison, they had to repeat the play and sprint the forty yards again.

"I don't want to see a typewriter, different keys going up and down at different times!" he shouted. "I want to see perfection!"

There was that word again. *Perfection.* The players realized that was Lombardi's ultimate goal, not only in this drill but also for the Packers in general. They grew accustomed to coming off the ball

95

and running forty yards downfield until they heard him shout angrily that one of them had flinched before the snap.

No! Do it again! No mistakes this time!

Over and over, they ran the play, hoping for the best.

No! Again!

Again!

Again! Again! Again!

Red-faced and exhausted, the players exhorted each other to avoid mistakes and end the misery.

Come on! Get it right! Everyone!

Hearing their desperation, Lombardi smiled inwardly. They're starting to understand what they have to do, he thought.

The practices were the toughest the players had experienced as pros, but many came from college programs in which tough coaches ran boot-camp-style workouts, so they had been through this before. Parilli had played for the brutal Bear Bryant; he could handle Lombardi.

It was, as the days passed, the mental challenge that became daunting, the fact that Lombardi refused to tolerate mistakes, demanding a standard they had never been asked to reach.

Perfection.

Jerry Kramer had mixed emotions about it. He enjoyed getting in shape and thought the team would probably win a few more games, but honestly, he wasn't sure he wanted to work this hard. Pro football had been, for him, kind of a lark until now. An affable, blond hulk with a quick wit and dazzling white smile, he had grown up in Idaho, far from the bright lights, and played for a school (the University of Idaho) that had never produced a drafted pro. But scouts noticed him — quick-footed 250-pound linemen tend to get discovered wherever they play — and he was drafted by the Packers and invited to play on the college all-star team in August. A coach at that camp, John Sandusky, a retired NFL lineman, told him he wasn't good enough to make the Packers, but Kramer ended up starting every game as a rookie, enjoying himself immensely in spite of the team's miseries. Scooter's practices were easy, the paychecks cashed, and the beer flowed all season. Hornung and McGee were a riot. It wasn't a bad life for a twenty-three-year-old country boy who had never expected to play pro football.

But now, Lombardi was rocking his pleasant little boat ride. The coach seemed to have it in for him in particular, calling him "a cow" and "the worst guard I've ever seen" after he jumped offside in a drill one afternoon. Kramer sat disconsolately at his locker after that workout until Lombardi approached, put his arm around Kramer's shoulders, and said, "Son, one of these days you're going to be a great guard in this league."

Some players couldn't take it. Alex Hawkins, the rookie back from South Carolina, loathed Lombardi's nonstop cursing and name-calling. A renowned college star with a cocky edge, he was unaccustomed to any criticism, much less hard-edged sarcasm. What a jerk, Hawkins thought as Lombardi lambasted him one day.

But most players realized Lombardi was just trying to make them better. Bettis lost twenty-five pounds in two weeks. Hanner dropped twenty. Forester dropped ten. Lombardi might be a madman, they thought, but if you didn't buy what he was selling, look out. Jerry Helluin, a Packer since 1954, had come to camp overweight and struggled through the grass drills and sprints. He was a popular veteran but failed to shed pounds quickly, and Lombardi called him into the office one morning.

Sorry, Jerry, we're letting you go.

One morning McGee and Hornung stood to the side during a blocking drill, breathing hard after a set of sprints. Watching Lombardi chastise the linemen, they shook their heads.

What an asshole. I can't believe him.

Yeah.

It's like he's never satisfied.

Then they noticed Lombardi's son, Vincent, standing close enough to hear their conversation.

Shit!

Did he hear?

Vincent smiled to himself. He was around the players every day, picking up towels, carrying buckets, doing whatever anyone asked on the field and in the locker room. Quiet and diligent, he had been a training camp fixture in New York when Lombardi was on Jim Lee Howell's staff, and he was excited to have the same job in Green Bay now that his father was a head coach.

The Packer players didn't trust him, fearing he would relay their private complaints to his father and the other coaches.

Nice kid. Nicer than his dad. But who knows what he's saying?

In New York the players had similar concerns until they discovered Vincent admired them, was on their side if any, and would never rat on them. From then on, they expressed themselves honestly in front of him.

But it was one thing to be an assistant coach's son and another to be the head coach's son, especially this head coach's son. The Packers shied away from Vincent until Emlen Tunnell stepped in after hearing several players complain about the youngster's continuing presence in their midst. Tunnell explained that the Giants also worried until they discovered Vincent would never betray them.

He's fine. He's good. He's a great kid.

The players began to speak freely in front of Vincent, complaining about his father's brutal practices and (in their mind) futile search for perfection.

Fucking guy jabbed his finger right at my chin. I'd like to slug him.

I don't know who he thinks he is.

One day, after leaning over to pick up a towel in the locker room as he listened to more complaints, Vincent stood up and eyed the players.

"You think you have it tough?" he said. "I have to live with him!"

Tim Brown, the rookie back, was opening eyes — in more ways than one. He was the quickest player in camp and consistently finished ahead of his teammates in the sprints at the end of practices. He gained good yardage on sweeps and could catch passes out of the backfield. He might be good enough to play in the NFL, it seemed.

But Lombardi was constantly on him, having decided he was a little too cocky and spirited for his own good.

Brown barked right back at him, startling the veterans who were terrified of their new coach.

"Don't they run through the hole at Ball State?" Lombardi shouted after Brown improvised on a carry during a drill.

"At Ball State we had holes, sir," Brown said.

Lombardi snorted. The linemen stared at Brown in the huddle.

No holes, huh? Fuck you!

Brown was one of four black players in camp, along with Borden, Tunnell, and A. D. Williams, a speedy young receiver just out of the Army. The two veterans were assured of making the team, and Brown had a shot. But Brown was different from the others. Borden and Tunnell were from a generation that was just happy to be playing and didn't want to cause trouble. Williams was too scared even to speak. Brown didn't mind speaking out and standing up for himself — and his rights. He had lived with segregation for as long as he could remember, and had a diminishing tolerance for it. Some of his new teammates didn't like that about him.

Brown had become acquainted with a young white girl from De Pere early in camp, nothing major, just a friendship, and she invited him over to her parents' house for dinner one evening. He went, and several veterans reported him to Lombardi.

Brown is dating a white girl.

The next day, wanting his position on such issues clearly known, Lombardi blew his whistle during practice and asked the players to gather around him.

"If I ever hear 'nigger' or 'dago' or anything like that, regardless of who you are, you're through here," he said. "You can't play for me if you have any kind of prejudice."

Everyone was adjusting to life with Lombardi. Executive committee members had attended the evening player meetings during camp when Scooter and Blackbourn were in charge, but Lombardi didn't want them around.

"What are you doing here?" he asked one night after spotting Dominic Olejniczak in the back of the room during a meeting.

Later, he told Ole that meetings were just for players and coaches now.

Nothing about the Packers was the same as before, it seemed. Lombardi even set new rules for the reporters covering the team. Previously, they could come and go as they wanted during camp; the *Milwaukee Sentinel*'s Bud Lea, a Green Bay native, had stayed with his parents when he covered the Packers the year before. Lombardi didn't want him doing that. "If you're covering camp, you stay with us here at St. Norbert," he told Lea.

"Why in the world do I have to do that?" Lea asked.

Lombardi explained that the reporters covering the New York Giants stayed with the team during camp.

"This is the rule here now," the new coach said with a shrug.

Lombardi was worried about controlling the press. Coming from New York, with its array of newspapers, he was used to aggressive reporters asking tough questions and competing for scoops. Although he respected their way with words, he saw them primarily as an annoyance and was gruff and intentionally bland around them.

It couldn't hurt to show them who was boss and corral them at Sensenbrenner Hall, he thought.

Lea, furious, considered leaving camp, but knew his editor wouldn't go for that. He was on assignment, had a job to do. And Lombardi wasn't the kind of coach you challenged. Most of the reporters acquiesced and moved into Sensenbrenner Hall, sharing double rooms just like the players. Lea gave in and moved into a room with a wire service reporter who snored.

Grumbling, he went about his business for a couple of days but then noticed that Lombardi, distracted by what was happening on the field, was paying no attention to the reporters. He moved out of the dorm, back in with his parents, and continued to cover camp, and Lombardi never said a word.

Lea initially felt he had won a power struggle, but soon realized that while Lombardi had yielded on this issue, the new coach was going to be much tougher on the press than Blackbourn or Scooter ever were.

Coach, are any players surprising you with their play?
A couple, I suppose.

Any names you care to give us?
No.
Are you pleased with the team's overall attitude?
What kind of a question is that?

Before practice one afternoon, Lombardi stopped in the doorway of the small room used by Bud Jorgensen, the Packers' trainer. A few players were sitting on the table in the middle of the room, having minor injuries checked out.

"Anyone in a bad way in here?" he asked loudly.

"No, sir," came a meek response.

"Good. See you on the field," Lombardi said.

He was as understanding as any coach about serious injuries, but had no tolerance for players who submitted to routine aches and pains. Football was a tough game; he wanted tough players. The Packers quickly learned to avoid Jorgensen's table and get on the field if all they had was a bruise or sprain. Lombardi wanted them to endure pain, and as he said, if you didn't like it, you could play elsewhere.

Living with pain and in fear of upsetting their coach, the players sought ways to relieve the stress. After the afternoon practices they raced to get on the first bus back to St. Norbert. Players on that bus had enough time to run across the street to a bar in De Pere and down a couple of beers before dinner, while those on the second bus arrived too late.

Sometimes after dinner, the veteran leaders ordered the rookies to stand up and sing — a pro football hazing tradition. Lombardi sat back with a bemused smile as the rookies croaked through off-key versions of their college fight songs and the veterans laughed and hooted them down.

When Tim Brown was called on, he stood up with a smile and asked what everyone wanted to hear. They didn't know he was a professional-caliber singer.

"Anything!" the veterans shouted.

Brown broke into a doo-wop classic, bouncing between high and low notes as he soulfully shook his shoulders.

"Sit down!!!!!" the annoyed veterans yelled.

And Lombardi doled out little perks along the way. If the players had small children, as many did, they could bring them to practice, he said, and the kids were encouraged to dash onto the field and hug their fathers after the final whistle. Determined to build a positive family atmosphere, Lombardi smiled when the players' wives thanked him for allowing their kids to experience that. It was hard to say who loved the moment more, the children, players, wives, or Lombardi himself, who turned from sarcastic to sentimental, shouting the children's names as they sprinted across the field.

The players also tried to find the humor in their situation when they could. One day Lombardi railed at them throughout the afternoon workout, complaining loudly about dropped passes, botched fundamentals, and forgotten assignments. Obviously in a foul mood, he picked back up during a meeting that evening, telling them they had a lot to learn. Dramatically, he held a ball aloft and said, "We're starting at the beginning. Gentlemen, this is a football."

McGee quickly raised his hand. "Coach?" he asked.

"What?" Lombardi barked, annoyed at the interruption.

"Can you not go so fast?" McGee said.

Lombardi couldn't help laughing. Practice went better the next day.

In the evenings Lombardi stood at a blackboard and slowly introduced his offense, painstakingly explaining every player's role on every snap. Lamar McHan was astounded at how clearly he presented the material. "I've always had coaches who told me to do things, but didn't tell me why. Lombardi tells you why," McHan said.

Lombardi's attention never strayed from his quarterbacks for long. Monitoring their performances in practices, scrimmages, and meetings, he wanted them not only to make plays but also to understand his offensive philosophy. They would be calling the plays on the field, so it was imperative that they understood what he wanted.

Privately, he shook his head at how easy some coaches had it with their quarterbacks; with a John Unitas, Bobby Layne, or Billy Wade on your roster, all you did was put them on the field and let the good things happen. But most teams didn't have that luxury and resorted to different approaches, often involving two quarterbacks. The Giants started games with Heinrich and finished with Conerly. Starr and Parilli had alternated in 1958, as had the 49ers' Y. A. Tittle and John Brodie, the Bears' Ed Brown and Zeke Bratkowski, and the Cardinals' McHan and M. C. Reynolds.

Lombardi hoped one of his four quarterbacks would make his job easy and emerge as clearly superior. McHan was the obvious candidate, having played so much more — and so much better — than the others as a pro. Lombardi liked what he saw of McHan so far. It was hard to believe the young man had run the single-wing offense at Arkansas; he could really sling passes. He seemed to be picking up the offense, too. Lombardi's affection for him was obvious. Watching McHan during a passing drill one day, he said, "Son, you're going to lead the league in passing."

The other three quarterbacks heard the comment and reasoned that McHan had the inside track on the starting job. McHan wasn't so sure. "I don't know. You guys are good. He doesn't need me here. He might send me back to Chicago," he said.

The others smiled at his concern. "Lamar, you're not only going to be here, but you're going to be starting," Parilli said.

"I'll believe it when I see it," McHan replied.

The other three also had their positive attributes, Lombardi thought. Parilli was smooth, calm, an accurate passer. Francis was a fast, elusive runner, almost a halfback more than a quarterback; he gained yardage when Lombardi, experimenting, let him run sweeps. And Starr excelled in the classroom, answering first when Lombardi took the quarterbacks alone into meetings and asked how to attack certain defenses.

OK, umbrella zone, and they come on a red-dog from the weak side. What do you do? Anyone?

Check off to Paul, sir. Send him where the linebacker came from.

Hmmm. Good, Bart.

There was no doubt Starr was a smart young man, Lombardi thought. But he ran into problems applying his knowledge on the field. It was almost painful to watch him hesitate and make mistakes, obviously thinking too hard.

During a scrimmage before hundreds of fans on a sweltering Saturday in early August, Starr retreated to pass, saw a defender moving toward his receiver, and threw anyway. The pass was intercepted.

"STARR!!! You could see that ball was going to be intercepted and you still threw it!"

Starr's shoulders sagged.

"Yes, sir."

"Well . . . throw one more like that and you're gone!"

Starr trudged to the sideline. It was so frustrating to make avoidable mistakes! Lombardi didn't tolerate them, he knew. He had to do better, he told himself — just had to, or he might be out of a job.

Come on, Bart, think!

Two days later, Lombardi approached Starr in the locker room and said he would start the Packers' first exhibition game against the Bears in Milwaukee on August 15.

"You deserve the chance," Lombardi said. "Your knowledge and preparation are outstanding."

Starr was astounded. Playing for this guy was like being attached to a yo-yo, he thought. He knocked you down so hard it made you dizzy, but he pulled you back up just as hard.

If I just stay calm and keep believing in myself, Starr thought, I think I can handle him.

Paul Hornung's life had turned inside out. On the field, where little had gone right for him in the NFL, he suddenly was flourishing; at halfback, his new position, he was an integral part of Lombardi's offense, running sweeps, catching passes, throwing options, making blocks. What a blast! But off the field, where he always enjoyed himself, he was cooped up in the dorm and adjusting to Lombardi's stricter rules.

Finally, he couldn't take it anymore and organized an escape. He and McGee and Kramer would wait until 11:30 P.M., tiptoe out, and drive across town to a pizza joint. Lombardi would never know, they thought.

As they crept down the hall that night, Jim Ringo and Dave Hanner heard them and came along. Bill Quinlan, who never missed a good time, also joined the group. They stayed out until 2 A.M., drove back to St. Norbert, crept into their rooms, and slept for a few hours before rising for breakfast. They thought they had gotten away with it, but at a meeting that night, Lombardi said, "People have been phoning me all day, saying they've seen some of you guys out after curfew. But I don't pay attention to those crank calls."

Hornung swore Lombardi knew precisely who had gone out and what had happened, but for some reason, chose not to punish them.

This guy is something else, the Golden Boy thought.

Lombardi had hoped some of the new players would help change the team's personality and erase the Packer defeatism that had been so obvious on film. He got his wish. One day in the locker room, Quinlan, who had played on a winning team in Cleveland, listened to several holdovers laughing about a loss the year before.

"No wonder you guys aren't champions. You talk like you enjoy getting beat," he said.

Turning to Hanner, Quinlan said, "You're not smart enough to be an end, Dave. You can't diagnose plays. You don't have the speed. You're not tough enough."

The redheaded Hanner flushed with anger. "OK, Quinlan, let's go on outside and settle this," he drawled.

Quinlan stared back for a moment, but then broke into a broad smile. "That's the way, Dave," he said warmly. "Now you're talking like a champion."

Jim Taylor was loving life. After a dismal rookie year, his second season was off to a terrific start.

As a rookie he had spent countless hours trying to make sense of Scooter McLean's complex playbook, and ended up on the bench.

105

Now, Lombardi's playbook was simple, the assignments made sense, and Lombardi had even sent Red Cochran to Louisiana during the off-season to tutor him, just so Taylor would completely understand what was going on. How nice was that? And then Lombardi had all but handed him a starting job by trading Howie Ferguson.

Taylor couldn't help thinking Lombardi liked him. The guy never said so, and Taylor certainly received his share of the coach's brutal criticism, from which, it seemed, no one was spared. *Taylor, you dumb ass, what in the hell are you doing?* But Taylor didn't mind; his skin was thick. And Lombardi didn't tear into him nearly as harshly as he did some of the others. Maybe, Taylor thought, the coach just liked the way he played, giving and taking punishment without saying a word. Built low and stocky with his sandy hair in a squared-off flattop, Taylor had bulging muscles in his arms, shoulders, chest, and trunk. When he broke into the secondary during scrimmages, he ran right at his pursuers rather than angling away. *You can dish it out but you're going to take it, too.*

Taylor felt Lombardi's offense, with its emphasis on straight-ahead football, had almost been devised with him in mind. He had sat, transfixed, as Lombardi explained the philosophy in an offensive meeting one evening in camp.

"Most plays last just three or four seconds," Lombardi said. "So you have to execute immediately, upon the snap of the ball. You have to know where you're going and move decisively. Linemen, you have to win that initial conflict, make the hit, drive your man, stay on your man. If you can move him back even just a foot or two, he doesn't beat you and the play can succeed. This is how we're going to win. Defenders want to penetrate. Once they cross that line of scrimmage, the play is destroyed. So our mentality is simple: 'Snap the ball, hit your man, move him back a step or two.' We win right there. We're going to go man on man, run it at you, send runners into the holes, pick up four or five yards, move those [first down] chains. And there isn't anything you can do about it because we're going to execute better."

Taylor wanted to stand up and cheer.

Damn! God damn! Now that's football!

Taylor's background was unusual for an NFL player. Growing up in Baton Rouge, Louisiana, as the middle brother of three, he was his family's only athlete. His brothers studied business (and would become, respectively, an accountant and a real estate developer). Taylor's first athletic love was basketball; he made the Baton Rouge High School varsity as a freshman and developed into a pounding forward who chased rebounds, sank jumpers, and made a national all-star team as a senior.

Unlike his brothers, he wasn't much of a student. But he was curious, open to new ideas, and that led him to Alvin Roy, a pioneering strength coach who lived in Baton Rouge. Roy had become a believer in weight training while in the Army in the 1940s and helped manage the gold-medal-winning U.S. weightlifting team at the 1952 Olympics. Returning to Baton Rouge, he convinced the football coach at Istrouma High School to put players on a weight-lifting program, no small feat when the football world believed lifting weights slowed players down. Istrouma, led by Billy Cannon, a future Heisman Trophy winner, won a state title, and Roy's influence spread. Taylor, while still in high school, went to Roy's gym, curious about this new way to get stronger. He became an avid weightlifter.

He didn't even go out for football until he was a high school junior, but he was so strong that he quickly became a two-way star, playing linebacker and fullback. As a senior he threw Statue of Liberty passes, kicked field goals, and attracted the attention of college scouts. But low grades limited his options and he wound up at Hinds Junior College in Raymond, Mississippi, where he played one season of football (he had given up basketball by now) and got himself together in the classroom. The University of Miami and University of Colorado wanted him, but he elected to stay home, play at Louisiana State, and continue to work with Roy.

LSU coach Paul Dietzel, another Red Blaik disciple, sat Taylor early in the 1956 season, but Taylor played his way onto the field as a linebacker, fullback, and kicker. He led the Southeastern Conference in scoring as a junior and played well enough in 1957 to earn

107

an invitation to the Senior Bowl, where, playing both ways, he butted heads with Ray Nitschke, then a hard-hitting fullback-linebacker from Illinois. Nitschke's team won, but Taylor was named the game's MVP.

Jack Vainisi attended the Senior Bowl and wrote Taylor, asking if he wanted to play pro football, and if so, what he thought his best position was. Taylor wrote back that, yes, he wanted to play pro ball and saw himself as a ball carrier. The Packers took him in the second round of the 1958 draft and selected Nitschke a round later.

At odds with the game's prevailing beliefs, Taylor prepared for the Packers' training camp by lifting weights and running up and down the steps at LSU's Tiger Stadium. He was a chiseled specimen when he reported to St. Norbert in July 1958, but his struggles with the playbook landed him on the bench next to Nitschke, who, the Packers had determined, was probably better at linebacker. Finally given a chance late in the season, Taylor ran the ball with abandon, startling his teammates.

After the 1958 season, Taylor went back to Baton Rouge and took the remaining courses he needed to graduate from LSU with an education degree, figuring he would coach football one day. He also ran the stadium steps and lifted weights under Alvin Roy's supervision, moving through an intense progression of squats, presses, and lifts. (Roy would formally introduce strength training to pro football in 1963 when the AFL's San Diego Chargers hired him and promptly won a title.) His hard work had paid off early in Lombardi's camp. The intensity had shocked some players and ended careers, but Taylor sailed through, smacking into defenders with fresh legs during the nutcracker drill, smiling as his teammates vomited during calisthenics.

Taylor was right that Lombardi liked how he played. In New York, Lombardi's offense had included fullback Mel Triplett, a tough, up-the-middle runner. Taylor was the same size, ran just as hard, and could catch passes out of the backfield. Twenty-three years old and married, with a small child, Taylor was, Lombardi felt, somewhat difficult to categorize. He was friendly but didn't seem to have many close friends, smiled a lot but didn't say much. He lifted weights before practices and was so strong that, as a joke, he went through the lunch line upside down one day, walking on his hands the entire way. His teammates, and Lombardi, stared in disbelief.

But boy, he ran hard with that ball.

There had been times during camp when Lombardi looked at the Packers' modest talents and dubious attitudes and wondered if they would win one game in 1959. But he always felt better when he watched Taylor take the ball, slam into a pile of humanity, and move it five yards.

Maybe we'll have something good here after all. Maybe we will.

★ 9 ★

I NSTEAD OF RETURNING to St. Norbert after their morning practice on Friday, August 14, the players boarded a bus, rode to Milwaukee, and checked into a hotel. The next night they would open their exhibition season with a game against the Bears at County Stadium.

The players felt like they were on vacation, even with a game to play; a hotel room seemed like the height of luxury after three weeks in Sensenbrenner Hall. Lombardi took a suite with Marie and received interview requests from Green Bay, Milwaukee, and Chicago reporters wanting to know how he felt before his first game as a head coach. To avoid spending all day talking to the press, he arranged a group session in his suite at 5 P.M.

The reporters arrived to find that an open bar had been set up and food put out. Marie buzzed around with a smile, graciously hosting. Lombardi, drink in hand, conducted his interviews and was looking at his watch within an hour. This worked out well, he thought. Seeing that he could satisfy reporters and control his message by doling out inoffensive quotes in a relaxed setting, he pledged to make the "Five O'clock Club" part of his routine.

Saturday was warm and cloudy, and a light mist started falling late in the afternoon. The Packers and Bears cast long shadows as they warmed up under the stadium lights. A charity promotion, the game would attract more than twenty-eight thousand fans, a larger throng than the Packers had drawn for any regular-season game in Milwaukee since 1956. Sports fans in Wisconsin's largest city cared much more about their winning baseball team, the Braves, than the stumbling Packers, but the football team, with its long history, still had support, and people wanted to see if this new coach from New York could make a difference.

Lombardi and Bears coach George Halas met, shook hands, and spoke on the field as their teams warmed up. Each wore dark slacks, a short-sleeved white dress shirt, and tie. Lombardi admitted he was nervous; even though the game didn't count, he wanted his team to make a positive first impression. In 1954 the Giants had lost miserably in their first exhibition game with Lombardi running Jim Lee Howell's offense. That had not helped them convince the players — or fans — they were on the right track. A similar scene could unfold now, Lombardi feared. The Bears were serious playoff contenders, winners of eight of twelve games the year before.

But Halas complimented Lombardi on how the Packers looked. At age sixty-four, after almost four decades in pro football, the Bears' crusty owner/coach could gauge an opposing team just by watching it warm up. Did the players hustle? Did they seem eager? Were they in shape? Halas could tell Lombardi's team was more fit and organized than Scooter's and Blackbourn's sloppy Packers. Green Bay would no longer be a pushover, Halas said. Lombardi nodded. He still had so much work to do, but things were moving in the right direction.

Starr warmed up by throwing passes and reviewing what had transpired in Lombardi's planning session with the quarterbacks earlier in the week. Lombardi would meet with them regularly, he said, to discuss how to attack their next opponent; Lombardi always had ideas but wanted the players' input, he said, since they called the plays. Somewhat startlingly, he dropped his taskmaster's persona and became a progressive schoolteacher in these meetings, encouraging dialogue and thought. Offensive theory was his specialty, he said. He showed them a reel of the Chicago defense in different alignments, stopping the film to discuss options as he went along.

Starr, what do you run when you see the safeties cheating forward like this?

I'd say a thirty-four, sir.

Good. McHan, look, they're clearly showing red-dog here. Do you check off to another play or try to beat it?

I'm checking to an R turn-in with Max, Coach. I think that works there.

Hmm. OK. Parilli, is this their base run defense disguised? Are they playing zone in the backfield?

Yes, sir. Look at the left end positioned where he is. That's the ti-poff.

Starr and McHan would split time in this game, he said, and should seek to establish the run, not an easy chore against the Bears.

Excited about being the first quarterback to see action under Lombardi, Starr contemplated which plays to run as he completed his warm-ups. He knew all four quarterbacks would take many snaps during the exhibition season, but he wanted to make the most of this opportunity. He was, after all, competing for a job.

The mist turned into a steady rain as Lombardi gathered the players around him on the sideline and urged them to play hard and smart. He sent out his coverage team, mostly rookies, for the opening kickoff. The crowd cheered as Paul Hornung booted the ball through the end zone.

The Green Bay defense that trotted onto the field included seven returning starters from the 1958 unit that had been beaten so mercilessly: Hanner, Borden, and Jim Temp up front, linebackers Bettis, Forester, and Dan Currie, and backs Hank Gremminger and Jesse Whittenton. The newcomers included Tunnell, Quinlan, and Bobby Freeman, a cornerback Lombardi had picked up from Cleveland.

The defense stopped the Bears and forced a punt. The starting Packer offense took the field with Starr at quarterback, Jim Taylor at fullback, Hornung and Don McIlhenny as the halfbacks, and McGee as the wide receiver. Gary Knafelc set up as the tight end, outside the left tackle. The line had Norm Masters at left tackle, Fred "Fuzzy" Thurston at left guard, Ringo at center, Jerry Kramer at right guard, and Gregg at right tackle. Thurston, a second-year pro whom Lombardi had picked up from the Colts in a minor deal just before training camp, was the only newcomer.

Playing on the baseball infield, which quickly became a mud pit in the rain, the offense sputtered on its first possession. Taylor gained just a couple of yards on a run up the middle, and Hornung was tackled for a loss sweeping left. After Starr's third-down pass to McGee fell incomplete, McGee punted.

But when the offense got the ball back and started a new series a few minutes later, it began to assert itself. Since February, Lombardi had pledged to emphasize simple, straight-ahead, physical football — effective blocking and determined running. The strategy seemed improbable given how badly the Packers had been manhandled in 1958, but Lombardi had spent months telling reporters and community groups the Packers would play that way, and now, under the lights at County Stadium, his offense began to crystallize. It became clear that what seemed impossible at first was, in fact, quite realistic — the Packers could pound the ball.

Facing a punishing Bears defense that included Bill George, a superb middle linebacker, and Doug Atkins, a brutal end known as one of the game's roughest players, the Packer linemen opened holes with forceful blocks. Kramer, Masters, and Gregg leapt quickly from their stances with elbows out and fists balled against their chests. Ringo vaulted forward after snapping the ball. Openings appeared as big bodies collided, and Taylor and Hornung slammed into them, legs churning. Taylor crashed through a hole to Ringo's right and gained six yards; the linebacker who hit him first was jolted back before steadying and holding on. Taylor then ran again, behind Gregg, and pushed the pile forward three yards. On third-and-one, Hornung swept carefully to his left, looking for a hole as he moved parallel to the line of scrimmage. Seeing a slim opening just past Masters, he dove into the hole and gained three yards, enough for the first down.

Lombardi beamed. It was amazing, he thought, that Taylor had barely played as a rookie. The first tackler never brought him down.

Taylor and Hornung gained just eight yards on the next three rushes, though, forcing the Packers to settle for a forty-five-yard field goal attempt by Hornung, which fell short. The game remained scoreless until late in the first quarter when Whittenton intercepted a pass thrown by Bears quarterback Ed Brown and returned it twenty-one yards to the Chicago 19. Three plays later, as the second quarter began, Hornung ran left out of the backfield and circled behind the linebackers, breaking open as the Chicago secondary focused on McGee and Knafelc. Starr's pass was on target and Hornung grabbed it as he crossed the goal line. The fans cheered, surprised to see their team ahead. An audible buzz sounded as Hornung added the extra point.

Lombardi sought out Starr as the quarterback trotted to the sideline.

Way to go there. Way to find the open man and hit him.

Starr nodded, satisfied and encouraged. The touchdown pass had unfolded just as Lombardi drew it on the blackboard.

The Bears responded with their first positive drive, a mixture of runs by fullback Rick Casares and halfback Willie Galimore, and passes to receiver Harlon Hill. They controlled the ball for seven minutes, but then the Packer defense stopped a pair of runs inside the 20 and a third-down pass fell incomplete. Bears kicker John Aveni booted a field goal, and the Packers led 7–3.

McHan took over in the second quarter; he wasn't thrilled about Starr playing first, but reasoned that the honor was largely symbolic and he would still win the number one job in the end. His first two series went poorly, as his receivers failed to get open and the Bears yielded little on the ground. McHan did lead a drive into field goal range just before halftime, but the Bears blocked Hornung's last-second kick. Green Bay took a 7–3 lead into the locker room. Lombardi was pleased, the lack of offense notwithstanding. His team was playing hard and competing with a winning opponent.

Starr returned in the third quarter. He handed to Taylor, who burst through a hole off right guard for sixteen yards, then found Lew Carpenter open in the secondary and passed to him for fourteen. The drive moved deep into Bears territory. On second-and-goal at the 9, Knafelc faked a block, dashed to the goal line, and turned around. Starr saw him and threw low, and Knafelc reached down and grabbed the ball at his knees as he fell into the end zone. Another touchdown pass for Starr!

Lombardi patted the quarterback on the shoulder as he came off the field after the sixty-two-yard scoring drive.

Excellent job! Way to use the halfbacks out of the backfield.

Starr nodded. *The pass to Lew was the same route that Paul scored on. It's there. It's open.*

Hornung's extra point bounced off the left upright, leaving the lead at 13–3. The fans stood, some trying to recall the last time the Packers led anyone by this much.

Halas lit into the Bears on the sideline, telling them to get their asses in gear. It was just an exhibition game, but this was ridiculous. His words had an effect. The Bears immediately drove seventy yards to a touchdown, looking crisper with Zeke Bratkowski playing quarterback. Galimore provided the big play, a thirty-yard dash up the middle. The Packer defense stiffened again near the goal line and appeared to force a field goal attempt when Bratkowski overthrew a receiver on third down at the 3, but Bobby Freeman was called for interference, giving the Bears a first down at the 1. Casares carried the ball over for the score, knocking Tunnell over and stepping on his hand.

Up by three as the fourth quarter began, Lombardi sent Starr back out with a pair of rookie halfbacks.

Brown! Hawkins! Get in there!

Both Tim Brown and Alex Hawkins had waited all night for a chance to play and wondered if they would touch the ball. Starr completed a pass to McGee for a first down at the Packer 49 and then called for a pitchout to Brown around right end.

On his first carry as a pro, Brown caught the pitch, zipped between two Bears, and sprinted down the sideline. The crowd shrieked, and for a moment it appeared Brown would go all the way, but a safety bore down on him at an angle and tackled him at the 5, water from the wet field spraying as the players tumbled to the ground together.

Brown quickly stood, tossed the ball to an official, and knocked the mud off his pants, his forty-six-yard gain by far the game's biggest so far.

Yeah. I knew I could do that.

On the next play Starr pitched to Hawkins going the other way, but the blocking failed and the play lost five yards. Then a holding penalty pushed the Packers back fifteen more yards. Lombardi, intolerant of mistakes, fumed as Starr tried to regain the lost ground with a long pass to McGee. The Bears' Pete Johnson intercepted at the 5 and returned the ball to the 33.

The game was on the line and both coaches wanted to win; even exhibition contests between the rival Bears and Packers stirred emotions. Galimore turned a pitchout into a thirty-yard gain. Bratkowski hit Hill with a pass for thirteen, moving the ball inside the Green Bay 20. When the Packers held, Aveni booted a field goal to tie the score at 13–13 with seven minutes to play.

Lombardi sent McHan in, telling the quarterback the rest of the game was his. Brown picked up a first down on a pitchout, McHan passed to McGee on the left sideline for nineteen. Brown, making something happen every time he touched the ball, took a pitchout on a fourth-and-four play and accelerated around left end for eight.

When the Bears held, Hornung sailed a forty-six-yard field goal toward the goalposts. The ball started out high and fell off sharply, but it had just enough oomph to clear the crossbar. The fans roared. The Packers led, 16–13, with two minutes left.

Galimore quickly quieted the cheers, returning the kickoff to the 50. Bratkowski went for the big play, hurling a long pass for Hill, who was briefly open near the goal line. The pass fluttered, giving Whittenton time to close and bat the ball away. Bratkowski dropped back again and hit a receiver across the middle for thirteen. The Bears were on the Green Bay 37 with less than a minute to play.

The next two plays produced a swing of emotions. Aiming a pass for Galimore in the right flat, Bratkowski threw right to Tunnell, but Casares had broken the veteran safety's right hand when he stepped on it earlier, and Tunnell dropped the easy interception. The Bears then made the most of their second chance. As Bratkowski faded to pass, the burly Casares slipped out of the backfield and circled undetected behind the linebackers, who didn't see him as a threat. Bratkowski threw him a pass at the 25, and Casares turned and ran for the end zone with blockers around him. He

Max McGee catches a pass against the Colts at County Stadium in Milwaukee in 1958. Tickets to Packer games were not hard to come by.

Curly Lambeau, the father of the Packer franchise, wanted to come back and run the team before Vince Lombardi was hired.

Publicist Tom Miller (holding plaque) and team president Dominic Olejniczak, the man who hired Lombardi.

ABOVE: Vince Lombardi, the new man in town in 1959, smoking a cigarette on the sideline.

RIGHT: Lombardi refused to let the Packers resume their many bad habits.

Emlen Tunnell (45) returns an interception. Lombardi talked the former New York Giants star into coming to Green Bay.

Bobby Dillon (44), the Packers' all-time interceptions leader, came out of retirement to anchor the defensive backfield for Lombardi in 1959.

Lamar McHan scrambles. He beat out Bart Starr and started at quarterback in Lombardi's first seven games in Green Bay.

A fan congratulates Lombardi as he leaves the field following the Packers' 9–6 victory over the Bears in the 1959 season opener. Joe Francis (right) looks on.

Bart Starr (15) spent the first half of the 1959 season on the bench. Then Lombardi gave him a chance.

Jim Ringo was the only first-team All-Pro on Lombardi's first Packer team.

Don McIlhenny runs the ball against the Colts. Lombardi came to rely on the veteran back.

Jerry Kramer (64) and Fuzzy Thurston (63) didn't meet until Lombardi's first season but became fast friends—and the best guards in the NFL.

Paul Hornung flies over the pile for a touchdown after Thurston (63, on ground) and Ringo (51) cleared a path. Lombardi revived the Golden Boy's career.

The Packer offense took off when Lombardi inserted tall, angular Boyd Dowler, a rookie receiver, into the starting lineup.

Bart Starr scrambles against the Colts in his first start of the 1959 season.

Fuzzy Thurston (63), Jim Taylor (31), and Bob Skoronski (76) clear the way for Paul Hornung (5). The Packers practiced the sweep until they ran it perfectly.

Jerry Kramer (64) knocks a Redskins defender out of the way as Hornung heads for the end zone in a 21–0 Green Bay victory on November 22, 1959.

Bart Starr hands off to Jim Taylor, and Jerry Kramer pulls to begin a sweep against the Redskins in the November 22 victory.

Ray Nitschke in the locker room. He was a raw project when Lombardi arrived, but he began to make plays late in the 1959 season.

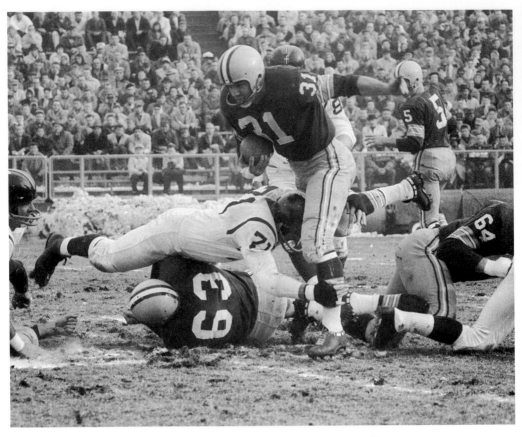

Jim Taylor blasts through a hole in the Redskins defense, opened by
Fuzzy Thurston (63) and Jerry Kramer (64).

Jim Taylor in the locker room. In
1959 he showed signs of becoming
a force to be reckoned with.

Once Hornung was established in Lombardi's
offense, he could beat you five ways—running,
throwing, receiving, kicking, and blocking.

scored without being touched. With forty-one seconds left to play, the Bears had their first lead of the night. The score remained 19–16 when Aveni missed the extra point.

The Packers had time for a final drive. McHan threw to Brown for nineteen, but the Packers were out of timeouts and, with the clock running out, McHan lobbed a prayer far downfield, again toward Brown. The Bears intercepted, sealing the outcome.

Lombardi and Halas met at midfield and shook hands. Both were pleased, Halas because his team had shown heart, scoring sixteen points in the fourth quarter to come back and win, and Lombardi because his team had competed. Lombardi was especially happy about his defense, which had stymied the Bears for most of the night. Improving the defense had been his top priority, and if this game was any measure, his additions had made a difference. Quinlan was a disruptive force all evening, and Tunnell and Freeman had been solid in the secondary.

"We showed we have a scrappy club," Lombardi told reporters. "It would have been nice to win, but we made too many mistakes offensively, like those penalties that set us back when we were in scoring position. We gave away points there that would have made the difference. But overall, I'm pleased. It is a good start."

What about Tim Brown? He certainly had looked good, one reporter said.

"We know what he can do," Lombardi snapped.

Halas, speaking in the Bears' locker room, also praised the Packers. "As you can see, they're already a much, much better team because they have Vince Lombardi as their coach," he said. "He is doing the kind of job we knew he would do."

Halas paused. In six weeks, the Bears and Packers would open the regular season on a Sunday afternoon in Green Bay. City Stadium would be packed, and the game, Halas knew, would bear little resemblance to the lopsided affairs that had marked this rivalry in recent years. The days of taking the Packers for granted were over.

"Once the season begins," Halas croaked with a crooked smile, "the Packers are going to give a lot of teams a lot of trouble, starting with us."

★ 10 ★

THE PLAYERS TOOK a bus back to St. Norbert after the exhibition game in Milwaukee, arriving after midnight. They had Sunday off, but most just relaxed around Sensenbrenner Hall and went to bed early, knowing two-a-days would resume Monday. Boyd Dowler and the three other rookies who had played for the college all-star team against the Colts (and lost, 29–0, the night before, in Chicago) arrived, having missed the first three weeks of camp. Their teammates warned them to get ready to run. *This guy is out of his mind. People have been going to the hospital.*

Lombardi's mood was sour after he watched film of the loss to the Bears. "We made an error on every play," he fumed Monday. "There's a lot of work to be done here. Someone would miss an assignment or a block, especially when we were close to the goal line. We should have scored thirty points."

That evening, he showed the films to the players. They were used to theater-like quiet when they watched game films; Scooter had typically just let the projector run, occasionally offering suggestions; he even fell asleep once as an assistant. Lombardi, conversely, was like a tuba player in a library. With his voice rising in anger, he pointed out mistakes, castigated the perpetrators, and frequently rewound film to show the offenses again.

He aimed his most caustic remarks at the starting guards, Jerry Kramer and Fred Thurston. Their blocks had helped Green Bay runners gain 190 yards against a tough defense, but they also had been flagged for holding and missed blocks that led to quarterback

118

sacks. Lombardi, the former guard, abhorred mistakes at "his" position.

What in the hell was that, Kramer? You call that a block? Damn! This is professional football! Are you a professional? Let's look at that again. There, that's a sorry excuse for a block, Kramer!

Yes, sir.

Kramer sunk lower in his chair and looked at Thurston. They shook their heads in dismay. It wasn't fair, they thought. They had played well but were getting crucified. When the session ended, they emerged with headaches and hollow expressions. Whew, what a nightmare.

The running backs also took their share of abuse.

Paul, we have to make that block there. Let's look at it again. See, Jimmy [Taylor] has no chance if you don't make that block. There's no excuse for not getting it done!

Yes, sir.

And Jimmy, you hit the wrong hole. That's just stupid. You need to think!

Yes, sir.

Obviously still annoyed, Lombardi halted practice the next morning after two receivers dropped easy catches. *Catching a pass takes just a little effort! If you want to stay around here, we've got to have full effort on every play!*

That day he ended practice with a goal-line drill. The starting units lined up opposite each other with the ball placed on the 5. Lombardi called out plays, mostly runs, and the offense tried to score while the defense dug in to make stops. Lombardi stood to the side with a thin smile, calling out plays and watching bodies collide.

The drill went on and on in the afternoon heat, lasting what seemed to the players like an eternity. The offensive linemen leapt forward to block as Taylor and Hornung slammed into the line behind them. As the defense held its ground, Lombardi grew agitated. *We're going to run the damn draw until you get it right! Again!*

The defense made another stop. Bettis and Hanner looked at each other as Lombardi chewed out the offense.

"You think he's going to run that draw again?" Bettis asked.

"Think so," Hanner replied.

"You think we should stop it?" Bettis asked.

"Yeah, we better," Hanner said.

After the defense made another stop, Ringo spoke softly to Bettis and Hanner in the middle of the line.

"We're all going to be here all day if we don't score pretty soon," he said.

Bettis and Hanner got the message. They quietly spread the word to the rest of the defense: don't make it obvious, but let them score.

The offense finally punched over a touchdown, then another. Satisfied, Lombardi blew his whistle. The exhausted players ran a set of sideline-to-sideline sprints to end practice. Then they raced to get on that first bus back to St. Norbert, thirsting to knock back a couple of beers.

The Packers' remaining five exhibition games would all be played either on the road or at a neutral site, in San Francisco; Portland, Oregon; Bangor, Maine; Winston-Salem, North Carolina; and Minneapolis, Minnesota. The players would awake in strange beds and practice and play on dim fields as they slowly got in shape for the regular season, earning a small per diem, barely enough to buy lunch. Their regular salaries didn't kick in until the regular season.

The schedule afforded the Packers just a few days at home in the month before their regular-season opener on September 27, but it wasn't unusual for NFL teams to barnstorm through the exhibition season. The league's owners still worried about their sport's popularity, even after 40 million TV viewers watched the 1958 championship game. Major league baseball still had more fans, as did boxing, horse racing, and college football. The NFL was popular enough in cities with teams, but it generated little interest in regions where it had no presence or history, such as the Southeast; when Dave Hanner left Arkansas to become a pro in 1952, some of his friends didn't even know what a Green Bay Packer was. The NFL's owners sent their teams on barnstorming trips before the season in hopes of attracting new fans in out-of-the-way places and cities without franchises.

Babe Parilli started at quarterback against the 49ers in San Francisco on Sunday, August 23. Lombardi told him to focus on the running game, and Parilli followed orders, handing off on thirty-seven of Green Bay's fifty-four plays as eighteen thousand fans watched under sunny skies. The play calling — and sound execution — left no doubt that Lombardi had replaced Scooter's complex offense with simple, straight-ahead power. The Packers punctured the 49ers' veteran defense with a mixture of runs, Taylor off right tackle, Hornung around left end, Taylor up the middle, McIlhenny around right end. Ringo won his share of tangles with Leo Nomellini, the 49ers' squatty All-Pro tackle. Jerry Kramer and Fred Thurston pivoted hard out of their stances, got out in front of sweeps, and delivered crunching blocks.

It had taken Lombardi a couple of years to build an effective line in New York, and he figured he would need at least that long now in the wake of Hank Bullough's retirement and his jettisoning of veteran starters Oliver Spencer and Jim Salsbury. He was basically starting from scratch, rebuilding with youngsters around Ringo. Lombardi marveled at his All-Pro center, so smart and agile his small size didn't matter.

Norm Masters, who had been the left tackle under Scooter, was playing well enough to keep his job; protecting the passer was critical for any blocker on the quarterback's blind side, and Masters had the strength to keep red-doggers away. But Bob Skoronksi, big and strong and back after two years in the Air Force, was also performing well at that position — so well that Lombardi wondered if they could split duties.

At right tackle, Forrest Gregg had surprised Lombardi more than any player. A tall, strong Texan, he had done little to distinguish himself in his first two seasons, bouncing between the offensive and defensive lines as he struggled to find a position. But suddenly he was playing up to his potential if not above it, relentlessly clearing holes and beating back pass rushers. There was no doubt he would start.

Stationed just inside Gregg, Kramer was also an obvious starter, easily the best right guard on the roster. Even though Lombardi pushed and berated him more than any player, the coach knew he had potential. Lombardi's system demanded a lot from the guards; they had to be strong enough to pass protect and quick enough to get in front of the end sweeps Lombardi loved to run. Kramer had the speed to get out there and knock people over, as well as the strength to pass protect.

The only line position Lombardi was unsure about was left guard. He had tried out a handful of players, and Thurston was the most effective so far. His pass protection was solid, but he was more chunky than chiseled, and Lombardi wasn't sure he was quick enough to get in front of sweeps.

Thurston was determined to make the most of the chance. He had already passed through the hands of three NFL teams (the Eagles, Bears, and Colts) in his one year in the league. If he didn't make it in Green Bay, he might be done. He radiated a devil-may-care approach to life, flashing a broad, white smile and making jokes under his breath, but in fact, had experienced his share of hardship. Growing up in Altoona, Wisconsin, he lived in a small house without an indoor toilet until he was a teenager. None of his seven older siblings finished high school because they had to work after their father died. Fred played basketball well enough to be recruited by Valparaiso University in Indiana, and didn't even start with football until his junior year in college, when the Valparaiso coach saw him battling for rebounds and thought he would make an effective lineman. Now he was a pro, but his future was in doubt.

In Lombardi's offense the guards had to know each other and play well together, and Kramer and Thurston were starting to become friends. They sat together as Lombardi showered criticism on them in the film session after the Chicago game, and they came away realizing they might be in this together and need each other's support. Before the game in San Francisco, they grimly nodded at each other in the locker room before kickoff.

Let's try to keep from getting our asses reamed this week.

Yeah. But I don't know if we can.

Lombardi liked what he saw from them early in the game as they led sweeps and kept rushers away from Parilli. Then, when the 49ers stacked more defenders up front to stop the run, Parilli threw over them, completing ten of eleven passes and thinking this offense worked pretty darn well. The Packers led at halftime, 10–3, and increased the margin to 17–3 midway through the third quarter when Hornung swept nine yards around right end for a touchdown behind Thurston and Kramer.

As the fourth quarter started, the 49ers suddenly awoke when veteran quarterback Y. A. Tittle replaced young John Brodie. With Tittle heaving long passes, the 49ers marched to a touchdown, cutting the Packer lead to 17–10 with ten minutes to play. But George Dixon, a Packer rookie, caught the ensuing kickoff two yards into his end zone, ran right, found a seam in the coverage, and broke into the clear. He sprinted ninety-six yards before being dragged down at the 6, and the Packer offense quickly pushed the ball into the end zone, with Don McIlhenny getting the score from the 2.

That should have settled the outcome, but Tittle was undeterred. He quickly passed his way to another touchdown, and his defense got him the ball again with four minutes left. With the sparse crowd cheering, aroused by the comeback, Tittle led his offense toward a game-tying touchdown until the Packers' Bobby Freeman read a sideline route, stepped in front of the pass, and grabbed an interception at the Green Bay 20.

By the time Tittle got his hands on the ball again, there was time for just one more play. He hurled an arching sixty-yard prayer toward receiver R. C. Owens, who somehow beat three Packer defenders to the ball and made a leaping catch at the Green Bay 1. But time expired before the 49ers could run another play. The Packers walked off the field as 24–17 winners.

Despite the shaky ending, Lombardi was pleased after his first victory as an NFL head coach. "We obviously still have a lot of work to do, especially with our pass defense," he said, "but the offensive line and Hornung and Taylor showed that we can move the ball."

Hornung sat at his locker with a satisfied smile, smoking a cigarette. What a pleasure to play for a coach who knew how to use him! The Golden Boy had rushed for thirty-five yards, scored a touchdown, and kicked a field goal and three extra points. And that was just an inkling of the load he figured to carry under Lombardi.

"We have a good, hungry ball club," Hornung said. "Our offense is

80 percent better this year. It's a pleasure to run behind a line that opens holes like that."

The next morning the Packers flew up to Oregon and set up a camp at the University of Portland. They would stay in dorms, hold a week of open-to-the-public practices, and play the Philadelphia Eagles on Saturday night. It was a typical "spread the word" NFL exhibition, but Lombardi declined to speak to a Portland reporter on Monday, saying he had to watch film of the San Francisco game. The reporter derided him in print, calling him "film fan," but Lombardi shrugged off the criticism; he was more concerned about his pass defense, which, if the San Francisco game was an indication, needed help.

He had thought it was a capable unit. Emlen Tunnell could survive on his wiles. Jesse Whittenton, an agile athlete, could cover top receivers (and beat anyone on the golf course). Hank Gremminger, a converted receiver, had started for three years. John Symank, a fearless tough, had intercepted nine passes as a rookie in 1957. Bobby Freeman seemed to have a knack for making plays.

But without Bobby Dillon or Tunnell, who was out with a broken hand, the secondary had been humbled by Y. A. Tittle in San Francisco. After watching films of Tittle hitting a slew of open receivers, Lombardi feared he had given the unit too much credit; the Packers might be in trouble even when Tunnell returned.

Lombardi asked Jack Vainisi to see if Dillon would consider coming out of retirement. Dillon, busy at work in Texas, said no.

But Lombardi, increasingly desperate, made Vainisi try again, stressing how much Dillon was needed.

"Oh, all right. I still love the game," Dillon said.

He was surely one of the NFL's unlikeliest stars, lacking vision in his left eye after a childhood accident. His parents wouldn't let him play football until he was a high school senior, but he showed such potential as a speedy pass defender that the University of Texas recruited him. (He had to sign a waiver freeing the school of responsibility for further eye damage.) He made up for his lack of depth perception with an intuitive knack for knowing where quarterbacks would throw, and after joining the Packers in 1952 had recorded fifty-one interceptions in seven seasons.

Lombardi was thrilled to have Dillon back but told Vainisi to make sure the returning player understood he would be fined for having missed training camp and the early part of the exhibition season. Lombardi fined anyone holding out one hundred dollars a day.

When he heard he would be fined several thousand dollars, Dillon blew up. "You can tell Lombardi to shove that fine up his ass, Jack," Dillon shouted over the phone. "This is totally ridiculous. You call begging me to come back, and then you fine me? Forget it. I'm not coming back."

Lombardi called Dillon himself and calmly explained he couldn't make exceptions to his policy.

"The fine money funds a team party at the end of the season. That's how I do things," Lombardi said.

"That's wonderful," Dillon replied, "but I never held out, I'm not paying the fine, and I'm not coming back."

Dillon started to hang up, but Lombardi shouted into the receiver: "Wait, wait! OK, if you come in, the team will pay the fine. We won't tell anyone. This will be a secret between you and me. But the money has to go into the holdout fund. I fined some other guys for coming in late. I have to fine you, too."

Lombardi asked Dillon to play that weekend in Portland, but Dillon said he would meet the team when it returned to Green Bay after the game. Lombardi would later tease Dillon throughout the season for having helped fund an extravagant end-of-year party, and Dillon would just smile and go along with the ruse, impressed by — but not quite sure what to make of — this feisty coach so intent on maintaining standards yet willing to bend them to get what he wanted.

One evening during the week in Portland, Lombardi summoned his four quarterbacks to a meeting room, turned off the lights, and turned on a film projector. They knew what was coming: their weekly planning session.

We're going to run the ball. I want to run the ball. And let me show you how we're going to run the ball.

As they talked about how to attack the Eagles' defense on Saturday, Joe Francis marveled at what his older teammates knew about football, and how they used their experiences to think their way through different situations. He was still learning how much went into being a pro quarterback. He had done his share of studying in his rookie season under Scooter McLean, but the team wasn't really serious and he mostly just enjoyed himself off the field with Hornung and McGee; he couldn't believe there was so much partying in the pros. But now, with Lombardi in command, the atmosphere was more businesslike and he spent so much time in front of a blackboard that he felt like he was in college again.

Known as Pineapple Joe, Francis had olive skin and dark features; he had grown up in Hawaii speaking Pidgin, an island language rooted in English but influenced by other tongues. A splendid athlete, he could outrun most of his Packer teammates and effortlessly hurl a ball sixty yards. But despite his athletic gifts, he sometimes wondered why he had been drafted; running the single wing at Oregon State hadn't prepared him to read NFL defenses or change plays at the line. Why, he was so raw that he was still getting used to speaking English all the time! (He had lived with other Hawaiians in college and continued to speak Pidgin.)

He marveled at how adroitly Starr, in particular, snapped authoritative answers to Lombardi's questions. McHan and Parilli had obviously experienced a lot, too. Francis felt like a beginner in their company.

But it was Francis whom Lombardi stopped as the film session ended and the quarterbacks left.

Come here for a minute, Joe.

Yes, Coach?

You're going to start Saturday night against the Eagles, Joe.

Really, Coach? That's fantastic!

Make the most of the chance, son.

Francis could barely contain his excitement. He was a hero in Portland, having worn an Oregon State uniform just two years earlier. His fans would flock to little Multnomah Stadium Saturday night to watch him oppose another local icon, Eagles quarterback Norm Van Brocklin, who had starred at the University of Oregon in the late 1940s.

The crowds at the Packers' daily practices increased in size after Lombardi announced Francis would be starting. Fans swarmed him after the workouts, asking for autographs.

Good luck on Saturday, Joe.

We knew all along that you could make it.

Francis studied his playbook in preparation for the game but also went out every night with friends, family members, and teammates, scrambling back to the dorm just ahead of curfew.

Lombardi was curious to see Francis perform. The young man was raw, but Lombardi wished some of the Packers' veteran stalwarts had his natural playmaking instincts. Francis wasn't afraid to hum a pass into a crowd of defenders or just take off running with the ball, hoping to create magic. It was difficult to thrive for long playing that way against disciplined NFL defenses, but Francis had made enough good things happen in camp that Lombardi wondered if he might have value during the season as a reserve who came in to provide a spark.

On Saturday, as the sun dropped on a cool late-summer evening, the crowd swelled under Multnomah Stadium's dim lights until every seat was taken. Not wanting to turn any customers away, event organizers allowed late-arriving fans to stand right on the sidelines, on either side of the benches. By the time the Packers kicked off, more than twenty-five thousand fans were crammed into the little stadium.

The Packers drove seventy-four yards to a touchdown on their first possession as Francis mostly handed to Hornung and Taylor, remembering what Lombardi had said about establishing the running game. The line opened plenty of holes and Francis didn't have to audible at the line. *Hey, this is easy.*

Van Brocklin, a seven-time Pro Bowl selection, lived up to his reputation in the next few minutes, zipping line-drive passes to open receivers as the Eagles struck for two touchdowns and took

127

the lead. Lombardi grimaced, relieved that Dillon would soon be on hand to rescue the pass defense.

Trailing 14–7 early in the second quarter, Francis got the offense moving again. Taylor and Lew Carpenter ran for first downs. Francis faded to pass but saw no one open, tucked the ball in, and scrambled for fifteen yards, breaking two tackles and lunging for more as his fans roared. Then he dropped back and hit Boyd Dowler for thirteen over the middle. The eighty-yard drive culminated with a short touchdown run by Carpenter. Francis was excited as he came off the field to cheers. *This isn't so hard. I can do this.*

At halftime Lombardi complimented him and told him the rest of the game was his. *I like your play-calling, your run-pass mix. Good job, Joe. Now keep it up.*

The Eagles fumbled on their first possession after halftime, leading to a short Hornung field goal that gave the Packers the lead, 17–14. Then Bobby Freeman, inserted into the secondary at halftime, picked off a Van Brocklin pass over the middle. The offense rolled to a touchdown in six plays, mostly rushes, and then Freeman intercepted another Van Brocklin pass, this time on the right sideline, and sprinted thirty yards to the end zone without being touched. Suddenly, the Packers had a 31–14 lead.

A few minutes later the Packer offense started a possession at its 3 after a long Philadelphia punt. Francis waited for Lombardi to tell another quarterback to take over, but the coach turned to him and said, "OK, keep going, Joe, just keep going." Francis nodded and trotted onto the field, adrenaline pumping, confidence soaring; how could he not move the ball with his line opening holes so easily? He commanded the huddle with a forceful voice. *Let's move it, guys. Let's keep hammering.* Taylor gained six up the middle. Hornung went for eleven around left end. McIlhenny gained five around right end. The offense crossed midfield and rolled deep into Philadelphia territory, Francis picking up a key third down on a twelve-yard toss to McGee. Just before the third quarter ended, Taylor took a handoff and bulled into the end zone behind Bob Skoronski. Hornung's extra point completed a quarter in which the Packers scored twenty-four unanswered points.

As Francis came off the field, Lombardi grabbed him by the shoulder.

Hell of a job, just a great job. That's it for the night.

Francis exhaled, took off his helmet, and moved down the sideline. Starr, summoned to replace him, gave him a pat on the back as their paths crossed.

Good job, Joe. Real good job.

Hey, thanks.

Van Brocklin filled the air with passes in the final fifteen minutes, leading two touchdown drives that made the score respectable; he ended the night with almost four hundred passing yards against the beleaguered Green Bay secondary. Starr, meanwhile, moved the Packer offense to a late touchdown, again mostly handing off. The final score was 45–28. The fans left having been enormously entertained.

Lombardi praised Francis after the game. "He surprised me. He really had a good game," the coach told reporters. "He hasn't done that well in practice, but maybe he's one of those 'gamer' players."

Francis had produced more than two hundred yards of rushing and passing. Reporters surrounded him in the locker room, and then he showered, dressed, and went out with friends and family. They bought him drinks and slapped him on the back. *It looked like you were back at Oregon State. Great game.*

Smiling, Francis admitted he had thoroughly enjoyed himself. The other Packer quarterbacks might be more polished, but Pineapple Joe could play this game.

★ 11 ★

ROWING UP IN Lake Village, Arkansas, a farming community of three thousand people, Lamar McHan learned to shoulder a heavy load of responsibility. His father drove a rural mail route but had lost the use of one leg after a bout with tuberculosis. McHan, the oldest child of four, took on part of the fatherly role, awakening before dawn to start the fire that heated the house, and helping farm cattle on the family's small acreage.

Ordinarily, a youngster with so many family commitments wouldn't have time for sports, but McHan was big, fast, and competitive, a star for all seasons, the eternal quarterback and shortstop. Widely recruited out of high school, he commanded the offense for three seasons at the University of Arkansas and then became an immediate starter in the NFL — still shouldering that heavy load of responsibility.

But now he was fighting for a job in Green Bay, and after the first three exhibition games, he was worried about his prospects. McHan was the only quarterback who hadn't started a game. In fact, he had barely played. Meanwhile, the other three guys had fared well, especially Babe Parilli in San Francisco and Joe Francis in Portland.

McHan had sensed that Lombardi favored him during the early weeks of training camp, but now he feared the coach might ship him back to the Cardinals. The other quarterbacks laughed when he expressed his concern, saying they wished Lombardi liked them as much as he obviously liked McHan. But McHan couldn't help feeling skeptical. His Arkansas and Chicago teams had never been big winners, and years of losing had spawned a negative inner impulse he constantly fought. Being a competitive young man of few words, he didn't always express himself gracefully and had gotten into trouble a few times as a result. He had butted heads with Cardinals owner Walter Wolfner, whom he didn't like or trust, and at Arkansas he complained so much about play selection during spring practice one year that he was moved to defense and told he wouldn't go back to quarterback until he shut up.

But his coaches generally understood that he just wanted to win, and in time, McHan had figured out that he needed to control his emotions and keep his opinions to himself. He shrugged when Bart Starr started the first exhibition game. He shrugged when Parilli started the second game. He felt his temper rising when Francis started the third game and McHan didn't get to play a down, but he didn't complain to Lombardi.

Now, as the Packers prepared for their next game, against the Giants on September 5 in Bangor, Maine, Lombardi approached McHan in the City Stadium locker room after a midweek afternoon practice.

OK, you've got this game, Lamar. Saturday night against the Giants.

Thanks, Coach.

Like to see you do well.

I plan on it.

McHan was pleased to get a chance, but shook his head ruefully as Lombardi walked away, his negative impulse rising. *Great. The other guys start against no one and I get the Giants, the best defense in the league.*

Maine had never hosted an NFL game, and Bangor city officials rented ten thousand folding chairs and situated them around tiny Garland Street Field to accommodate the crowd. The Packer offense drove crisply on its first possession. Lombardi had spoken to McHan about mixing runs and passes — you can't just cram the ball down the Giants' throats, he said — and McHan heard the coach's voice in his head as he called plays in the huddle. Jim Taylor picked up one first down around left end. Paul Hornung ran up the middle for another. McHan threw to Gary Knafelc for thirteen yards.

On a first down at the New York 28, Hornung slipped out of the backfield and into the middle of the secondary, finding an open spot. McHan threw him a strike, and the Golden Boy grabbed the ball and lunged across the goal line for a touchdown. McHan punched the air in triumph as the fans rose from their folding chairs and cheered, but then everyone spotted the flag on the ground — a referee had whistled the Packers for being offside, nullifying the score. A few plays later Hornung lined up for a thirty-two-yard field goal, but it was blocked.

The Packer defense, fortified by Bobby Dillon's return, forced a punt. Dillon had practiced with the team all week and quickly played his way into shape as Lombardi, having grudgingly yielded on the fine issue, made him run extra laps after every practice, just so Dillon knew who was boss. With Emlen Tunnell, back after a broken hand, at one safety spot, and Dillon at the other, the pass defense suddenly looked solid.

On its second possession the Packer offense again drove into New York territory. McHan threw a pass to Steve Meilinger, a veteran reserve tight end, open over the middle. But the ball bounced off Meilinger's hands and into the arms of Giants safety Jim Patton. McHan muttered as he walked off the field. *Why do they drop my passes?*

After failing to capitalize on those early chances, the Packer offense began to struggle. Rushing plays still gained yardage but penalties and the Giants' pass rush undermined drives. With opposing players bearing down on him, McHan became flustered and missed open receivers. Parilli took over in the second quarter but immediately threw an interception on a sideline route. Starting from the Green Bay 16, the Giants pushed the ball over the goal line in five plays.

The Giant defense clamped down hard after that, yielding little ground. McHan returned to the game but missed more passes (he would end the night with just five completions in fourteen attempts), and Parilli also couldn't move the ball. Meanwhile, the Giants drove eighty-six yards to a touchdown in the third quarter.

Lombardi gave Francis a shot in the fourth quarter, and Pineapple Joe moved the offense to four straight first downs with his running and passing. But then he lost a fumble at the New York 14, and the game ended moments later. After scoring sixty-nine points in their two wins on the West Coast, the Packers had been shut out, 14–0.

Lombardi wasn't upset in the locker room; he tended to be in a better mood after losses, for whatever reason. He said he was pleased to see the defense yield so little, and noted that Green Bay rushers had gained 136 yards. "It's been a long time since anyone moved the ball that well on the Giants," he said. "We hit very hard in this ball game. We still have a lot of work to do, but I like how we're moving the ball."

McHan, frustrated by his performance, sat quietly at his locker, his shoulders sagging.

With their exhibition record now even at 2-2, the Packers barnstormed on, flying to North Carolina for their next game, against the Washington Redskins on Saturday night, September 12, at Wake Forest University in Winston-Salem. They would practice in the outfield of a Class B minor-league baseball park for a week before the game.

This was the fifth straight year in which the Packers had played an exhibition game in Winston-Salem against Washington. The southern site posed no problems for the Redskins, the only NFL team with no black players, as mandated by owner George Preston Marshall. But the Packers' four black players couldn't stay at their team's segregated motel. Unhappy with the situation but unwilling to fight it, Lombardi arranged for Tunnell, Borden, Tim Brown, and A. D. Williams to stay in dorms at North Carolina A&T, an all-black college nearby.

Brown, the youngest of the four, was furious. He railed at Tunnell as they sat up late in the dorm one night.

"This is bullshit. We're supposed to be a team and we can't even stay with our teammates? It's embarrassing. It's not right. It shouldn't be," Brown said.

Tunnell talked him out of making a scene.

"You're right, Timmy, it's bullshit," Tunnell said. "But you might make this team. Don't blow it now. Sit tight. Vince will get things under control here."

Brown kept his mouth shut.

Ray Nitschke joined the team in North Carolina after missing training camp and two-thirds of the exhibition season because of a military-service commitment. Lombardi was unsure of the role he would play. Nitschke had made a strong impression, but not always positively, as a rookie under Scooter McLean. It was hard to say whether he was wilder on or off the field.

Prematurely bald with piercing, close-set eyes and a pointed chin, Nitschke lived on the edge. Raised by his older brothers in a working-class Chicago suburb after his parents died, he ran wild, becoming a drinker and brawler, the human version of a pair of brass knuckles. Openly seething at what he believed was the bad hand he had been dealt in life, he took out his anger on the football field, knocking opponents senseless as a fullback and linebacker in high school and at the University of Illinois.

Jack Vainisi knew he was drafting a headache when he took Nitschke in the third round in 1958, but he couldn't pass up a young man who played a violent game so violently. If Nitschke ever learned how to harness his aggressiveness, he could be a brutal force.

The experiment had not gone well in Nitschke's rookie season. He struggled to master the signals, and when given a chance to play, just ran around hitting people. Unable to supplant starters Tom Bettis, Bill Forester, and Dan Currie, the latter a more polished rookie drafted ahead of him, he took to calling himself the Judge because of all the time he spent on the bench. Lombardi wondered if he would ever mature enough to be helpful.

After the Wednesday practice in Winston-Salem, Lombardi informed Bart Starr that he would start against the Redskins.

"That's great, sir," Starr replied with a smile, his elation obvious. "I look forward to playing well and beating the Redskins."

Starr hadn't played much since the first exhibition game against the Bears. Understanding that the other quarterbacks also needed to play, he had done all he could to impress Lombardi in the meantime, memorizing the playbook, studying hours of film, and brain-storming about when and how to change plays at the line. He loved the coach's clear-eyed, clinical approach and felt it suited him, but he had no idea where he or any of the quarterbacks stood with Lombardi. The coach offered no hints.

Alex Hawkins, the rookie halfback, also was told he would start Saturday, and like Starr, had no idea what to think. His introduction to the NFL had not gone well. Lombardi mostly just yelled at him, it seemed, and while that approach inspired some players, Hawkins had retreated into a shell and performed poorly.

Now, he was being given a chance.

Starr also realized the upcoming game was his chance to prove himself as a starting quarterback. The regular-season opener was in two weeks. Lombardi would be making decisions about jobs soon. Starr asked him for film of the Redskins' defense and watched it at the motel instead of going out to dinner. He hoped he would see something he could take advantage of, a linebacker who gave away a red-dog, or a safety who cheated in one direction. By Saturday night he was confident he could move the ball on the Redskins, who weren't one of the NFL's top teams.

The college stadium was half-full as the game kicked off, with most of the fifteen thousand fans supporting the Redskins, the NFL's southernmost team. A national television audience was watching on ABC, giving fans around the country their first glimpse of Lombardi's rebuilding project.

After the Redskins drove to a touchdown on their first series, the Packers' first series began with Starr kneeling and calling plays in the huddle. He started with a pass. Max McGee dropped it. Then he badly overthrew Taylor, who was open in the left flat. An offside penalty moved the ball farther back, and Starr gave up on the possession, calling for a pitchout to Hawkins on third down. Red-dogging linebackers nailed the rookie for a loss. McGee punted the ball away.

After the Packer defense forced a punt, Starr started the next possession by throwing over the middle to Gary Knafelc, his road roommate, for nineteen yards.

Nice pass.

135

Nice catch, let's move that ball.

But the drive ended when Taylor lost a fumble, and after the Packer defense got the ball right back, Starr dropped it while scrambling for a first down, and the Redskins recovered. The rash of mistakes infuriated Lombardi. *Damn, why can't we hold onto the ball out there?!*

Shocking Starr, the coach turned to the bench and hollered, "Francis! Get warmed up, you're going in!" Joe Francis grabbed a ball and started to throw, and Lombardi turned his back on Starr. That was that. Starr was being pulled.

Francis drove the offense into scoring range on his first series and Hornung kicked a short field goal. The Packers were on the board. Francis would stay in the game, Lombardi said. Starr sat down at the end of the bench, wondering if he had played himself off the team. This had been his chance, and he had prepared hard, but things had spiraled in the wrong direction.

Tears welled in his eyes, which he closed as he quietly choked back sobs.

"What in the hell are you so upset about?" a nearby voice sounded.

It was Hawkins, who had also been pulled from the game and was sitting next to him on the bench.

"He . . . took me out," Starr stuttered.

"Well, he took me out, too," Hawkins replied.

The rookie knew his time with the Packers was over and he would be cut when the team returned to Wisconsin after this game. (As it turned out, he was waived, then pulled from waivers and traded to Baltimore for a draft pick. "I'll see you around," he told Lombardi, and sure enough, went on to play ten years in the NFL, mostly with the Colts.) Starr, meanwhile, sat and watched Hornung lead the Packers to a 20–13 victory in Winston-Salem. The Golden Boy, adapting to the Frank Gifford role, rushed eight times for forty-nine yards, caught two passes for twenty yards, threw an option pass, and scored every Green Bay point on two touchdowns, two field goals, and two extra points. Francis, unlike Starr, didn't turn the ball over.

On the charter flight back to Green Bay, Starr stared out the window, wondering if he was about to be cut. Lombardi had pledged to keep three quarterbacks, and with McHan more proven, Parilli more experienced, and Francis having a great exhibition season, Starr figured he was in trouble. When Knafelc, sitting next to him, told a joke, he pretended to laugh.

The fall semester at St. Norbert had started, so instead of returning to Green Bay, the Packers set up a final training camp near Milwaukee beginning Sunday, September 13. For the next ten days they would practice at St. John's Academy, a military school, and room at Oakton Manor, a secluded resort on Pewaukee Lake. They would briefly leave camp for their sixth and final exhibition game, against the Pittsburgh Steelers, in Minneapolis, on September 20.

Lombardi invited the players' families to join them at the resort, but he closed the camp to the public, wanting the players to himself with the regular season so close now. The Packers would open their twelve-game league regular-season schedule against the Bears at City Stadium on September 27.

Lombardi's first day at Oakton Manor was busy. He made another trade with Paul Brown, his third since March, sending a draft pick to Cleveland for Henry Jordan, a defensive tackle in his third NFL season. Small but quick, Jordan wasn't starting in Cleveland, but Lombardi immediately penciled him in. With the pass defense more secure now thanks to Bobby Dillon and Emlen Tunnell, the line was Lombardi's chief defensive concern; the Giants and Redskins had combined for more than 250 rushing yards in the past two games. Hopefully Jordan would help.

Next, Lombardi made a big move that rocked the Pewaukee camp — he cut quarterback Babe Parilli. The veteran was enormously popular in the locker room and had played well in his only exhibition start, but in Lombardi's view, Starr was younger and better prepared, McHan more experienced and talented, and Francis a more natural playmaker. Parilli just didn't stand out in any way. Lombardi couldn't envision missing him.

After the coach called in Parilli and gave him the news, word spread quickly through camp. *He cut Babe? Are you serious?* Starr, though relieved to be spared, was sad for his friend and boyhood idol. Francis, likewise, had admired Parilli as a youngster and couldn't believe he had been kept over the better-known player.

Parilli shook hands with Lombardi and walked away believing he had blown his prospects when he took a dollar off Lombardi in that golf bet at the Oneida Golf and Riding Club back in the spring.

I should have let him win. What was I thinking?

Lombardi still hadn't announced which quarterback would start the regular-season opener, but he had an idea. He had brought in McHan to take control of a murky situation, and the other two quarterbacks had their positive qualities, but McHan was farther along in his career. McHan hadn't done much in the exhibition season, but in the end, he probably gave the Packers their best chance of winning. Starr? He was an ideal backup. Francis? Let's face it, he probably didn't pass well enough to beat top teams such as the Colts or Giants. McHan had started in the league for five years, battled playoff teams, won some games. The choice seemed obvious, actually.

Still, Lombardi started Francis in the sixth and final exhibition game on September 20, rewarding the second-year man for his surprising play. But Francis struggled. The Packer running game was stymied by Pittsburgh's rugged defense on a humid Sunday afternoon, and Francis misfired in must-pass situations, confirming Lombardi's concerns about him.

Starr took over in the second quarter, immediately spotted Tim Brown open on a deep route down the middle, and hit the rookie with a strike. Brown dropped what would have been a touchdown, summing up Starr's hard-luck career. But Bobby Layne, the Pittsburgh quarterback, couldn't dent a Packer defense that suddenly didn't seem to have many holes, and the game remained scoreless until just before halftime, when Forrest Gregg cleared an opening that Taylor ran through for a long gain, setting up a Hornung field goal. The Packers led at halftime, 3–0.

McHan took over in the third quarter, and after several stalled drives, hit Lew Carpenter with a short pass in the left flat. Blocks by

Norm Masters and Jim Ringo freed the veteran back, and he sprinted fifty-eight yards down the sideline before a Pittsburgh safety brought him down. But Taylor fumbled on the next play, and after the Packer defense held, Tim Brown, having a rough day, fumbled a punt at midfield. The Steelers converted that mistake into a field goal that tied the score early in the fourth quarter.

The fumbles angered Lombardi.

Jimmy Taylor, one more fumble and you're on the bench.

Come on, Brown, you think you're so great. Hold onto the damn ball!

What in the hell is going on here?

He calmed down when McHan led the offense on a long touchdown drive, hitting four passes, including a touchdown throw to Hornung, who drifted into the left flat, beat the defender covering him, and grabbed McHan's tight spiral right at the goal line. Hornung added the extra point to give the Packers a 10–3 lead.

The Steelers then misplayed the ensuing kickoff, the ball bouncing out of bounds at the 1, putting Layne in a seemingly impossible situation. But Layne, thirty-two, was a daredevil who loved a challenge. He led a ninety-nine-yard touchdown drive with his passing and running — and help from Nitschke, whose ill-timed roughing-the-passer penalty negated a fourth-down incompletion deep in Green Bay territory.

With the score tied at 10–10 and twenty seconds left, the Steelers tried an onside kick that failed, the ball rolling out of bounds at the Green Bay 46. McHan led the offense onto the field and hit McGee over the middle for a seventeen-yard gain. McGee alertly called a timeout as he went down, stopping the clock with three seconds left. Lombardi sent in Hornung for a forty-three-yard field goal attempt, and the Golden Boy's kick split the uprights as the final gun sounded, giving the Packers a 13–10 win.

Finally, after six games in six states and more than ten thousand travel miles, the exhibition season was over. The Packers had gone 4-2, faring better than anyone who saw them in 1958 could have expected. Speaking to reporters after the Minneapolis game, Lombardi said he was pleased overall. He still needed better talent at some positions and saw numerous mistakes when he reviewed game films, but his players were in shape, blocked and tackled hard, and ran the ball effectively, this last game notwithstanding. It was encouraging, he said, to see them buy into his stricter program. When he came to Green Bay he had thought he would need five years to turn the Packers around, he said, but now he could see it happening in three.

"Remember what I said when I took this job? You have to have a good defense to start with," he said, his smile indicating he believed he now had one.

Indeed, the Packer secondary had been solid since Dillon and Tunnell returned, and the linebackers had been tough and consistent through the exhibition season. Forester, the veteran on the right side, was seldom out of position; a drawling Texan (one day he ordered a steak at a restaurant and the waitress brought him pancakes, thinking he had said "stack") nicknamed Bubba, he was the unit captain. Currie, the second-year man on the left side, was an athletic first-round pick with the speed to cover receivers and a knack for making plays. Bettis, in the middle, loved to flatten opponents.

Up front, Phil Bengston had tried different tackle-end combinations throughout the preseason, but the guesswork was over now that Henry Jordan was around. Jordan and Bill Quinlan, teammates in Cleveland, would start on the left side. Quinlan, as advertised, was a wild man — rumors abounded about his off-day drinking escapades — but he played with a relentless motor, chasing ball carriers and delivering jarring hits. Dave Hanner, in the best shape of his career after surviving training camp, would team with Nate Borden on the right side. This "front four," playing together for the first time, had held Pittsburgh to sixty-nine yards rushing while pressuring Layne on passing plays.

"We had our share of problems last year, but I think we're just a much better defense this year," Bettis said. "I'm looking forward to playing the Bears."

A few days before the game in Minneapolis, a tall, slender athlete knocked on Lombardi's door at Oakton Manor. The coach answered and broke into a smile.

140

"Hi, Coach," Ron Kramer said, extending a hand.

"Great to have you back. Are you ready to go?" Lombardi replied.

"I think so," Kramer said.

A twenty-three-year-old tight end, Kramer was the best athlete Vainisi had ever drafted, lineman-sized at six feet four and 235 pounds, but possessing a receiver's speed and hands. At the University of Michigan, he had been a two-time football All-American, the leading scorer on the basketball team, and ran track. The Packers had made him the fourth overall pick in the 1957 draft, and he had caught twenty-eight passes and blocked hard as a rookie. Having Kramer out there was like having an extra player on the field, Lisle Blackbourn had said.

Near the end of the 1957 season, though, Kramer went down with a terrible injury during a game in California — three torn knee ligaments and a broken leg. A team doctor repaired the damage but Kramer's doctor in Michigan told him he would never play football again. Kramer didn't tell the Packers about that prognosis. He went into the Air Force for a year and tried to rehabilitate his knee on his own. Day after day in Washington, D.C., where he was posted, he wrapped a hundred-pound weight around his ankle, sat on a table, and kicked up the leg over and over.

Lombardi had been told to expect a major contributor when Kramer was discharged, but Kramer arrived at Oakton Manor in rough shape. His knee was better but he weighed just 212 pounds, well below his usual playing weight. He had suffered from ulcers during the year off, he explained. Still, he dressed for practice, and Lombardi immediately ordered him to run pass routes, curious to see him move. Kramer caught some balls, but later, with his room door closed, raised his foot on a pillow and applied ice packs to his sore knee. It had swelled badly.

Gary Knafelc welcomed Kramer back; they had become friends standing next to each other in the huddle throughout the 1957 season.

Great to see you, Ron. Hope you're ready. You won't believe how things have changed.

So I hear.

But Knafelc couldn't help wondering what was in store for him now that Kramer was back.

Knafelc had fretted about his future since the day in February when Lombardi told him he was moving from receiver to tight end, Kramer's position. Knafelc had gone home and told his wife, "We're in trouble, honey. I'm going to have to start blocking people, something I've never done!"

Knafelc, twenty-seven, really wanted to stick with the team. His lopsided grin, high cheekbones, quick wit, and dashing sweep of dark hair had made him a fan favorite. Unlike many of his teammates, who fled Wisconsin as soon as the season was over, he had built a year-round life in Green Bay with his wife and two young sons, purchasing a home and a business. Everyone in town knew him. He had hosted one of the Packers' weekly television shows several years earlier.

After being ordered to switch positions, he worked hard to become a tight end. Lombardi taught him the ABCs of blocking, how to take a quick first step, fire into an opponent, and pop the man in the chest. Knafelc hurled himself at defenders in the nutcracker drill, his easygoing nature masking a tenaciousness that had helped him make it in pro ball after a career at the University of Colorado. His tight-end competition included Kramer, a star, and Steve Meilinger, a low-key veteran who blocked well. Lombardi had alternated Knafelc and Meilinger during the exhibition games, but Meilinger had broken an arm in Winston-Salem, putting him out for the season. Now Kramer had returned. Knafelc glumly watched the bigger, stronger, younger tight end in practice, thinking his chance to start had evaporated.

After the Minneapolis game, Lombardi brought the team back to Pewaukee Lake for a few final days of hard practices before the regular-season opener against the Bears on Sunday at City Stadium. A palpable sense of excitement coursed through the camp. Lombardi initially opened the practices to the public, but when more than one hundred fans showed up on Tuesday, the coach eyed them nervously, knowing George Halas was famous for spying on opponent practices. Fans who returned to watch the Wednesday and Thursday practices were shooed away by police.

Lombardi drove the offense relentlessly in these final workouts, zeroing in on his beloved sweep, the heart of his running game. It looked simple, just a handoff to a back running wide, but was actually a complex dance in which every player had a crucial assignment. It failed unless every player did his job, making it the perfect play for emphasizing the importance of limiting mistakes and playing well together, key commandments in Lombardi's football faith. His Giants had mastered the sweep, and his Packers would, too, he vowed.

The play call was "twenty-eight" or "forty-nine," depending on which back carried in which direction, but either way, its identifying marker was the "pulling" of the guards, who, instead of driving forward on the snap, stepped back, pivoted in the direction of the play, and raced parallel to the line until they passed the tackle and turned upfield ahead of the back, who had taken a handoff and was just behind them, looking for openings. The goal was to create mismatches between the guards and opposing linebackers and defensive backs. For that to happen, the other Packer blockers had to keep the rest of the defense away. Ringo had to handle the middle linebacker. The tackle on the side where the play was directed had to control the defensive end. The back that didn't carry the ball had to take on the defensive tackle the pulling guard ordinarily took.

And the tight end, after lining up wide of the tackle, had to shoot out to the inside and seal off the linebacker, whose area the play went through. That was the most important block. The sweep was doomed if the tight end missed it.

Lombardi wanted his players so comfortable with the sweep that they ran it perfectly, never making a bad read, missing a block, or hitting the wrong hole. He drove them toward that goal in Pewaukee, running the play again and again. The linemen made their reads, the guards pulled, the back took a handoff, and for it all to work, the tight end made the key sealing block.

"Come on, make the reads!" Lombardi shouted. "Hold your blocks! Drive your man!"

Early in the workout, Knafelc and Kramer alternated, but then Lombardi ordered Knafelc to stay on the field. Knafelc lined up and blocked Forester for ten straight plays, Lombardi standing right beside him, voicing a stream of criticisms. *Come on, Gary, move your arms! You can do better than that!* Then Knafelc lined up against Currie for ten straight plays. *Drive, drive, drive, Gary! Hit him harder! More, more!* Finally, Knafelc lined up against the crazed Ray Nitschke for ten straight plays. *No, Gary! The play fails if you can't make that block!*

Knafelc knew he was being tested. He looked over to the sideline and saw his young sons, who had accompanied him to practice. They could hear their father being lambasted.

After blocking on thirty straight sweeps, Knafelc rose wearily from a pile, turned to Lombardi, and said, "Coach, Ray knows what is coming." Moments later, Lombardi ended practice. Knafelc's sons ran to him and hugged him, and they walked across the field to the locker room. Knafelc's oldest son looked up and said, "It's OK, Daddy, we still love you."

The players spent a final night at Oakton Manor before returning to Green Bay Friday morning. Knafelc and his wife and sons were eating an early breakfast at the coffee shop before heading out when Knafelc's wife's face went ashen.

"Honey, he's walking toward us . . . Coach Lombardi," she whispered.

"Oh, no. He's going to cut me or something," Knafelc muttered.

There was a pause and his wife continued, "Yes, here he comes. He's walking right to us."

Moments later Lombardi arrived at their table. He greeted Knafelc's wife and children, put his hand on Knafelc's shoulder, leaned close, and whispered in his ear.

"Gary," he said, "you're starting Sunday."

Knafelc nodded. He was speechless, stunned, and electrified. Lombardi had challenged him, humbled him, frightened him, helped him, and in the end, rewarded him. He didn't know if he could keep the starting job for long, but he had it now.

Suddenly, he couldn't wait for Sunday. He would play harder for this demanding coach than he had ever played before. And he knew his teammates would, too.

* * *

Before breaking camp in Pewaukee, Lombardi made his final cuts, paring the roster down to thirty-six men. It was a long, emotional day as he gave bad news to some players and good news to others.

Tim Brown fully expected to get cut when Lombardi called him in; he thought he had played well enough to earn a job, recent drops and fumbles notwithstanding, but he had probably run his mouth too much, and NFL teams just didn't keep that many black players, especially ones who chafed at the status quo.

But Lombardi stunned him.

"Congratulations, Brown. You're on the team. You had a hell of a camp," he said.

It took every ounce of Brown's limited self-restraint to keep him from breaking into song as he walked out of the room.

The final roster had three quarterbacks (McHan, Starr, and Francis), five offensive backs (Hornung, Taylor, Carpenter, Don McIlhenny, and Brown), seven offensive linemen (Ringo, Kramer, Thurston, Gregg, Skoronski, Masters, and John Dittrich), five offensive ends (McGee, Knafelc, Kramer, Dowler, and A. D. Williams), six defensive linemen (Quinlan, Hanner, Jordan, Borden, Jim Temp, and Ken Beck), four linebackers (Bettis, Forester, Currie, and Nitschke), and six defensive backs (Dillon, Tunnell, Symank, Whittenton, Gremminger, and Freeman). Lombardi had delivered on his promise to shake things up, adding three rookies and eight other players who had not been with the Packers before. But still, twenty-five of the thirty-six men had played for Scooter and, in most cases, experienced at least several years of Packer misery.

Basically, Lombardi would be playing a new game with a pat hand.

His last move in camp was to name McHan the starting quarterback. The news didn't generate big headlines or stir a dramatic response. Francis had played the best of any of the quarterbacks in the exhibition season, but Lombardi wasn't about to start him against a defense as savvy and hard-hitting as Chicago's. Starr excelled in film sessions, but alas, the game was played on a field. McHan hadn't stood out until the last quarter in Minneapolis, when he led a touchdown drive and then completed a clutch pass to set up Hornung's game-winning field goal — just the kind of playmaking Lombardi had hoped for when he obtained McHan.

McHan exhaled inwardly when Lombardi gave him the good news, having never stopped worrying that he might get shipped back to the Cardinals and that dingbat Wolfner. Now he could relax and play ball, once again bearing a heavy load of responsibility, just as he always had and always preferred.

He thanked Lombardi for the chance and pledged to reward the coach for having faith in him.

Let's go out and win on Sunday, Coach. We can do it. We can beat the Bears.

The other two quarterbacks reacted differently to the news, which they heard from teammates. (Lombardi, like most coaches, informed only those who would be playing, not those who wouldn't.) Francis shrugged; he had never really expected to start. Starr took it hard. He was glad to make the team, but having been the Packers' primary starting quarterback for the past two seasons, disappointed about being passed over. McHan had beaten him out.

He packed for the trip back to Green Bay with dull eyes and an impassive expression, saying little. As the team bus rolled out of the Pewaukee camp under gray skies on Friday, carrying the players toward Green Bay and the start of the regular season, he stared out a window and kept his thoughts to himself.

But he wasn't sulking. It simply wasn't in Starr's makeup to sulk.

I am going to keep working hard.

I am going to prepare myself to play as if I'm the starter.

And one of these days, I will be.

PART II

★ 12 ★

WO HOURS BEFORE kickoff on September 27, Lombardi was at City Stadium. It had rained on and off during the night, and he wanted to check on the grass. He put on his tan overcoat and dark fedora in the locker room, walked down the tunnel, and stepped onto the field. A light mist fell and a breeze blew the tails of his coat as he tapped a shoe into the thick green turf.

Good, it's firm. We should be able to run the ball.

Looking up, he envisioned the now-silent stadium as it soon would be, filled with cheering fans. But would the damp conditions limit the passing game? McHan was experienced, having made fifty-three starts for the Cardinals, but he was prone to self-doubt. *The Bears are tough on defense. I hope his confidence doesn't sag.*

Lombardi and Marie had entertained friends the night before, but amid the laughter, clinking ice, and cigarette smoke, his mind seldom strayed far from the looming occasion, his first regular-season game as an NFL head coach. He had awakened early, collected Vincent, and driven across town to the stadium, stopping at St. Willebrords for mass. (Vincent, whose high school football season had started, would watch the game from the end of the bench. Marie Lombardi would sit in the stands with the wives of the other coaches.) The rain, wind, and chilly temperatures gave the day a wintry feel, and it wasn't even October. Welcome to Green Bay.

The game had been sold out for more than a month, with all but

149

a few of the 32,500 tickets in the hands of Packer fans curious to see if this coach could succeed where Scooter McLean, Lisle Blackbourn, and Gene Ronzani had failed. Could Lombardi make the Packers respectable again? He believed he could. His players were in better shape and more disciplined and confident, and although most had played on the horrid 1958 squad, Lombardi had added talent, especially on defense. If the exhibition season was any indication, the Packers would at least no longer lose by 56–0 scores.

Of course, Lombardi knew better than to attach significance to meaningless contests. Even though the Packers had won four exhibition games, *Sports Illustrated* and *Sport* magazines had still picked them to finish last in the Western Division — they had so far to climb. Even the ever-optimistic *Press-Gazette* had predicted they could win "three or four games, maybe more."

The Bears, meanwhile, were expected to challenge the Colts for the Western Division title. They had won eight of twelve games in 1958 and had a bruising defense led by Bill George, regarded as the game's best middle linebacker along with the Giants' Sam Huff and Detroit's Joe Schmidt. Smart, quick, and almost impossible to block, George had started out as a lineman until Halas discovered that, with his agility and reactions, he could make plays all over the field when positioned just behind the line instead of on it. His supporting cast included Doug Atkins, a vicious, tackle-tossing 260-pound end, and veteran pass defenders Erich Barnes and J. C. Caroline.

The Packers had almost beaten Halas's team in August, but now, Wally Cruice, the Packers' advance scout, told Lombardi that Halas had played with his hands tied behind his back that night, using just a few of the many defensive alignments he employed to confuse opponents, changing them from play to play as expertly as a major league pitcher mixed a fastball, curve, and changeup. Cruice was a former Northwestern halfback whose job, since the early 1950s, was to study Green Bay's next opponent and prepare a report. He knew his stuff. The Packers would have a tough time.

Lombardi had huddled with his quarterbacks during the week, debating which plays to run. Taylor off right tackle? Hornung around left end? McGee over the middle? As always, he wanted input from the quarterbacks themselves, especially McHan, who would be calling the plays. Starr, despite having been relegated to the bench, had studied film of the Bears — more than McHan — and made several astute suggestions. As always, his intelligence and work ethic impressed Lombardi.

The stands began to fill ninety minutes before kickoff. Fans came in their cars, on city buses, by foot. Politicians and paper mill owners came through the turnstiles, found their seats next to shift workers, hailed each other, and discussed the game. Years of losing hadn't dulled Green Bay's love for the Packers, especially early in a season, before the losses started piling up. Women dressed in their best clothes and paraded to their seats in the single-tier bowl. The Lumberjack Band, a flannel-clad marching band that had played at Packer home games since the 1920s, played a brief show.

In the press box, which hovered over the home-side stands, every seat was taken. Television and radio broadcast crews tested their equipment. A statistical crew, composed of moonlighting *Press-Gazette* business and news reporters, got ready to chart the game. Reporters from wire services, radio stations, and smaller papers sat at desks and prepared to cover the game alongside beat writers Art Daley and Lee Remmel of the *Press-Gazette* and Bud Lea and Chuck Johnson from the Milwaukee papers.

Halas took a walk on the field as his players dressed. He was pleased to see the Packers looking better, not that he would admit it. He usually just wanted to crush them; the Bears and Packers had the NFL's oldest and angriest rivalry, having traded low blows and broken bones since the 1920s while their fans brawled, bet, and threw liquor bottles at each other. At one time Halas had valued nothing more than a victory over Curly Lambeau, but the heat had gone out of their games since the Packers fell apart, and as much as Halas craved victories, he was a businessman first, and bitter games between the Bears and Packers were good for business. They made news, sold tickets, made seasons more interesting. Halas wanted the fire back in the rivalry. In 1956, when the Packers were campaigning to win funding for their new stadium, he had stumped on their behalf just before the election. More recently, when Packer president Dominic Olejniczak had asked him to recommend replacements for Scooter, he suggested Lombardi, whom he'd gotten to know at league events. Now that Lombardi was here, the Packers surely would be tougher. Halas smiled to himself and shook his head ruefully.

I need to whip his Italian ass today.

In the Packer locker room, players quietly went through their pregame rituals, anticipating the hard hitting ahead. They took off their street clothes and put on their uniforms, which the team's equipment manager, Dad Braisher, had arranged on hangers in their lockers. Then they went to Bud Jorgensen's training table to get their ankles taped. Jim Ringo, as always, also wanted tape on all ten fingertips.

They looked at each other with smiles as they put on their uniforms, which Lombardi had redesigned. The Packers had worn an assortment of different uniforms in the 1950s, seemingly unable to find a design they liked — navy blue jerseys with faded gold pants; all-white tops and bottoms with a single navy stripe down the side of the pants; and recently, dark bluish-green jerseys with three gold bands on the ends of the sleeves. Lombardi had gone with dark forest green jerseys with gold and white stripes on the ends of the sleeves, white numerals, and gold pants and helmets.

At noon, both teams went out to warm up as the Lumberjack Band played and fans shouted encouragement to the Packers and booed the Bears. Lamar McHan, Bart Starr, and Joe Francis threw passes to receivers running square-outs and crossing patterns. The backs and linemen ran through plays. The stands continued to fill.

After a half hour outside, the players returned to their locker rooms. Lombardi asked the Packers to gather around him. He was more nervous than he wanted to admit. He hadn't been in charge of a team since St. Cecilia's.

You're prepared. Go play like you can. Be physical. This is football. Do your job. Represent the Green Bay Packers. We can win. We can beat this team.

The players jumped up, crowded through the doorway, and

sprinted down the tunnel to the field. *Let's go! Come on!* Lombardi had been encouraging and humiliating them since July. It had been an exhausting and, at times, discouraging process, and some players still weren't sure they wanted to play for him. But he had pushed them beyond what they thought their athletic limits were, and that was exhilarating. Unlike Scooter or Blackbourn, he had truly prepared them to compete.

This first game was critical for any team in any season, but especially so now for the Packers. Lombardi understood that. If the players lost after working so hard, they might rebel, thinking he was just a louder version of Blackbourn, just another guy destined to lose in Green Bay, and start resisting what he was teaching. All hell could break loose. But if they won, they would see the benefits and work even harder.

Jim Ringo and Bill Forester, the team captains, went to midfield and won the coin flip. Lombardi chose to kick off; the wind was gusting to twenty-five miles per hour and he wanted the conditions in his favor early. The crowd rose and cheered as Johnny Morris, a Bears rookie, caught the opening kickoff at the goal line and ran forward. Ray Nitschke, the first man downfield for Green Bay, slammed into him at the 18-yard line. The ball popped loose and Nitschke pounced on it. *What a start!*

McHan exchanged a glance with Lombardi as the offense headed to the field. He knew what the look meant. *Go ahead. This is a gift. Take a shot.* McHan kneeled in the huddle and called for a halfback option. He took the snap and handed to Paul Hornung running right on what appeared to be a sweep. The defense came up to stop him, but Hornung slowed, looked downfield, and arched a pass toward his backfield mate, Lew Carpenter, who had circled behind the defense and was open at the goal line.

The crowd sent up a piercing roar, but Hornung, in his excitement, put too much on the pass. The ball sailed above Carpenter, who leapt and got one hand on it but couldn't control it as he fell. It bounced away, incomplete, as the crowd groaned.

Ooooooooh.

The near miss seemed to deflate the offense. The Bears stuffed

Jim Taylor up the middle and McHan's third-down pass for Max McGee was incomplete. Hornung then missed a nineteen-yard field goal attempt, hooking the ball left. The crowd groaned again and Hornung's shoulders slumped as he jogged off the field. *After all that, no points.*

The Bear offense took the field for the first time with Ed Brown, a veteran quarterback, calling the plays. He sent Rick Casares off right and left tackle on the first two plays. Bill Quinlan and Nate Borden held their ground, and Forester and Dan Currie delivered strong hits to knock the sturdy Casares over. A third-down pass fell incomplete and Lombardi clapped as his defense came off the field. *How to go there! That's some football!*

The Packer offense fared better on its next possession. Hornung gained five yards on a sweep. Taylor picked up six up the middle. Hornung drifted out of the backfield and caught a short pass for five. In the game's first seven minutes Hornung had run, caught, kicked, and thrown the ball. He couldn't believe how drastically his fortunes had changed. He had gone from the end of the bench to the middle of everything.

The drive continued. Taylor gained seven behind Forrest Gregg and four behind Norm Masters. Lombardi paced, pleased to see his blockers winning battles. At midfield, McHan dropped back and looked to his left and right as Gary Knafelc got behind J. C. Caroline deep over the middle, around the Chicago 20. An on-target pass would have resulted in a touchdown, but McHan threw too hard and the ball sailed over Knafelc.

One play later, Boyd Dowler, the rookie, also got behind Caroline deep, around the 15, and McHan threw a perfect pass. Dowler dropped it. Lombardi kicked the ground, frustrated by the missed opportunities. Dowler would pay for his mistake.

Halas subbed in the younger Zeke Bratkowski at quarterback near the end of the first quarter, and the Bear offense perked up. Bratkowski completed two passes, moving the ball to the Green Bay 26. Three plays later, Halas went for it on fourth-and-one at the 17. The Packer defenders exhorted each other in the huddle, taking deep breaths to steel themselves. It was early in the game but their uniforms were already caked with mud. Bratkowski took the snap and tried to lunge across the line, but Dave Hanner and Henry Jordan outmuscled their blockers and stood him up. No gain!

Midway through the second quarter, Bratkowski drove the Bears just far enough into Packer territory for their kicker, John Aveni, to try a forty-six-yard field goal. Aveni put it through to give the Bears a 3–0 lead.

Lombardi and McHan spoke on the sidelines before the next series. As much as he wanted to run the ball, Lombardi noticed Packer receivers were getting open.

Mix it up, Lamar. Don't be afraid to go deep.

Yes, sir.

After Taylor gained twelve yards behind Gregg on first down, McHan called for an option pass. Hornung took the pitchout, swept right, and stopped to throw. McGee, his deep target, was covered, so he arched a pass back over the middle to Knafelc, who grabbed the ball for a nineteen-yard gain. McHan, emboldened, threw deep on the next play for Dowler, the rookie receiver, who had gotten behind Caroline on a "streak" route, a straight downfield sprint. Caroline, a veteran, knew he had been beaten, and grabbed Dowler, intentionally interfering to keep the rookie from scoring.

The penalty gave the Packers a first down at the Chicago 17. Knafelc ran a square-out pattern and broke open in the end zone, but Richie Pettibon, at safety, gave him a subtle shove to the hip as McHan's pass neared. Knafelc stumbled without a referee's flag falling, and the ball sailed beyond him. A holding penalty on the next play moved the ball back fifteen yards, and then McHan, just looking to move the ball close enough for a field goal attempt, badly overthrew Hornung in the left flat. The ball sailed right to Bill George, who intercepted.

The half ended moments later, and McHan limped noticeably as the teams jogged to their locker rooms with the Bears ahead, 3–0.

"What's wrong?" Lombardi asked.

McHan explained that he had taken a hard hit from Atkins on his left thigh midway through that last drive. There was a bruise that kept him from planting solidly, he said, which might be why he had missed that last throw so badly.

The quarterback said he would understand if the coach took him out, but Lombardi shook his head no. *I like what I'm seeing. The offense is moving the ball. You're changing plays at the line. Do your best.*

McHan walked away determined to play well despite his injury. He couldn't remember a coach showing such faith in him, especially after a half in which the offense had been shut out. His prior coaches mostly just told him to play better.

Lombardi spoke optimistically to the squad. *You're playing a hell of a ball game. The defense is doing a good job, a great job. We should be in good shape if we cut down on our offensive mistakes.*

Early in the third quarter the Packer offense continued to move. Taylor swept around right end, hesitated as Jerry Kramer and Fred Thurston opened a hole, and dashed through for a twenty-one-yard gain. Then he went for twenty up the middle as Ringo sent George sprawling with a leg block. The fans implored Lombardi to take a risk on a fourth-and-one at the Chicago 19, but he felt it was important to score points and sent in Tim Brown to hold a field goal attempt by Hornung. The rookie hadn't been on the field all day.

The snap was perfect, but Brown mishandled the wet ball and dropped it. As he desperately tried to right it for the kick, he was smothered by the opposition.

The fans groaned as they sat. *Another chance wasted! Damn!*

This one annoyed Lombardi. He didn't mind the Bears stopping the Packers, but he loathed the sight of the Packers stopping themselves.

The Packer defense eased everyone's frustrations, again stopping the Bear offense cold to force a punt. Halas, nothing if not stubborn, was convinced he could run on the Packers; Chicago's rushing offense had been among the league's best the year before, and the Packers hadn't stopped anyone. He kept calling for Casares to slam into the middle of the line, expecting holes to open. But Hanner and Jordan held their ground, fending off blocks and crashing into the burly fullback, knocking their helmets askew as they rolled to the ground in a heap. Then Halas tried sending Willie Galimore wide on sweeps, but Forester and Currie sniffed them out, moving laterally down the line and tackling Galimore at the waist before he could find a hole, hitting him so hard that he lay on the ground for several seconds before wearily rising and returning to the huddle.

Lombardi clapped his hands as the defense came off the field, having again forced a punt. Tom Bettis, his bright-white uniform numerals gone dark with mud, stopped to talk to Phil Bengston, the quiet defensive coach, who, like his boss, wore a hat and overcoat.

They keep running it. I'm sticking with the base defense.

Yes, do that for sure. But be ready for when they open it up. They aren't going to run forever.

McHan kneeled in the huddle and called another long pass, came to the line, surveyed the defense, and didn't change the play — his receivers had been getting open against the Bears' man-to-man coverage. McGee faked a square-out and sprinted past Erich Barnes at midfield. McHan lofted a spiral toward him, and McGee caught the ball on the run at the Chicago 40. The crowd screeched as McGee raced for the end zone, his long legs churning. Barnes pushed him out of bounds at the 13 after a sixty-seven-yard gain.

Surely, Lombardi thought, this time the Packers would score. McHan sent Taylor into the line, but the Bear defense held him to a short gain. Then Taylor ran off left tackle, behind Masters, and Atkins slammed him to the ground. On third down McHan overthrew Dowler, his bruised thigh affecting the throw. Tim Brown came back out for another field goal try, and this time the snap and hold were flawless . . . but Hornung stubbed the kick and the ball sailed left of the uprights. The Golden Boy put his hands to his helmet in disbelief as the crowd buzzed. *Maybe it's just not meant to be.*

A shiver ran through the stands as Galimore finally punctured the Packer defense on the next series, turning a short pass into a thirty-two-yard gain that moved the ball past midfield. The drive stalled after that, but the Bears' Aveni sailed a forty-two-yard field goal attempt high into the mist and between the uprights. Despite having been badly outplayed and outgained, the Bears now led, 6–0, as the third quarter ended.

The fans grumbled. *This game would be so different if we had their kicker.*

As the fourth quarter began McHan misfired on two passes and

McGee dropped back to punt. He kicked the ball, but an onrushing defender ran into him and an official dropped a flag, signaling a roughing penalty. The Packers would retain possession with a fresh set of downs. But even better, Pettibon fumbled as he returned the punt, and Ringo, having sprinted downfield after the snap, fell on the ball at the Chicago 26. Lombardi declined the penalty, and the Packers had a first down deep in Chicago territory.

As the offense broke its huddle and approached the line, the fans stood, drawn to their feet by the tension. *If we don't score now, we probably won't.* Lombardi walked down the sideline toward the action as the Bear defense dug in. Moments such as this were why he had put players through all those sprints and grass drills. Being in shape could make all the difference at the end of a rough ball game.

McHan fretted that he couldn't throw effectively, so he kept the ball on the ground. Hornung gained six around right end as Kramer and Thurston cleared a path. Taylor, going the other way behind Masters, slammed into a hole and gained five for a first down at the 15. Hornung swept right again for five. Taylor went for two up the middle, and George, making a critical mistake, hit the runner late and was flagged, the personal foul giving the Packers a first down at the 4.

There were eight minutes left in the game. The crowd was shouting, the wind gusting, a light mist falling. Lombardi stuffed his hands deep into his pockets. He couldn't do anything. He just had to hope his guys came through.

Hornung ran right on a sweep, but George cut through Kramer's block and tackled him for a one-yard loss. On second down at the 5, McHan knelt in the huddle and called for Hornung to run up the middle behind Ringo, but he changed his mind when he reached the line. The Bears wouldn't expect the Packers to run right at Atkins, their right end — not now, with the game on the line.

McHan barked an audible signaling that Taylor would now carry around left end.

One, thirty-four!

Two months of chalkboard sessions and on-field practices had prepared the players for this moment. They heard McHan and adjusted to the new play call. When the ball was snapped, Kramer and Thurston pivoted and ran to their left down the line as Knafelc carried the outside linebacker toward the sideline — a sealing block that created a lane. Taylor took the ball from McHan, saw the opening, cut sharply inside Knafelc, and slammed into the hole. His forceful push sent the pile toward the end zone, and Taylor rode it across the goal line like a surfer catching a wave.

The fans erupted. *Touchdown! At last!* The cheers were so loud the stadium's concrete underpinnings vibrated.

The stands quickly quieted as Hornung stayed on the field for the extra point, ordinarily a sure thing but not on a day when he had missed three field goals, including two from inside the 20. The fans prayed he wouldn't give them one more reason to criticize him. *Come on, Golden Paul! Don't blow this one!*

The snap, hold, and kick were perfect. The ball sailed through the uprights. Horning exhaled. The Packers led, 7–6, with six minutes to play.

The Bears started a possession at their 34 after the kickoff return, needing to gain around twenty-five yards for Aveni to have a shot at a field goal. The Packer defense dug in. Galimore swept right for nine yards and picked up six on a swing pass. Halas tried a piece of trickery, a reverse. Ed Brown handed to Casares running left, and Casares handed to Galimore coming the other way. The deception didn't fool Hanner. He saw the play unfolding, waited for Galimore, and slammed the runner to the grass for a six-yard loss. That put the Bears in a hole. Brown's second-down pass was dropped, and a third-down throw to Galimore gained just a yard, as Forester hounded the elusive Bears back and brought him down. The Bears punted.

Trying to run out the clock, McHan kept the ball on the ground, and Taylor and Hornung picked up two first downs before the Bears stopped them and forced a punt with slightly more than a minute left. McGee dropped back, took the snap, and sent a booming kick far downfield. The ball landed on the Chicago 10 and rolled out of bounds at the 2. The fans chanted McGee's name as he came off the field. He had sailed a sixty-two-yarder at the perfect moment.

Halas sent Brown out, hoping for a last-gasp miracle, but when Brown dropped back on first down, Hanner and Jordan beat their blockers and swarmed him in the end zone. A referee ran up with his hands clasped over his head, signaling a safety, worth two points. The linemen rose from the ground and smiled at each other over the fallen quarterback. Green Bay led, 9–6, with forty-six seconds left.

The Bears' only hope was to recover an onside kick, but Nitschke fell on the ball when they attempted it. The fans sent out thunderous cheers as the offense trotted onto the field for a final play. Partaking in a Packer tradition seldom seen in recent years, the fans counted down the final ten seconds and threw their programs and seat cushions into the air when time expired.

Ringo grabbed the ball, raced over to Lombardi, and handed it to him. "Here, you deserve this more than anyone," he said. As noise rained down on them, the players followed Lombardi as he walked across the field to shake hands with Halas. The Bears coach managed to smile and offer congratulations. As Lombardi walked away, Lew Carpenter and Emlen Tunnell picked him up and ran toward the locker room with him on their shoulders. Lombardi, still holding the game ball, was too stunned to speak. McGee, Bobby Dillon, and Bill Quinlan trotted along behind him, whooping and hollering. They finally let Lombardi down as they crossed the goal line and neared the tunnel.

Fans marveled at the scene. The Packers had played hundreds of games over the years and won a half-dozen championships, but no one could remember their coach being carried off the field.

In the locker room, the players shouted as Lombardi held the game ball high and thanked them for their hard work. When he was finished, he sought out McGee, whose long punt had sealed the victory. Lombardi grabbed the receiver by the cheeks and kissed him right on the lips.

When reporters were let in, they found Lombardi in the coaches' quarters, just off the main locker room. He wore "a smile that refused to come off," the *Press-Gazette* reported.

"As I told you when I got here, you have to have a defense to win in this game, and our defense did a tremendous job," he said. "And our boys were so determined. Even when all those breaks went against us, they stayed right in there."

McHan, standing at his locker, told reporters he had played the second half with a thigh bruise; he had connected on only three of twelve pass attempts. Lombardi said McHan stayed in the game because he was running the offense so well. "I don't know if it was apparent from the stands, but he changed the play at the line many times, including on the winning touchdown Jimmy ran," Lombardi said.

McHan said he appreciated Lombardi keeping him in after he was injured. "I checked with him and he told me to keep going. When a man displays that kind of confidence in you, you'll do anything to keep from letting him down," McHan said. "This was a great team effort, especially on defense. If they can keep that up and we can iron out a few of our mistakes, we will have a tough ball club."

No one knew that better than Halas, who was glum but gracious when he spoke to reporters. "The better team won, no question," he said. "You have to hand it to Vince. He did a splendid job. He had a fine team out there. The Packers have made a great transition under him."

A steady rain fell as daylight ebbed, but it couldn't douse the excitement that swept through Green Bay. Fans left City Stadium and crowded into downtown bars and restaurants, anxious to celebrate. The Packers dominated conversations.

McGee won it with a punt!

Taylor and Hornung ran right through the Bears!

You had to see it!

Lombardi collected Vincent and drove home to dry off and warm up. He thought about taking Marie out to Jimmy Manci's for an Italian meal, or to Zeider Zee's, where they had a piano bar. But his house quickly filled with friends such as Jack Koeppler, Tony Canadeo, and Dick Bourguignon — the people who had brought him to town wanted to celebrate with him. Lombardi laughed and manned the bar. When Jerry Atkinson, another board member, called to congratulate him, he grabbed the receiver and roared into it.

Jerry, why aren't you here?

He was a long way from New York and just one game in, but already, indisputably, at home.

★ 13 ★

HORNUNG WAS TOO TIRED to celebrate that Sunday night. He enjoyed a night out more than anyone, but all that action had exhausted him. *Lombardi wore my ass out!* He had loved every minute, even when he missed those short field goals and almost ended up as the goat. He was in the middle of things again, a key player in the game. Scooter and Blackbourn had taken that from him, and Lombardi had given it back. Nothing could please him more. Packer fans didn't understand how much he loved to play and win. The closer his offense got to the goal line, the more he wanted the ball; he saw himself as a difference maker, a winner. He had been miserable when Notre Dame went 2-8 in his senior season and the Packers won just four games in his first two years. But those miseries made this win that much sweeter. They had beaten old man Halas!

By Monday afternoon he was rested and ready. The players had the day off, and he and Max McGee headed to Appleton, twenty-five miles south of Green Bay, for an evening of fun. Since Lombardi had declared their favorite Green Bay haunts off-limits, they had to leave town to shake loose in their customary style. Fred Thurston, Ron Kramer, and Jerry Kramer were coming, and there was talk of Bill Quinlan also joining them.

People at the bar bought them drinks and slapped their backs, still elated a day after the game.

We really did beat the Bears, didn't we?

The players would pay for their fun the next day when Lombardi

163

started practice with a longer-than-usual grass drill. But they didn't regret celebrating.

The Packers' victory shocked the rest of the NFL. Other players and coaches paused when they heard the score. *Huh? Whaaat?* How could the lowly Packers beat the mighty Bears?

It wasn't the result of a lucky bounce or single, crazy play, either. The Packers had played better, controlling the ball for nearly forty of the game's sixty minutes, and rushing for 176 yards to Chicago's 75. Casares had gained just 29 yards on the ground, seldom finding running room in the middle of the Packer defense. Taylor and Hornung, meanwhile, had combined for 159 rushing yards, repeatedly charging through holes cleared by their blockers.

Yes, the Packers had blown a handful of scoring chances and needed a gift, a fumbled punt by a rookie, to set up the winning touchdown. But they had worn the Bears down physically, especially in the fourth quarter.

As the fans and players celebrated on Monday, Lombardi and his assistants were back at work, watching game film and grading individual performances. Lombardi didn't hold a news conference, just spoke — briefly — to any reporters who called. And unlike Scooter McLean, he didn't walk to the Northland Hotel to absorb a noontime grilling from the executive committee. Those days were over. Although Lombardi had only been in charge for one league game, it was laughable to think of him being second-guessed in such a way. The committee wouldn't dare.

Lombardi was back to his grouchy self when practice resumed on Tuesday, wanting to review what had gone wrong, not right, in the Chicago game. The players split into offensive and defensive groups to watch film. The defensive session, led by Phil Bengston, was calm and quiet; the players could hear Lombardi through the walls, voice rising in anger as he showed the offensive mistakes he had unearthed.

Fuzzy, you need to feint to the left there, not the right. Didn't we go over that?

Yes, Coach. I will, Coach.

Max, you need to sell that route much better than that. No one is going to buy that fake.

I'll do that from now on, sir.

Paul, catch the damn ball!

I will, sir.

There was no chance of self-satisfaction setting in. When the players hit the practice field that afternoon, they focused on correcting mistakes and avoiding Lombardi's ire. Their big win was behind them. It was time to move on to their next game, against the Detroit Lions at City Stadium on Sunday.

The Lions had lost their opener, 21–9, to the Colts, in a matchup of the two most recent NFL champions, the Lions having won their third title of the decade in 1957 before the Colts won in 1958. The once-mighty Lions had fallen off sharply since then, going 4-7-1 in 1958 with Tobin Rote playing quarterback after Bobby Layne was traded. Rote, the former Packer, had thrown four touchdown passes in the 1957 championship game, but now, at age thirty-one, seemingly was slipping. He had thrown four interceptions in the Baltimore opener and there was talk of him being replaced by Earl Morrall, a twenty-five-year-old journeyman.

Like the Bears, the Lions depended on their defense to stay in games. They had one of the league's tougher fronts, led by end Bill Glass, tackle Alex Karras, and Joe Schmidt, the brilliant middle linebacker. Lombardi publicly said the Lions "looked more solid than the Bears" on defense, but privately believed they were vulnerable in the secondary, a notion Wally Cruice seconded. Cruice had watched them shut down Baltimore's running game in the opener but succumb to Johnny Unitas's passing.

When he met with the quarterbacks on Wednesday, Lombardi suggested McHan pass more; the Packers had rushed on forty-eight of their sixty-two plays against the Bears.

"I was hurting. And we were running well," McHan explained.

Lombardi nodded. That was fine. He never minded pounding the ball on the ground. And obviously, it had worked out in the end.

But remember, the Lions will see the films of the game. They'll be ready for the run. We need to prepare for that.

Starr, who had studied film of Detroit's defense at home, suggested plays that might work. McHan nodded. What a pleasure all

165

this was, he thought. In all his time with the Cardinals, he had never gone into such detail preparing for games.

Surely it would pay off.

Early in the week Lombardi made a tough decision. Tim Brown had alternately impressed and annoyed him; the speedy, self-assured rookie could make big plays and had done so at camp and early in the exhibition season, but lately he had mostly made mistakes, dropping passes and punts. The botched field goal attempt on Sunday was, for Lombardi, the last straw. Role players had to be more dependable than that.

He summoned Brown to his office and soberly delivered the bad news.

Brown, we're going to have to let you go.

Brown quietly nodded, turned in his playbook, and went back to Indiana, figuring his football career was over and it was time to find a job singing. Getting cut would mark him as a fringe player, a tough label to shake, especially if you were black. Brown knew he was as good as, if not better than, many white NFL halfbacks — he had seen them and knew he compared favorably — but teams obviously still didn't want too many black players. *This is just how it is. I don't like it, but I have to live with it.*

Lombardi replaced Brown with another rookie, Bill Butler, a tough little defensive back from Berlin, Wisconsin, who had played at Tennessee-Chattanooga. He could return kicks and had better hands, Lombardi felt. Lombardi had cut him during camp but kept him around, thinking such a hardnosed player might eventually make the team.

Before the end of the season, Brown would catch on with the Philadelphia Eagles as part of their "taxi squad" reserve of signed players who didn't play on Sundays unless a starter was injured.

In time, he would become known as perhaps the best player Lombardi ever cut.

When the players came to practice on Thursday, they found a paper tacked to the locker room bulletin board. Lombardi had posted their individual grades for the Chicago game.

166

An 86! I knew I did a hell of a job.

Shit, I'm toast.

A 68? What film did they watch? I did better than that.

The assistants herded the players into a meeting room, which fell silent as Lombardi entered and cleared his throat.

"We had some people play some damn fine ball on Sunday," he said. "You've seen the grades. Forrest, come on up and get paid."

He had their attention now. Get paid? What was the crazy bastard talking about?

Gregg rose from his seat with a sheepish smile and ambled up to Lombardi, who handed him a crisp twenty-dollar bill.

"Nice game, son," he said.

The other players clapped and hollered, but seeing their baffled faces, Lombardi explained what was happening. Players who graded above certain levels or made big plays would get paid, in cash, out of Lombardi's pocket. Ten dollars for a quarterback sack or a thirty-yard run. Twenty when a guard made his block on 60 percent of the running plays and 85 percent of the passing plays — 65 percent and 85 percent for tackles.

Lombardi made a show of calling up players who had qualified and presenting them bills as the rest of the squad clapped.

Hornung was irritated not to earn a bill and left the room grumbling. *I played my ass off. This doesn't seem right.* He didn't care about the money; ten dollars wouldn't cover one night at a bar. But he wanted those kudos from Lombardi. He wanted the hard-ass coach to have to shake his hand and say, "Good job, Paul."

I'm going to play even harder this Sunday. I'm going to do what I need to do.

I'm getting paid next week.

The Packers dominated conversations around Green Bay during the week. *Can we do it again? Heard anything about McHan's thigh?* The Detroit game would reveal a lot, it was believed. The Packers had seldom won back-to-back games in recent years.

Sunday's weather was overcast but drier and warmer. Another sellout crowd packed City Stadium. The Packers started their first possession at their 45 after a Detroit punt. McHan handed off to

167

Don McIlhenny, who swept around left end, cut through an opening forged by a Bob Skoronski block, and broke into the clear along the sideline. He angled back across the field as he ran, throwing off his pursuers, and gained forty-six yards before a pair of Lions dragged him down at the 9.

An early score seemed likely, but McHan fumbled the snap on the next play, and the Lions recovered. The fans groaned, wondering if another long day of frustration loomed. But the Packer defense pulled them back to their feet. Phil Bengston had devised a plan calling for linebackers to red-dog blitz the relatively immobile Tobin Rote — wait until the snap and then charge into the backfield, hopefully catching the blockers off-guard. Bill Forester came at Rote on second down, forcing the quarterback to scramble to his left and throw hurriedly toward his safety receiver. Bobby Freeman read the route, intercepted the pass, and raced down the sideline until he was pushed out of bounds at the 9.

One play later, McHan dropped back to pass and looked for McIlhenny over the middle, but the back was covered so he checked his second option, Knafelc, who was open in the end zone along the near sideline. McHan fired the ball low and Knafelc reeled it in, hugging it to his midsection as he fell. Touchdown, Packers.

Lombardi slapped McHan on the shoulder as the quarterback came off the field. *How to go, Lamar!*

The offense was back on the field within minutes. Hornung, sprung by a Thurston block, ran for twenty-two yards around right end. McGee ran a deep sideline route, eluded Detroit cornerback Terry Barr, and caught a spiral from McHan for a forty-seven-yard gain. At the Detroit 5, McHan rolled right and threw for McIlhenny, who caught the ball just over the goal line with a linebacker on his back. Hornung's extra point put the Packers up 14–0 with three minutes left in the first quarter.

The crowd cheered, the Lumberjack Band played, and the Lions were stunned; they had won fifteen of their last eighteen games against the Packers, usually by a wide margin, and still saw themselves as contenders despite their fading fortunes. Most of their players had won at least one championship; several had won three.

It was inconceivable to them that the Packers could push them around.

They responded to the challenge. Their defensive front rose up, stopping the run and forcing punts on every Green Bay possession in the second quarter. Meanwhile, Rote completed three passes to move the Lion offense into scoring range, and Nick Pietrosante, a rookie fullback, bulled over for a touchdown, the first the Packers had allowed all season. With his team ahead 14–7 at halftime, Lombardi was perturbed. The Packers had started quickly but stalled like a temperamental car engine.

The Packer offense kept sputtering after halftime as the Lions focused on stopping the run, putting seven defenders on the front line to overwhelm the Packer blockers. Taylor and Hornung found defenders plugging the holes they had run through against the Bears. (Taylor would end the game with sixteen yards on ten rushes, Hornung forty-four on fourteen.) "We should have passed more," Lombardi would say later. "We knew they had that [seven-man front] defense but didn't expect them to use it like they did."

But the Packer defense didn't yield. After an interception gave the Lions the ball at midfield early in the third quarter, Forester and Currie came on an all-out rush that forced Rote to throw into coverage. Bobby Dillon intercepted. Later in the quarter, after the Lions drove to the Green Bay 37, Forester red-dogged again and drove Rote to the ground, breaking the quarterback's nose. Rote rose shakily and was helped off the field, replaced by Morrall.

Late in the third quarter, the Lions' Jim Martin kicked a fifty-yard field goal to narrow Green Bay's lead to 14–10. The crowd had been given little reason to cheer for two quarters, and it grew quieter when Morrall drove the Lion offense to the Green Bay 40 as the quarter ended. But the Packer defense made a stop with a red-dog rush. Forester bore down on Morrall, who turned and ran backwards, but Forester caught him by the shoulders and slung him down for a seventeen-yard loss. On the next play, Pietrosante fumbled and Jesse Whittenton fell on the ball at the Detroit 41.

That one play awakened the sleeping Packers. McGee ran a deep crossing route, running from right to left across the secondary ahead of Terry Barr, the Lions' top cornerback. McHan's pass was on target and McGee caught the ball in stride and raced untouched to the end zone as the fans rose and shouted. Hornung booted the extra point to put the Packers up, 21–10.

The defense sustained the Packers' sudden momentum on the next series when Henry Jordan beat his blocker off the snap and sacked Morrall at the Detroit 1, just missing a safety. After Morrall punted the ball to the Detroit 36, the Packers went for the knock-out. McGee told McHan to look for him; Barr, normally dependable, was clearly struggling. (Barr would reveal after the game that his right knee had been injured in practice.) For the second time in minutes, McGee raced past Barr into the open. McHan, behind air-tight blocking, slung the ball at McGee, who juggled it at the 5, brought it to his chest, and crossed the goal line. McHan's fourth touchdown pass of the game and Hornung's conversion gave the Packers a 28–10 lead.

The rest of the game consisted mostly of the Packer defense harassing Morrall and Rote, who briefly returned with a bandage across his nose. The fans again went through their happy ritual of counting down the final seconds and tossing their programs and seat cushions into the air. Two wins, no defeats!

In the locker room, Lombardi praised the defense, which had played superbly again, limiting the Lions to eighty-two rushing yards while throwing Rote and Morrall for sixty yards in losses. He would be handing out a lot of bills when the grades were posted.

He also praised McHan for taking advantage of what the Lions gave him. They had dared the quarterback to beat them, he said, stacking their front and leaving the pass defense short-handed and vulnerable. McHan had responded by throwing four touchdown passes in a game for the first time in his pro career.

"And he changed the call at the line on both of those late touchdowns to McGee," Lombardi said, "so he took a look at the defense and hit the weakness. That's precisely why we do that. And don't forget that he's still learning our system and our plays, so he's going to get better as he learns more."

McHan told reporters he had won back-to-back games only a couple of times in five years with the Cardinals. "It's a pleasure to play in a system like this," he said. "Everything is organized and thought out. There is a reason for everything we do."

He left with Whittenton and Dowler, fellow bachelors with whom he shared a rental house on the east side of town. Their car poked through streets clogged with cars filled with fans headed for bars, clubs, and restaurants. Nothing electrified Green Bay like a Packer victory. The town would be hopping.

That afternoon, the San Francisco 49ers also scored their second straight victory, pounding the Los Angeles Rams, 34–0. Red Hickey, the 49ers' voluble new head coach, had predicted his team would beat the Rams, telling reporters, "We'll rip them up. Go print that so they can put it on their bulletin board." His players had backed him up, and now the 49ers and Packers, two teams predicted to do little, would play for sole possession of the Western Division lead at City Stadium the next Sunday.

The few hundred tickets that had not been sold went quickly; a third straight sellout crowd of 32,150 would be on hand.

On Tuesday the Packers watched film of their game and also of the 49ers' win over the Rams; the 49ers had played almost perfectly, registering the first shutout of the offensive-minded Rams in a decade. That afternoon, as the players went through calisthenics before practice, Lombardi approached Tom Bettis.

"You OK?" Lombardi asked.

Bettis glared at him. Lombardi had blistered the veteran after Bettis missed a tackle late in the Detroit game. *What the hell are you doing, Bettis? Do I need to find someone else to make a tackle?* After the game, Bettis told Bud Jorgensen he was experiencing shooting pains in his abdomen, and x-rays showed that two small rib-bone chips had become lodged in his transverse muscle — no doubt having been jarred loose by a hit.

"Why didn't you say you were hurt?" Lombardi asked now, on the practice field.

Bettis glared again. Like all the Packers, he now heeded Lombardi's exhortation that players practice Spartanism and play through injuries.

"I was out there, Coach," Bettis huffed while running in place.

171

Lombardi nodded, walked away, and never again belittled his defensive signal-caller in front of the team.

After practice, most of the married players went home to their families. Jim Taylor, his wife, and their two-year-old daughter lived in a small apartment behind a bar at the edge of downtown. A grease fire erupted as his wife fried potatoes in a skillet. Taylor grabbed the skillet, ran to the front door in his bare feet, and tossed the burning grease outside, but it sloshed as he ran and drops landed on his right hand and right foot. Taylor howled. The grease had caused severe burns.

His wife drove him to the emergency room, where doctors put ultraviolet paste on the burns to seal the skin. Taylor didn't know how many games he would miss, but he wouldn't be playing for several weeks. Lombardi heard the news Wednesday morning. He was relieved Taylor wasn't more seriously injured, but disappointed to have to play without his fullback. Lew Carpenter would replace Taylor in the lineup, but Paul Hornung would pick up most of his rushing load — and it would be a heavy load against the 49ers, who had given up more than 150 rushing yards in their exhibition game against the Packers in August.

Lombardi pulled Hornung aside to discuss the situation.

We're going to try to exploit something there, Paul. I think we can run the ball on them.

Yes, sir. I agree.

But Jimmy can't go. I'm going to need you to fill in. You're going to carry the ball a lot.

Yes, sir. You can count on me.

Lombardi smiled. Hornung annoyed some of the assistant coaches with his casual attitude and playboy lifestyle, but Lombardi loved the way he played on Sundays. The Golden Boy would be filthy and exhausted by the end, having given his all.

Lombardi wanted tough guys, and Hornung was plenty tough.

No one ever doubted Lombardi's work ethic. He had worked long days as an assistant under Earl Blaik and Jim Lee Howell, and he felt compelled to attend to every detail now that he was an NFL head coach and general manager. He was gone from the rented house in Allouez by 8 A.M. on most weekdays, and often didn't return until long after dinner. Even when he made it home in time to sit down and eat with his family, he was quiet and distant, his mind on football.

Marie kept the family running. Fortunately, their kids had adjusted to living in a new place. Susan, after shedding tears initially, had plenty of friends. Vincent's senior year at Premontre was going well; his grades were good and the football team was winning. Marie wasn't seeing much of her husband, but that was typical during the season. And being the head coach's wife had its advantages. The assistant coaches left town after practice on Fridays to scout a college game the next day, flying back to Green Bay late Saturday night in time to get up and coach the Packers on Sunday. Their families had no time together on the weekends. Marie and Vince Lombardi went out every Saturday night.

Marie felt responsible for the assistants' wives; her husband had brought their husbands to town. Knowing they would be alone on the Saturday before the San Francisco game, she invited them over for lunch with their young children. Her quiet house suddenly filled with shouts and laughter.

Lombardi, meanwhile, oversaw a light "walk through" practice on Saturday morning and then headed for the Oneida Golf and Riding Club. He teed off at noon with his regular golf buddies, including Jack Koeppler, the insurance man. The weather was chilly and he only played nine holes, but the brief break from football relaxed him. That night he and Marie went out with friends.

By the time he rousted Vincent for their weekly drive to St. Willebrords and City Stadium early Sunday morning, he was anxious to coach some football.

A cold front moved in that Sunday. The sky darkened and a light mist fell around noon as the temperature dropped into the thirties and a twenty-mile-per-hour wind blew. If the temperature fell much more, there would be snow — on October 11!

City Stadium's press box was packed for the NFL's biggest game

173

of the week. Aside from the Packer press contingent, reporters from seven West Coast papers, the *Washington Post,* and the *Minneapolis Star* were present, as was Tex Maule, the pro football writer for *Sports Illustrated,* covering a game in Green Bay for the first time.

The Packers were taut and focused. They won the coin flip and Lombardi took the ball. On the game's first snap, at the Green Bay 20, McHan retreated to pass, found no open receivers, eluded two rushers, and ran upfield. Gregg cleared a path for him, and he gained nineteen yards before being tackled. On the next play, Carpenter swept left for ten behind Kramer and Thurston. Then Hornung swept right for fourteen.

The 49er defenders dug in, annoyed to be getting trampled a week after shutting out the Rams. They were led by thirty-five-year-old Leo Nomellini, a crusty stump of a tackle, and Jerry Tubbs, an agile twenty-four-year-old middle linebacker who had never lost a game as a Texas high school player or in college at the University of Oklahoma. But the Packers continued to move, picking up another first down on three runs as Jim Ringo effectively blocked Tubbs. At the San Francisco 30, McHan dropped back as the line gave his receivers time to run their patterns. McGee faked inside, faked outside, and sprinted past a cornerback for the end zone. McHan lofted the ball high and far ahead of him — too far, it first appeared — but McGee caught up with it, grabbed it with his fingertips, and held on as he crossed the goal line and tumbled.

The crowd thundered. What a start!

The Packer defense took the field with high hopes, having played brilliantly in the first two games, blunting rushes, pressuring quarterbacks, and allowing just one touchdown. But the 49er offense posed a stern challenge. Y. A. Tittle had a strong arm, and his receivers included Billy Wilson, a five-time Pro Bowler who ran precise routes, and R. C. Owens, a big-play specialist. The backfield featured versatile halfbacks J. D. Smith and Hugh McElhenny, both of whom could run and catch, and rugged fullback Joe Perry.

The 49ers had scored seven touchdowns in their first two games, and they rolled toward another on their first possession. Perry earned a first down on a run up the middle. Tittle hit Wilson for fifteen. Perry picked up another first down up the middle, as Hanner and Jordan yielded. Then Bettis, playing with those bone chips, stopped a run to put the 49ers in a third-down situation at the Green Bay 21. Tittle changed the play at the line but his receivers didn't hear the audible and the play fell apart. The 49ers settled for a twenty-eight-yard field goal by their rookie kicker, Tommy Davis.

The Packer offense picked right back up on its next possession. Four straight runs by Hornung and Carpenter produced twenty-two yards. McIlhenny, seemingly trapped off left tackle, kept his balance, found a seam, and gained twenty to the San Francisco 38. Then McHan began to lean on Hornung. The Golden Boy ran around right end for six, off left tackle for five, and up the middle for four. After a short run by Carpenter, McHan passed to Hornung in the left flat for eight and a first down. A pass moved the ball to the 8, and McHan called for Hornung to sweep right. Kramer and Thurston pulled together, Knafelc sealed off the linebacker, Gregg took the end down, and Hornung raced to the end zone between sprawled-out defenders — the perfect execution Lombardi had demanded. Hornung's extra point gave the Packers a 14–3 lead. The offense left the field to sustained cheers.

"How to go there!" Lombardi shouted above the din.

The Packer defense made stops on the next two 49er series when Bettis and Currie red-dogged and tackled Tittle for losses. But the 49er defense also began to assert itself, as Nomellini and Tubbs battered Hornung, and McHan misfired on third downs. The Packers led at halftime, 14–6, and Lombardi saw little to correct. The Packers were throwing hard blocks, harrying Tittle, and stopping Perry and Smith, yet they led by just eight points, a deficit easily overcome. Lombardi told them to limit their mistakes and not let down. *This game could tighten up in a flash.*

His fears were realized in the third quarter. The Packers made a first down to get started, but then McHan floated a pass for McGee on the right sideline and the 49ers' Dave Baker grabbed it and sprinted untouched down the sideline until Hornung pushed him out of bounds at the Green Bay 12. On second down, Wilson, the crafty receiver, ran a zigzag route and got behind John Symank.

Tittle threw the ball on a low, hard line, and Wilson grabbed it in the corner of the end zone. The extra point cut the Packers' lead to 14–13.

The Packers came back with a drive dominated by Hornung runs, but it stalled at the San Francisco 45 and Hornung's field goal attempt flew wide. The 49ers started a series at their 20 with five minutes left in the third quarter. On third down, Tittle faded to pass and could hardly believe what he saw. Owens had slipped behind the defense and was all alone at midfield. Tittle lobbed the ball to him, and Owens caught it and turned for the end zone. Whittenton, who had blown the coverage, chased Owens and went for the tackle at the 25, but Owens wiggled his hips, slipped free, and continued on to the end zone, completing a seventy-five-yard scoring play.

The crowd went silent as the 49ers whooped and celebrated on their sideline. The fans could barely fathom the sudden change in the game — and for that matter, neither could the Packers. The extra point put the 49ers ahead for the first time, 20–14. Snowflakes began to swirl in the crosswind as the temperature dropped. It was hard not to sense the Packers' early-season magic suddenly dissipating, and the gloomy mood in the stadium worsened when a linebacker tackled McHan for a loss on the next series, forcing a Packer punt. The 49er offense zoomed downfield again, mixing runs and short passes to move into Packer territory.

On a first down at the Green Bay 28, Tittle faded to pass and surveyed the field for open receivers. But he didn't have time to plant and throw, as Forester, rushing hard, forced him out of the pocket. Tittle ran right, but Forester grabbed him and threw him down for a twelve-yard loss. The third quarter ended before the 49ers could run another play, so Tittle went to the sidelines and conferred with 49ers coach Red Hickey, who called a trick play. Tittle would hand off to Perry going up the middle, but Perry would stop before he reached the line, turn, and lateral the ball back to Tittle. Meanwhile, the receivers would go deep and hopefully pass Packer defensive backs rushing to the line to stop the run. Tittle would toss the ball to an open receiver for a touchdown.

The fake fooled the defensive backs, who charged up to stop

Perry as the receivers slipped beyond them, but Dave Hanner sniffed out the ruse, burst past his blocker, and slammed into Perry just as the 49er back was turning to lateral. Jolted, Perry dropped the ball, and Hanner scrambled to it and fell on it. The fans cheered, relieved that the 49ers' momentum had been blunted. But could the Packer offense get going? It hadn't scored since the first quarter.

Hornung had been carrying the ball all day, filling his usual load as well as Taylor's. McHan sent him left on a sweep, good for six yards. Then Carpenter ran behind Masters for five, moving the ball into San Francisco territory. McIlhenny had gone out with a shoulder injury, so Hornung and Carpenter were the Packers' only healthy backs. On first down, Hornung absorbed a searing hit to the right side of his helmet as he swept right. He stayed down as the other players returned to their huddle. A timeout was called and the Packers' trainers trotted out to tend to him.

My neck is stinging! Damn! My shoulder is stinging!

Hornung couldn't get up. The trainers called for a stretcher, but then the Golden Boy slowly rose and walked off the field without assistance.

After a run by Carpenter picked up two yards on second down, Hornung trotted back onto the field. He had told Lombardi he could play. *Let me go back out there, dammit! I can go!* On third down he drifted into the right flat and McHan threw him a soft pass. He started to run, broke a tackle, and fell forward just far enough to pick up a first down. The ball was now on the San Francisco 39.

The Packers had lived by their running game all day, but now the passing game suddenly opened up. McHan faked a toss to Hornung, retreated, and searched the field. Knafelc, after faking a run block, ran straight downfield and turned. As he did so, McHan's line drive hit him in the chest, and he held on for a twelve-yard gain. On the next play, Knafelc again faked a block and ran downfield, this time cutting across the secondary. He got one step ahead of the safety and McHan's pass led him perfectly. The fifteen-yard gain put the ball on the San Francisco 12.

The crowd was on its feet, urging the offense on. McHan tossed to Hornung, who ran left on a sweep. The 49ers' Matt Hazeltine smelled out the play and brought Hornung down for no gain. Hornung rose slowly and walked off the field holding his neck. On second down McHan dropped back and threw for McGee on the goal line, but a cornerback broke it up. That left the Packers facing third-and-ten at the 12. Hornung came back onto the field, and McHan faked a toss to him, dropped into the pocket, and searched the field. Knafelc ran straight downfield, faked left, and cut right. McHan's throw led him perfectly, and Knafelc grabbed it for the touchdown.

With the crowd roaring, Bart Starr, the forgotten man, trotted onto the field to hold for the extra point — his only duty these days. Hornung knelt in the huddle, exhausted and sore, knowing he needed to make this kick. Ringo's snap was perfect, the blocking held, and Starr grabbed the ball and put it down. Hornung's kick split the uprights. The Packers had the lead, 21–20.

The score inspired the Packer defense, which stopped the 49ers on two straight possessions as the final quarter ticked down. The Packers started a series on their 26 with five minutes to play. Hornung carried for four and thirteen yards. Carpenter went for eleven behind Ringo. But just when it seemed the Packers would run out the clock, Carpenter fumbled when hit at the San Francisco 46, and the 49ers recovered. They would have one final shot.

The crowd quieted. Tittle, who had been in many similar situations, rolled left and passed to receiver Clyde Conner for eleven yards, and then, after Smith ran for three, found Billy Wilson open for nine. The ball was on the Green Bay 30 with two minutes to play. The crowd mustered a cheer, imploring the defense to hold. Hanner smothered Smith for no gain up the middle. Tittle dropped back, but Currie, red-dogging from the left, forced him to unload the ball for an incompletion. On third down, Jordan broke through a block and pressured Tittle into throwing the ball away.

On fourth down, Hickey sent in his rookie kicker, Tommy Davis, to try a thirty-seven-yard field goal — a probable game-winner if he made it, which seemed possible, as he had already put kicks of twenty-eight and thirty-two yards through the uprights. The crowd quieted. The snap and hold were perfect, and Davis approached and swung his right leg forward. Like a golfer attempting a wedge shot, he dug up a small divot as he brought his leg through, taking up too much grass. The ball sailed into the twenty-mile-per-hour crosswind toward the uprights, but it lacked the necessary thrust. The wind pushed it to the right and it fell short of the end zone.

He missed!

The crowd sent out a giddy yowl. Lombardi smiled. Phil Bengston pounded him on the shoulder.

Our ball game, Vince, our ball game.

Heh, yes sir.

McHan handed off to Hornung twice as the 49ers, out of time-outs, watched the clock tick down. The Golden Boy's final carry was his twenty-eighth of the afternoon. He had rushed for 138 yards, caught a pass, scored a touchdown, and kicked three extra points. His neck and ribs were so sore he would spend that night in a hospital.

But he had earned his ten-dollar bill.

Exhausted by the game's dramatic ebb and flow, the fans stood for the final seconds, counted down the clock, and, for the third straight week, hurled their cushions and programs into the air as the final gun sounded. The Packers pounded each other as they ran up the tunnel to the locker room. Lombardi shook hands with Hickey. They agreed that their surprising teams had played one hell of a game. Lombardi walked on with a broad smile, listening to the cheers, watching his players celebrate. Three weeks into the season, the Packers were the NFL's last-remaining unbeaten team.

Three wins, no losses.

Not even Lombardi, in his most optimistic moment, had expected that.

★ 14 ★

LOMBARDI'S EUPHORIA DIDN'T last long. In the locker room he was told that NFL commissioner Bert Bell had suffered a heart attack and died while watching the Eagles in Philadelphia. Lombardi slumped into a chair.

Bell, sixty-five, had ruled the league with dignity and class and was as responsible as anyone for the pro game's growing popularity. He had been loyal to Green Bay, telling newsman Art Daley that the city would always have a team as long as he was commissioner. He had helped the Packers, too, encouraging them to build a new stadium and advising them to hire Lombardi. If the Packers had continued to play at the old City Stadium, failed to hire the new coach, and continued to lose, their future in Green Bay could have become tenuous, and Bell, had he lived, might have been forced to break his promise. But the Packers appeared to be on the upswing now, thanks in no small part to Bell.

Lombardi gathered his thoughts as reporters entered the locker room. "I don't know how the National Football League is going to replace Bert," he said. "He has been the backbone of the league for years. We just lost the strongest member of our family. He truly cannot be replaced. We all loved him and he loved all of us."

His demeanor brightened when the subject changed to the 21–20 victory the Packers had just scored.

"The biggest thing was we came from behind to win," he said.

"We had to overcome some obstacles, and we did. We have a battling group of players."

His eyes bulged when an assistant handed him a copy of the game statistics. The Packers had rushed fifty-five times for 284 yards, their highest single-game total in six years. Besides Hornung's 138 yards, Carpenter had gained 62, McHan 45, and McIlhenny 39.

"We knew we could run on them," Lombardi said. "We learned it in the [exhibition] game in August."

Paul Hornung sat on a metal folding chair by his locker, too tired to take off his uniform. "I hurt all over," he told reporters. "Someone was really popping me, and there were three or four guys on me every time I went down. They're a tough defensive club. I'm just glad we hung in and won."

In the visitors' locker room, Coach Red Hickey shook his head when he saw the statistics. "We gave up too damn many rushing yards," he said. "That allowed them to control the ball. They did a fine job, but our tackling wasn't good at all."

Regarding Hornung, Hickey said, "He played a fine all-around ball game. I didn't know he could run like that."

As they dressed, the 49ers obviously believed they had let a winnable game slip away, despite the Packers' statistical dominance. "It was a great ball game but I'm not sure the best team won," R. C. Owens said. Tittle added, "They were tough, but we will see them again on the coast [in December] and see what happens."

The Packers' locker room slowly emptied as the players dressed and left to celebrate. Lombardi was so pleased with the win against San Francisco, he addressed *Press-Gazette* reporter Lee Remmel's question about next week's game against the Rams at County Stadium in Milwaukee with uncharacteristic nonchalance. "Oh, let's let next week take care of itself," he said.

But by the next morning he was focused on the Rams, who had recovered from their horrid loss to the 49ers by beating the Bears in Chicago on Sunday. With one win and two losses so far, the Rams were enigmatic but dangerous.

On his drive to work, Lombardi picked up the Green Bay and

Milwaukee papers, wanting to see what his players had said, what the 49ers had said, what the writers were saying about the Rams. Nothing was more eye-popping than the standings. The Packers were the NFL's only unbeaten team.

The national sports media jumped on their improbable turnaround story. Tex Maule interviewed Lombardi on Monday and wrote about the Packers in his *Sports Illustrated* column that week. The *Sporting News,* which focused on baseball but also covered other sports, also published an article about the Packers.

Maule's column recounted Lombardi's career and explained that the fans owned the Packers and felt that that gave them the right to second-guess the coach. Lombardi told Maule that improving the defense had been his first priority, and that Lamar McHan and Paul Hornung had made a dormant offense productive. The headline on the column read, "Vince Brings Green Days to Green Bay," with a subhead saying, "Under the analytical eye of Vince Lombardi, the Packers head for better times."

The publicity pleased Lombardi, but by the middle of the week it — and the expectations it generated — began to make him nervous. Yes, the Packers were 3-0, but they hadn't played a road game, hadn't faced real adversity, and hadn't taken on the Colts, New York Giants, or Cleveland Browns, the league's top teams.

Lombardi railed at Tom Miller, the Packer publicity director.

"Dammit, people are going to expect us to win now! And we're not anywhere close to being as good as those other teams!"

The press was just making his job harder. He hated those bastards!

His eyes flashed with anger as he stormed through the halls of the Washington Street offices, bristling with nervous energy.

"Do something about this, Miller!" he thundered like a Brooklyn streetcar.

The calm, lanky publicity director towered over Lombardi but was still intimidated.

"What do you want me to do, Coach?" he asked.

"Oh, go on those shows of yours. Tell people not to get so excited," Lombardi finally said with resignation.

Miller hosted popular television and radio shows about the Packers during the week.

"I'll do that," Miller said.

That night, on his weekly radio show, Miller stated, "Don't raise your hopes, fans. This can't continue indefinitely."

Lombardi wasn't the only one who believed the Packers weren't as good as their record. Red Hickey, still frustrated about the 49ers' loss that Sunday, told reporters he expected the Rams to beat Green Bay, as they had in twenty of the past twenty-six games between the teams. And oddsmakers in Las Vegas favored the Rams by four points even though the Packers were undefeated and playing at home. Clearly the Packers had doubters.

This would be the first of Green Bay's two 1959 regular-season "home" games in Milwaukee, and they hoped for a big crowd. They had played eighteen games at County Stadium since it opened in 1953, with the average attendance a disappointing 23,038. Sports fans in Milwaukee were more excited about their own winning baseball team than Green Bay's losing football team. But the 1959 baseball season was over, the Braves having failed to win a third-straight National League pennant — they had finished second, two games behind the Los Angeles Dodgers — and the Packers hoped their surprising start would bring out more spectators.

Tickets sold briskly during the week, the total surpassing 23,000 on Wednesday, 28,000 on Friday, and 32,000 by Saturday afternoon. With sunny, mild weather predicted, the *Milwaukee Journal* speculated the crowd might top 40,000, a threshold reached only once before, at an August 1955 exhibition game against the Colts and then-rookie Alan Ameche, a Wisconsin native who had won the Heisman Trophy as a University of Wisconsin fullback.

While the midweek conversation in Milwaukee focused on ticket sales, the Packers were in Green Bay, getting ready to play. Practice resumed Tuesday with Packer scout Wally Cruice delivering his report. He had watched the Rams beat the Bears in Chicago the previous Sunday, and he warned the Packers to prepare for a challenge. The Rams had an array of electric offensive players such as Ollie Matson, the halfback who had been obtained from the Chicago Cardinals in a trade for nine other players; runner/receiver Jon Arnett, a former Southern Cal star who had been the second overall pick in the 1957 draft; wide receiver Del Shofner, the league leader in receiving yards in 1958; and veteran quarterback Billy Wade, who had led the league in passing yards the year before. Matson had rushed for 199 yards against the Bears on Sunday, embarrassing Halas's proud unit. Orchestrated by head coach Sid Gillman, an offensive innovator, the Rams' attack figured to give the Packers' resurgent defense its toughest test yet.

Offensively, Lombardi encouraged McHan to continue to rely on the rushing game even though the Rams had injuries in their secondary and planned to start two rookie cornerbacks and a backup safety. "We do what we do best, regardless of the circumstances," Lombardi said. And what the Packers did best, indisputably, was run the ball. In their three wins, they had stayed on the ground on 136 of their 181 offensive snaps — an astounding 75 percent — and picked up more rushing yards than any team in the league. Word had already spread that Lombardi's Packers would mostly just try to cram the ball down the opposition's throats.

After practice on Friday afternoon the Packers took a bus to Milwaukee and checked into the Astor Hotel. The Rams, who had stayed in Chicago to practice during the week instead of commuting back and forth to the West Coast, checked into the Schroeder Hotel that evening. Both teams practiced at County Stadium on Saturday. The players and coaches shook hands and chatted between the workouts. Lombardi and Gillman were both Earl Blaik disciples (Lombardi had taken Gillman's spot on Blaik's staff when Gillman left Army to become the head coach at the University of Cincinnati in 1947) and had many mutual friends. The Rams' line coach, Lou Rymkus, had worked in Green Bay with Jim Ringo and Forrest Gregg.

With reporters from New York, Los Angeles, and Chicago in town to cover the game, along with the usual Packer press, Lombardi wanted to show that the Packers were a classy operation now. He told Tom Miller to invite the reporters to his suite at the Astor for a cocktail party late Saturday afternoon — a renewal of the Five O'clock Club he had started in August.

The Green Bay coach, dressed in a dark suit, greeted the reporters as they arrived. He introduced them to Marie, chatted with them, and made sure the hired bartender fixed what they wanted. He was different around his wife, more jocular than the driven coach who barked at his players and habitually cut off reporters' questions.

Think you can take the Rams tomorrow?

Normally intolerant of such simplistic questions, Lombardi simply smiled. *We'll have to play our best game. They have a fine team.*

The players registered surprise when they came out to warm up the next day and saw fans sitting in sections of the stands that always had been empty before. The sun-splashed crowd of some thirty-six thousand fell short of the hoped-for forty thousand but was still the second-largest for a Packer game in Milwaukee. The date was October 18, the press contingent so large some reporters were elbowed out into the baseball press box overlooking the end zone.

The Packers' locker room was quieter than usual before kickoff; Lombardi sensed the players feeling extra pressure. That wasn't a good sign, and neither was Don McIlhenny's discovery that he couldn't lift his right arm above his shoulder in warm-ups. He had injured the shoulder against San Francisco and thought all week he would be able to play Sunday, but now he couldn't.

With Jim Taylor also still out because of burns on his hand and foot, the Packers were down to just two healthy running backs, Hornung and Lew Carpenter — and Hornung had been sluggish in practice all week after carrying the ball almost thirty times against the 49ers, battling fatigue and pain in the dramatic final minutes.

Lombardi, concerned about his team's running game, huddled with McHan before heading out to the field.

Lamar, I think we're going to need to pass more today.

Yes, Coach.

Let's get that going early.

Hornung carried on the game's first play but was slammed for a loss by Lamar Lundy, a young defensive end for the Rams. On second down, McGee ran a square-out route and broke open near midfield, but McHan's on-target pass slipped between the receiver's hands. McHan stewed in the huddle before third down. *Why is it always my passes that get dropped?*

Hornung gained six yards on a third-down sweep, and McGee dropped back to punt. Standing on the Packer 15, he caught the chest-high snap and stepped forward. The Rams' Sam Williams, a rookie defensive end, rushed in untouched from the right side and smothered the kick. The ball ricocheted off Williams's chest and sailed behind McGee, landing in the end zone and rolling through it. The referee clasped his hands together over his head, signaling a safety — two points for the Rams.

The crowd, which had cheered loudly at the game's outset, sat quietly. As the rules for a safety dictated, McGee punted again from the Packer 20. The Rams began a drive at their 40. Matson ran up the middle for six. Wade passed to Arnett in the left flat for seven and to Shofner on the ride sideline for fifteen. Matson barged up the middle for seven. The Packer defense hadn't seen this kind of speed. Wade passed to Shofner for twelve. Arnett gained eight around left end. Every play the Rams tried worked.

Linebackers Tom Bettis and Bill Forester implored their teammates in the huddle. *Come on! Let's play!* They made a stand, finally stopping the drive inside the 10. The Rams lined up for a short field goal try, and Forester broke through the line and blocked it, bringing the crowd to its feet. Maybe that would get the Packers going.

It didn't. The Rams stopped the Packers on three downs again, and McGee punted, this time successfully kicking the ball away. The Rams took it and drove deep into Packer territory, niftily blending runs and throws. The Packer secondary finally knocked away a couple of passes near the end zone, and the Rams settled for a field goal and a 5–0 lead.

As the next Packer possession began, McHan kneeled and looked around the huddle. *OK, we start now. Let's catch the passes.*

But the Rams' defensive ends, Lundy and Lou Michaels, and linebacker Jack Pardee — three young players — broke down the Packer blocking, leaving Hornung and Carpenter nowhere to run. McHan had little time to throw when he dropped back, pressured by red-dogging linebackers. McGee punted for the third time, and the Ram offense went to work again. Their quick guards opened holes on sweeps and runs up the middle. Matson and Arnett ripped past the line and into the secondary. Wade had plenty of time to throw, as rushes by Forester and Dan Currie were blunted at the line.

On the last play of the first quarter, Rams wide receiver Del Shofner lined up wide right at the Packer 26 and ran a square-out, and Wade tossed the ball in his direction as he neared the sideline. Bobby Dillon saw the play developing, went for the ball, and grabbed it just as Shofner got his hands on it. They wrestled for possession but Shofner had a better grip and pulled it away. Dillon fell and Shofner jogged to the end zone with the ball, completing the scoring play. The holder fumbled the snap on the conversion, leaving the Rams' lead at 11–0.

The Packer offense finally got going on its next series. Hornung gained eighteen on a right sweep through a hole opened by Fred Thurston, who knocked Pardee over. McHan flipped successive passes to the Golden Boy and picked up fifteen. McGee ran a crossing pattern and reeled in a pass from McHan for twelve. The fans cheered as the drive neared the end zone, thinking the Packers were waking up and getting into the game. But McGee slipped and dropped a sure touchdown on second down from the 7, and Boyd Dowler dropped a pass on third down.

McHan was furious as he left the field. *Damn! What is it with everyone dropping my passes?*

A field goal by Hornung narrowed the margin to 11–3.

On the first play of the Rams' next possession, Arnett charged through a gaping hole by his left guard, Hanner having been shoved aside, shook off an attempted tackle by Currie, and sprinted for thirty yards. The Rams just kept coming. Matson picked up a first down on a pair of runs. Wade threw for twenty-two yards to Rams receiver Jim "Red" Phillips. The drive ended in a field goal, which the Packers matched as Hornung booted a forty-six-yarder to make the score 14–6 at halftime.

In the locker room Lombardi said he was encouraged that the

Packers weren't further behind after having been so thoroughly outplayed. The defense had not stopped the Rams from driving on any possession, and the offense hadn't moved much.

Bettis gathered the defense around him. *We're better than this. Come on, make your reads.* The speech worked. The defense stopped the Rams early in the third quarter, but the Packer offense couldn't take advantage, a sack ending one possession and a holding penalty on Thurston scuttling another. Lombardi berated Thurston as the offense came off the field.

Damn, Fuzzy, that just kills us. Concentrate out there!

Thurston cursed Lombardi under his breath, knowing he would hear about the mistake again Tuesday morning when the team watched film of the game.

Midway through the third quarter the Rams started a series at the Green Bay 49 after a short punt by McGee. On first down defensive coach Phil Bengston smelled a pass and sent Currie rushing in, but Wade countered by retreating to pass and handing off to Matson on a draw. Matson charged into the secondary through a huge hole up the middle, shook off a tackle by Whittenton, and broke into the clear. Packer safety John Symank chased him but Matson, a former Olympic sprinter, was too fast. Legs pumping, he reached the end zone without being touched. The conversion gave the Rams a 21–6 lead.

Frustration swelled on the Packer sideline. The Rams were just so quick, and not just at the skill positions but throughout their lineup — on the lines, in the secondary, everywhere. The Packers couldn't match that speed.

Suddenly, this felt like a 1958 game, the score spiraling out of control as the Packers failed to make stops or generate offense.

On their next possession, a run by Hornung gained just two yards and Rams safety Ed Meador blanketed McGee and Knafelc on second and third downs, forcing another McGee punt. Lombardi shook his head in frustration, thinking McHan needed to do a better job of finding ways to move the ball.

The Ram offense began driving again. Arnett gained six around left end, twisted his ankle, and left the field limping, but his replacement, Tommy Wilson, was just as effective. He caught a screen pass and weaved through defenders for twenty yards, then zoomed around right end for twenty-nine. The Rams rolled deep into Packer territory and right into the end zone, taking a 28–6 lead as the fourth quarter started.

The Packer defense came off the field battered and frustrated, simply unable to stop the speedy Rams.

Fuck those guys!

We're better than this.

Lombardi shouted at the offense as it waited to start a new possession. *We still have time. Let's score and put some pressure on them.* Scooter McLean never had faith in the team's ability to rally in such situations. Lombardi's positive attitude had an effect. Symank returned the kickoff to midfield, and for just the second time all day, the Packer offense drove deep into Ram territory. Using rollouts to avoid the pass rush, McHan passed to Knafelc for fifteen, ran for six, and passed again to Knafelc for ten. At the Los Angeles 21, he dropped back, found McGee open in the end zone, and hit him with a perfect pass.

Again, McGee dropped the sure touchdown.

McHan lost his composure. *What is it with you people?* But he steadied himself and kept playing, picking up a first down on a swing pass to Hornung. The offense rolled to the 2-yard line, seemingly set to score. But Jerry Kramer jumped offside, moving the ball back five yards, and McHan was chased out of the pocket and lofted a hurried, wobbly pass for Dowler. Meador cut in front of the rookie receiver and made a diving interception.

Lombardi stopped Kramer as the offense came off the field. *You're making enough mistakes by yourself to lose the game. Can't you think?*

Then the Packers fell apart. Tired and sore, Hornung fumbled twice as the game wound down. Wade found Red Phillips open behind the secondary for a fifty-three-yard touchdown, and then, a few minutes later, hit Shofner for a twenty-seven-yard score. The Rams added a field goal to push the score to 45–6. This was a massacre.

The fans headed for the exits. The stands were nearly empty by the final minutes. Lombardi removed McHan, who had not performed that poorly, completing thirteen of twenty-two passes in spite of all those drops. Starr finished up, completing one pass to rookie end A. D. Williams and then misfiring on three attempts before ending the game by throwing an interception.

When the gun sounded, Lombardi walked across the field and congratulated Sid Gillman. The Rams had played superbly. They had traded nine players for Matson because they believed they were a championship contender, and if this game was any indication, they were.

But what about the Packers?

"We had a bit of a flat game," Lombardi understated when he spoke to reporters. "I don't know why, but we seemed to be extremely tense today for some reason. It's hard to understand because this was our fourth game so it shouldn't make any difference. But the Rams are a good team, the best we have played, and they had a hot game. We have no excuses. We just got rapped hard."

He paused and continued: "They put us in a hole in the first quarter and we just couldn't climb out. We dropped some key passes that would have made a difference, and we also had some penalties. So, lots of mistakes like that. I saw some good things, and we competed. And, this isn't an alibi, but we only had two healthy backs. We should be in better shape next week."

The locker room was almost silent. The players were taking a team bus back to Green Bay as soon as everyone was ready. The ride would be quiet.

"We were flatter than a pancake. We just have to bounce back," Bettis said.

"I never thought we'd get beat like that. Everything we did was wrong," McHan added.

What about the lopsided final score? Lombardi actually mustered a smile when a reporter asked.

"It makes no difference," he shrugged, "if you lose by one point or a hundred. It's still a loss."

On the ride back to Green Bay Lombardi took the right front

seat, opposite the driver, and said little as the bus rolled along. As he feared, the Packers had gotten ahead of themselves with their 3-0 start. They had shortcomings, which the Rams had exposed. They were slow, inconsistent, and just mediocre in places. Their secondary had been embarrassed today. Bobby Freeman didn't cover anyone, and frankly, neither did Bobby Dillon. And what about all those dropped passes? That was just a lack of concentration.

If we don't have receivers who can catch, I'll find some who can.

The feel-good party was over. The Packers' next games were on the road against the Colts, Giants, and Bears.

In a way, their season was just beginning.

★ 15 ★

SINCE THE MERGER between the NFL and All-America Football Conference in 1950, the Packers' league-season schedule had followed the same pattern every year. They played most of their home games early, before the weather in Wisconsin turned nasty, and spent most of the rest of the season on the road, ending with a game at Detroit on Thanksgiving and a December trip to California to play the 49ers and Rams.

What little success the Packers had experienced during the decade had occurred early in seasons, when they were playing at home. Since 1950 they had a .425 winning percentage (17-22-1) during the first third of their schedule and just a .250 winning percentage (18-53-1) the rest of the way. In other words, it wasn't unusual for them to begin a season respectably but then fall apart.

The specter of that recent history hung in the air after the loss to the Rams. The Packers had just two home games remaining now, compared with six on the road. For the holdovers on the roster, it was impossible not to reflect on how they always stumbled at this point in the season, never more sadly than the year before, when they absorbed that 56–0 beating in Baltimore and went into the worst tailspin in their franchise's history. Now, heading back to Baltimore to play the Colts on Sunday, they wondered if it would all happen again.

Lombardi knew the defeatism he had tried to eradicate from the team was still lurking, capable of reemerging. He thought about

192

how to handle the players in the aftermath of a bad loss, with so many tough games ahead.

His natural instinct was to give them hell. After watching films of the 45–6 loss with his staff on Monday, he knew he wouldn't be giving out any crisp bills.

Look at that, Red. What in the hell was Max thinking about there?

It's hard to say, Vince. He certainly couldn't catch the ball.

Bill, the next good block Kramer makes will be his first.

I don't know what the problem is.

Is something wrong with Dillon? He isn't the player I expected.

But as horrid as the loss had been, Lombardi could rationalize it. His design for a winning team was built around having a strong running game that controlled the ball, and the Packers couldn't mount much of a ground game with Jim Taylor and Don McIlhenny out and Paul Hornung banged up. That had put more pressure on the passing game, and the receivers had an off day, dropping balls all over the place. It was left to the defense to keep the Packers close against a Rams offense undeniably on its game — sometimes you have to give credit to your opponent. And even with all that going against them, the Packers trailed by just eight points at halftime and by fifteen going into the fourth quarter. The final score made the game appear more disastrous than it really was.

This was not the time to tear down the players' confidence, Lombardi decided. It was a shaky confidence to begin with, and with so many difficult games looming, the players needed to be supported more than ripped apart. There would be a time to lay into those who deserved it, he thought. And he would make sure the players who screwed up Sunday knew it. But he wouldn't push the gas pedal all the way to the floor. Not now.

On Tuesday morning the players slunk into the film room expecting to be destroyed. Lombardi surprised them. They had played better than the score indicated, he said calmly. Instead of reviewing their mistakes, he spent much of the hourlong film session pointing out what they had done well.

"You're good enough to beat the Colts on Sunday," he concluded.

He believed it, too. McIlhenny would be back, Taylor's burns were almost healed, and the Colts, champions though they were, didn't have the Rams' all-around speed, which had caused the Packers so much trouble.

The players walked out of the film room shaking their heads. This guy was unpredictable, to say the least. Sometimes you just wanted to slug him, but other times he inspired you to dig down and play harder.

Jerry Kramer and Taylor quietly discussed Lombardi as they dressed for practice.

I thought he was going to blow the roof off in there. What's he thinking?

Hell if I know.

Like a lot of the players, they still weren't sure they believed in the new Packer coach. Even though Lombardi had them playing competitively, he could be enough of a sarcastic jerk that you wondered if you were being paid enough to put up with him. And it remained to be seen if he really had turned the team around.

That afternoon, after easing up in the film room, Lombardi turned up the pressure on the practice field. He added five minutes to the grass drill, shouted until he grew hoarse during position drills — *dammit, Max, catch those on Sunday!* — and ended the workout with an extra set of sprints.

You could tell which players had spent Monday night in Appleton's bars and clubs. They were throwing up.

Lamar McHan was pleased, all things considered. Playing on a new team, in a new town, for a new coach, he had won three of four games as the number one quarterback, throwing six touchdown passes and just three interceptions. The Packers were tied for first place in the Western Division. You couldn't ask for a better start.

During training camp and the exhibition season, when he didn't play well or often, he had worried about being sent back to the Cardinals, the one scenario he didn't want. It seemed clear, at least to him, that he had more going for him than any of the other quarterbacks, but you never knew what a coach might do — the Cardinals had asked him to split time with a rookie who wasn't half as good. Lombardi gave him the shot in the end, though, and now McHan was getting a chance to establish himself.

The loss to the Rams had been a major disappointment, no question; a team wasn't supposed to go into a game undefeated and lose by thirty-nine points. And McHan had lost his cool for a few minutes there, no question about that, either. But he hadn't done much with his arm in the first three games other than throw those four touchdown passes against Detroit, and he had wanted to show Lombardi what he could do in a tough situation. But guys dropped passes all over the place, and his emotions just got the best of him. He kicked himself later for letting it happen.

The season was just one-third over, though. There was plenty of time for him to show what he could do, starting with this next game against the Colts. He had never played them, not once in six years in the league. They had some superb defensive players, starting with Gino Marchetti, and obviously would be tough to beat. But if the Packers could run the ball like they did in their first three games, they could compete with the Colts. They could compete with anyone. McHan believed that.

The Packers took a charter flight to Baltimore on Friday afternoon. On this trip a year earlier they had stayed at a motel far from town as the front office cut costs. Lombardi had put a decisive end to such penny-pinching. This time, they checked into the Lord Baltimore, a French Renaissance–style landmark in the heart of downtown. They wore green blazers, ate team meals together, and went through a light workout at Memorial Stadium on Saturday before meeting a curfew that night.

The Colts had not played especially well so far in 1959 but still had won three of four games, leaving them tied with the Packers and 49ers for first place in the Western Division. They were coming off a road victory over the Bears in which they were outgained in yardage but forced six turnovers.

Bart Starr awoke Sunday morning, attended a church service near the hotel, and took the team bus to the stadium. He had spent the week preparing to play the Colts, knowing he probably wouldn't leave the sideline unless the score got out of hand, as it did against the Rams, when he got in and threw a few passes at the end. Lombardi seemed set on McHan as his number one quarterback, through good times and bad. Starr couldn't do anything about it except practice and prepare hard and keep his spirits up, all of which he did regardless of what his coach thought of him. It was disappointing, but Starr was a team player, and if his job was to back up McHan, so be it.

Still, he felt jealous as the Baltimore game started in front of fifty-seven thousand fans in sunny, fifty-degree weather — a pleasant surprise for October 25. He wanted to be on the field. His best game as a pro had come against the Colts in 1958, when he passed for more than three hundred yards as the Packers narrowly lost. Yes, the Colts had batted him around a few times, too, intercepting five of his passes in a 1957 game and swallowing him whole along with the rest of the Packers in the 56–0 rout. But his one good performance had showed him he could succeed against the NFL's best teams, and he longed for another opportunity.

Instead, he stood next to Lombardi and offered play-calling opinions as McHan tried to get the offense going.

I think Paul can get open in the L zig-out, Coach.

Think so?

I do. And when they go heavy up front, run the sixty-one.

Lombardi didn't mind having Starr around offering suggestions. The young man spent a lot of time studying film and thinking of ways to attack defenses. It was too bad Starr was so quiet, polite, and mistake prone, Lombardi thought. He could really think his way through a game.

The crowd was frenzied in the first minutes. Colt fans had not forgotten about John Symank sending quarterback Johnny Unitas to the hospital with a knee to the ribs the year before. Unitas never blamed Symank, but local fans believed the Green Bay player had delivered a cheap shot, and now held up signs reading, "We Want Packer Blood."

A McHan fumble stopped one Packer drive in Colt territory, but on the first play of the second quarter Lew Carpenter ran left on a sweep, and when Jerry Kramer and Fred Thurston opened a hole with devastating blocks, Carpenter broke into the clear, accelerating past several bunched-up Colt defenders. He didn't slow down until he crossed the goal line, completing a fifty-five-yard touchdown run that silenced the crowd.

The score seemed to motivate Unitas, who promptly started pitching balls to Raymond Berry and Lenny Moore. Phil Bengston had switched around his secondary assignments, putting Bobby Freeman on Berry, but Berry confused Freeman with his precise, impossible-to-predict routes, and Bobby Dillon, who was supposed to help Freeman, went out with a concussion. The Colts moved eighty-one yards to a touchdown, got the ball back, and moved seventy-nine yards to another touchdown.

After trailing 14–7 at halftime, the Packers started the third quarter with the ball. On second down from their 19, McHan dropped back as Max McGee faked a square-out route and burst past his defender, Ray Brown. McHan arched a long pass seemingly too far ahead of McGee, but McGee sprinted all out and caught it on the run at the Baltimore 40. With only grass in front of him, he dashed to the end zone ahead of Brown as the noisy crowd abruptly fell silent.

The players on the Packer bench shouted and clapped. McGee jogged to the sidelines, smiling broadly through his single-bar face mask, still panting after the eighty-one-yard scoring play, and as always, ready with a joke.

Damn, Max! Hell of a play!

Yeah . . . yeah . . . guy didn't catch me, did he?

Lombardi whacked McGee on the shoulder. *Way to sell that fake, Max! Beautiful!* He then turned to the defensive regulars and implored them to maintain the momentum. They stopped the Colts on three plays, forcing a punt. *That's the way! That's some Green Bay Packer football!*

McHan and the offense trotted onto the field, taking possession on their 35. A score would put the Packers ahead, and the fans were plainly uneasy about the possibility, shifting in their seats and making little noise. The Packers sure were improved from a year ago, they thought.

Hornung ran right, behind Forrest Gregg, for two yards, and McIlhenny gained four going left. On third down, McHan called for an option pass, a play he hadn't used since the first game. He handed to Hornung, who swept right behind Kramer and Thurston, pulled up, and lobbed a pass for Gary Knafelc, open twenty yards downfield. A completion would have moved the ball into Baltimore territory, but the pass sailed well beyond Knafelc, incomplete. Hornung stood with his hands on his hips, upset to have missed such an open receiver. *Damn, it was there!*

McGee punted on fourth down, and the Colts' John Sample caught the kick, found a seam in the Packers' coverage, and sprinted twenty-five yards before being shoved out of bounds at the Green Bay 36. The fans awoke, encouraging Unitas to regain control of the game. He turned the good field position into a touchdown in seven plays, the score coming on a short pass to Alan Ameche. Baltimore led, 21–14.

Lombardi, McHan, and Starr debated what to run on the next series, deciding passing plays could work. On second down, McHan dropped back, looked right, and saw Knafelc open on a sideline route, but threw an abysmal pass, well short of his target. The ball flew right to Colts linebacker Bill Pellington, trailing the receiver. Pellington intercepted on the Green Bay 30, eluded the lunging Knafelc's grasp, and raced untouched to the end zone.

Lombardi kicked the ground in frustration as the crowd cheered and McHan walked off the field slowly, almost dazed, wondering how he could have thrown a ball so poorly.

Starr moved away on the sideline, avoiding what he thought might be a confrontation between the coach and quarterback, but Lombardi didn't say a word as McHan walked past on the way to the water cooler.

The offense was right back on the field after the kickoff, now down by two touchdowns. McHan, trying to stay clam, handed to Hornung and McIlhenny and picked up a pair of first downs. At midfield, he dropped back, saw no one open downfield, and threw a swing pass for Hornung, stationed in the left flat. But he threw errantly again, leading Hornung by too much, and the Colts' Ray Brown grabbed it and took off with blockers in front of him. Weaving around several tacklers, Brown appeared set to go all the way, until Carpenter tossed him to the ground at the Green Bay 18.

The crowd howled, thrilled by the big plays and dramatic momentum shift, as Brown and Carpenter fell in a dusty heap on the sideline. The game had been tied a few minutes earlier, but the Colts had blown it open. The noise swirled around McHan, who was on his knees near midfield, having failed to tackle Brown during the return.

Shit! What is wrong with me?!

As the Colts celebrated on their bench, McHan slowly rose to his feet, dusted off his pants, and trudged toward his sideline. Lombardi, palpably stewing, again didn't say a word as McHan reached the bench. They stood together, watching in silence, as Unitas quickly turned the mistake into points, hitting Berry for a touchdown.

The game had gotten away from the Packers, 35–14.

McHan tried to pass the Packers back, scrambling, improvising, boosting his yardage total, and throwing a late touchdown to Boyd Dowler to make the final score more respectable, 38–21. The Packers had given away five fumbles and four interceptions, ruining their shot at an upset.

Furious, Lombardi slammed the locker room door shut after the game. He picked up a towel and slammed it down.

We're as good as they are and you damn well know it! You better start showing some guts and desire!

He kicked a metal locker, the hollow clang echoing in a silent locker room.

If you don't there are going to be a lot of changes around here! I can guarantee you that.

Speaking more calmly to reporters a few minutes later, Lombardi praised Unitas, who had also beaten Lombardi's team in the championship game a year earlier. "He's the greatest I ever saw," Lombardi said flatly. "He does everything well and he had himself a great day today." Asked if he wanted to elaborate on his "greatest I ever saw" statement, Lombardi shook his head no. "That speaks for itself," he said.

He also complimented McHan, who had compiled more passing yardage than Unitas but also thrown four interceptions.

"He's going to be a great one for us someday," Lombardi said. "He's starting to take charge despite the fact that he's not entirely familiar with his team yet."

But Lombardi was less charitable about the quarterback in private when he discussed the game with his assistants.

Four interceptions! We just gave it away! We can't have that! We have to be more sound at that position!

When Lombardi watched films of the Baltimore game back in Green Bay on Monday, he saw a lot of mistakes — penalties, fumbles, blown assignments. McHan had thrown into heavy coverage on interceptions.

He lashed out at the quarterback in the film session on Tuesday.

Did you think your arm was so strong you could throw the ball right through all those defenders, McHan?

No, Coach.

Did you see them? I'm asking, did you see them?

Yes, Coach.

Well, dammit, read the play! Read your keys! Read the coverage! Think out there, McHan! That was just dumb. We can't afford to be dumb.

Yes, Coach.

Of the many mistakes, one especially infuriated Lombardi. On the interception in the third quarter that changed the game, Lew Carpenter was supposed to run a downfield pass route out of the backfield, occupying the linebacker on his side, the Colts' Bill Pellington. But when the ball was snapped, Carpenter, fearing a reddog, stayed in to block. That left Pellington without anyone to cover, and he slid sideways to help cover Knafelc. McHan's toss was off-target and sailed right to Pellington, but the linebacker wasn't supposed to be near the play.

Lombardi blistered Carpenter with sarcasm in the film session.

Carpenter, do you think we design plays because we think you might want to try it our way?

No reply.

Do you think it's a good idea to ignore your assignment and just make up some goddamn thing to do?

No, sir.

Well, it sure looks like you do think that's a good idea. Because you did it on this play, and because you did, a man intercepted a pass and ran it in and we lost a game we could have won.

Silence.

So the next time you're inclined to ignore your assignment and make up some half-assed thing, do you think you will?

No, Coach.

I'm not sure I believe you. Let's look at this play again, everyone. Let's look at the interception that killed us because Carpenter thought he was so smart and didn't do his job.

The room was silent except for the clicks of the projector buttons Lombardi manipulated to rewind the film and show the play again.

Are you watching, Carpenter?

Yes, Coach.

Later, after the film session, Carpenter, a quiet veteran, was consoled by his teammates as he dressed for practice.

Hang in there, Lew. We've all been there.

Yeah. He acts like I was intentionally trying to lose the game or something, the asshole.

Yeah.

What a prick. He can shove that projector right up his ass.

Lombardi had circled the Packers' next game as a special occasion from the moment he saw it on the schedule. They would play in his hometown, New York, against his former team, the Giants, on Sunday, November 1, at Yankee Stadium. He told reporters it was just another game, but no one believed him. He had lived and coached in and around New York for his entire life until now. He wanted to go back and show how well he was doing on his own. Earl Blaik would be watching. Jim Lee Howell and his former players would be on the other sideline. His father, Harry, and other family members would be in the stands. How could it be just another game?

The Giants, he knew, would be a tough opponent, especially at home. Still running his offense and Tom Landry's defense, they led the Eastern Division with a 4-1 record. Their defense hit hard and yielded grudgingly, as the Packers had discovered when the Giants shut them out in their exhibition game in Maine. Frank Gifford was out with broken ribs, but thirty-eight-year-old Charlie Conerly was having another strong season at quarterback, and he was surrounded by playmakers.

The Packers, meanwhile, had issues — a growing list. McHan had emerged from the Baltimore game with a sore right shoulder; Lombardi kept him out of throwing drills all week, expecting the soreness to disappear by Sunday. The secondary had been picked apart in the past two games. And although Jim Taylor's burns were healed enough for him to practice and suit up on Sunday, his doctor said he couldn't carry a heavy load. The backfield was still shorthanded.

Lombardi drove the players hard during the week, shouting in practice and jamming his chalk into the board so violently it shattered. His players sensed he was uptight. When Hornung moved before the snap during a drill, he stopped practice to berate the Golden Boy, loudly making a scene.

Can you count to three, Hornung?

Yes, sir.

Let's hear it.

Hornung didn't respond, unsure if the coach was serious.

He was.

COUNT TO THREE, HORNUNG!!

One, two, three, Coach!

Good. That's easy, right? Don't get confused when we're running a damn play.

Early Sunday morning in his suite at the Hotel Manhattan, Lombardi stared at his image in a mirror and adjusted his tie. Everything had to be just right. It was a big day. He remembered the Packers and Giants playing NFL championship games in the late 1930s and early 1940s, when he was coaching at St. Cecelia's. The rivalry had diminished with the teams now in different divisions, but it was still a couple of old lions.

He had put on a dark worsted wool suit, one of his favorites. His camelhair overcoat would go on top. Nice. Looking good.

Get that tie just right.

He had enjoyed his weekend, hosting a Five O'clock Club party in the suite, entertaining Big Apple writers with tales from Green Bay, and visiting with Blaik before Army played Air Force at Yankee Stadium on Saturday. Marie had enjoyed herself immensely. They had eaten well, seen family and friends. The game might not be as much fun, he feared. The Giants could batter his young team. The Packers had some good things going for them, but he needed more time to put together a team that could go on the road and beat a winning veteran team like this.

Lombardi took an elevator down, strode purposefully across the lobby, and boarded the team bus. On the twenty-minute ride out to the stadium, he sat upright in the front row, opposite the driver, staring ahead with a stern expression, like a general leading his army into battle. No one dared speak to him.

During warm-ups he chatted on the field with Gifford, who wasn't dressed, and also visited with Landry, a good friend. They agreed it would be an interesting day. Before kickoff, Lombardi told the players they would need to give their best physical effort of the season.

The Giants are damn tough. But so are we. Hit them!

McHan tried to run the ball on the first possession. Hornung swept right, but Sam Huff, the Giants' agile middle linebacker, broke through and tackled him for a loss. Then Carpenter ran between Gregg and Jim Ringo, but Rosey Grier, the massive defensive tackle, shed the blocks and stood Carpenter straight up before slamming him to the ground. The crowd of sixty-eight thousand loved the big hit, sending up a cheer.

On third down, McHan dropped back, saw no receivers open,

turned, and tossed an outlet pass toward Hornung in the left flat. The Golden Boy was wide open but McHan threw the ball over his head.

McHan shook his head and trotted off the field, chalking up the mistake to jitters. Lombardi shouted at him. *Come on, McHan. Hit those passes. Take what they're giving us.*

The Packer defense started well. Dave Hanner and Henry Jordan stopped fullback Mel Triplett for no gain. Dan Currie fought off a block and tackled halfback Alex Webster on a sweep. Tom Bettis red-dogged and forced Conerly into a hurried incompletion.

But the Packers' second offensive possession went no better. McIlhenny ran left on a sweep but Huff and Harlan Svare shot past Kramer and Thurston and tackled the runner for a loss. Hornung tried to find a hole by Forrest Gregg, but the Giants' Jim Katcavage eluded the block and slammed into Hornung. On third down McHan again missed an open receiver, forcing another punt. Lombardi paced the sideline, his frustration evident. *We have to hit those throws. We have to do something.*

He started to think about pulling McHan, who looked like a quarterback who hadn't thrown all week because of a sore shoulder.

Late in the first quarter, with the game still scoreless, a Giant punt rolled deep into Packer territory, stopping at the 3. On second down, McHan handed to McIlhenny on a slant play off left guard. Svare beat Kramer and hit McIlhenny in the chest. The ball popped loose and Giants tackle Dick Modzelewski fell on it. It happened so quickly some fans didn't see it. They clapped, surprised, when a referee signaled that the Giants had the ball. What a gift! Just three yards from the end zone!

Conerly knelt in the Giants' offensive huddle and called for a left sweep, still using Lombardi's terminology. Webster took the handoff and rolled into the end zone behind a pair of clearing blocks. Kicker Pat Summerall's extra point put the Giants up, 7–0. The crowd didn't make much noise. It was so easy.

Early in the second quarter McHan tried Hornung, Carpenter, and McIlhenny going left, right, and up the middle. Defenders filled every hole. As Lombardi had feared, Grier and Andy Robustelli were too quick for Thurston and Norm Masters, Gregg couldn't budge Katcavage, and Huff read plays and moved to stop them before Ringo could get to him. And without a running game, McHan looked lost. The Giant secondary blanketed his receivers, and McHan either threw into coverage or misfired on outlet tosses. It was a miracle he wasn't intercepted.

Increasingly agitated on the sideline, Lombardi finally had seen enough by the middle of the second quarter.

Francis!

The reserve quarterback raced up, helmet in hand.

Yes, Coach?

Get warmed up. You're going in for Lamar.

"Pineapple Joe" grabbed a ball and began to throw on the sideline. McHan nodded when told of the change, knowing he wasn't one hundred percent.

Standing near Lombardi, Starr sagged. He couldn't believe the younger, inexperienced Francis was getting the shot before him.

Lombardi stared out at the field, jaw set. Francis had faded into the background recently, but had played well in the exhibition season. Lombardi had kept him around for a situation such as this, when the offense was stymied and needed a spark. Francis, with his natural athleticism, might be able to make a play and get things going. The circumstances called for his boldness more than Starr's deliberate approach.

When the Packers got the ball back, Lombardi sent not only Francis onto the field but Jim Taylor, seeing action for the first time since the second week of the season. Francis tried a different tactic, throwing to the backs rather than handing the ball to them. A pair of completions to McIlhenny picked up a first down. Then Taylor gained eleven yards off left tackle, as Masters opened a hole. Francis scrambled for seven after finding no receiver open. Lombardi nodded. *Yes, yes, just what I thought might happen.* Francis moved the offense deeper into New York territory than it had been all day. But the Giant defense finally made a stop, cutting through blocks to bring down runners before they got going. Hornung kicked a twenty-nine-yard field goal.

Lombardi nodded at Francis as the offense came off the field.

Good job, excellent, way to get things going.

After Summerall kicked a field goal to put the Giants up, 10–3, Francis again moved the offense. Hornung made a lunging catch to gain twenty yards. Francis passed to Knafelc on a square-out for seventeen. A tripping penalty moved the ball to the New York 17 with a minute left in the half. A touchdown would tie the score, giving the Packers a huge lift considering how badly they had been outplayed.

Hornung and Francis ran the ball down to the 8. On third down, Francis rolled right and threw for McGee on a curl route just over the goal line, but the pass sailed high, incomplete. Hornung stayed on to try a fourteen-yard field goal with a few seconds left. Lombardi counted on the three points, but the Golden Boy banged the easy kick off the left upright. The crowd gave its loudest roar of the day as the teams jogged to the locker rooms. *All that work for nothing, ha!*

The Packers were relieved to be just seven points down at halftime. Lombardi, encouraged by the spark Francis had provided, sat with the young quarterback and discussed how to get the offense into the end zone. Coming back onto the field for the second half, the Packers thought they had a shot at an upset.

But the Giants came out with a renewed sense of purpose. Howell and Landry didn't want to lose to Lombardi. The Giant offense drove downfield on its first series of the second half, using Lombardi's plays to crush him. Webster sprinted behind Bobby Freeman on a swing route, caught Conerly's pass in stride, and picked up thirty-two yards. Then Webster got behind Freeman again and the frustrated defender grabbed the receiver. The interference penalty moved the ball to the Green Bay 7, and Webster swept to a touchdown around right end. The Giants had a 17–3 lead.

The Packers were in trouble, needing two touchdowns against a defense they had barely dented. When Francis missed two passes, Lombardi yanked him for McHan, going with the better thrower. But the Giants, knowing McHan had to pass, fiercely red-dogged him, forcing him to scramble and throw hurriedly. Quickly realizing McHan wouldn't be leading any comebacks, Lombardi went back to Francis, hoping the athletic youngster could make plays.

Starr, bypassed again, moved away from Lombardi and watched Francis spray incompletions. Summerall booted a forty-five-yard field goal late in the third quarter to put the Giants up 20–3.

Lombardi was a forlorn figure on the sideline in the fourth quarter, the brim of his hat pulled low, his hands shoved deep into the pockets of his overcoat, his team knocked cold. The Packers weren't ready for Broadway.

Starr was beyond disappointed. It had crushed him to see Lombardi sub in Francis for McHan — not once but twice!

A loyal team guy and military officer's son, Starr believed in the chain of command; you didn't second-guess your coach, especially one as shrewd as Lombardi. But as he watched Francis try to rally the Packers, he couldn't help entertaining dark thoughts. Did he belong in pro football? If, in his fourth season, he couldn't even beat out a raw, second-year guy for a number two spot, maybe he needed to accept that he just wasn't going to have much of a career.

He was the straightest guy on the Packers, didn't go to clubs, barely swore or touched alcohol, but the players had several hours to themselves before their charter flight back to Green Bay departed Sunday evening, and Starr ended up in a Manhattan bar. Ron Kramer, the tight end, whose season also wasn't going well, wanted to drown his sorrows with a few beers. Starr went along. He was in that kind of mood.

Kramer, the former number one draft pick, was playing only on special teams. His knee was sore and he hadn't caught a pass all season. Lombardi and the assistants didn't know what to make of him, having expected a major contributor.

But Kramer wasn't so fond of them, either.

I don't know, Bart. This season is totally for shit.

Starr was just as glum as he quickly downed three beers.

Jeez, I was ready to go in, Ron.

His teammates laughed out loud when they heard he had gone to a bar.

Bart! What's gotten into you?!

But they were just trying to cheer him up. They knew things must be pretty bad if Bart Starr needed a drink.

★ 16 ★

LOMBARDI ENUNCIATED each word clearly, his rumbling Brooklyn voice suddenly resembling that of a snippy college professor.

Twenty-six pass attempts. Seven completions.

He paused to let the players reflect on those numbers. Then he repeated them for emphasis, speaking even more slowly.

Twenty-six attempted. Seven completed.

Another pause.

Can we win a ball game when we pass like that?

The room was filled with offensive players who had known their Tuesday morning film session wouldn't go well. None answered Lombardi's question, so he answered it himself.

No. We cannot win a ball game when we attempt twenty-six passes and complete seven. That's what we did in New York. And we got our asses kicked all over the field!

He paused again for emphasis, then continued.

They beat us up front. They manhandled us. We looked like we'd never learned how to block. Kramer, what were you doing out there? When you figure that out, please let me know.

And our passing attack was just miserable, awful, you name the description. McHan, Francis, we have to make better throws; a lot better. Max, we have to run better routes.

We have to give the defense more of a challenge.

He paused before making his final point.

If the people here now can't challenge a defense any better than we did in New York, I will find people who can.

Lombardi was irritated about his offense, his baby. It hadn't scored a touchdown in two of the past three games. Yes, Taylor had been out and McHan was banged up, but the air game was as lame as an old racehorse. McGee had caught just eleven passes all season, and of the backs, only Hornung seemed to pose a receiving threat.

As much as Lombardi favored the running game, he knew he had to have a better passing game. After listening to Wally Cruice and studying film of the Bears, whom the Packers would play next, on Sunday in Chicago, he decided to shake things up. He would switch from his beloved three-back formation to a more spread-out alignment featuring two backs and a second wide receiver. Hopefully, the passing game would be more formidable with a second receiver replacing the second halfback. Taylor and Hornung could still carry the ground game.

Who would start as the second receiver? Boyd Dowler was the only choice, Lombardi felt. Towering over the huddle at six feet five, with legs as long and taut as stretched rubber bands, the rookie ran crisp routes with a graceful stride, eating up ground. Lombardi had lost some faith in him after he dropped a touchdown in the opener against the Bears, but he had a knack for getting open. A. D. Williams, the other rookie receiver, was faster, but A. D., struggling with the playbook, became lost whenever the quarterback changed plays at the line.

Starting a rookie was risky, but Dowler was a genuine long-ball threat and would just go back to the bench if he flubbed, Lombardi figured.

Lombardi called in Dowler and gave him the news. Dowler was shocked but ecstatic. He had barely played on Sunday against the Giants. He knew Lombardi was having trouble forgetting his drop against the Bears. He had replayed the moment in his head countless times, the pass slipping through his hands, the crowd groaning, Lombardi grimacing. Since then, he had just tried to play well enough in practice to change Lombardi's opinion of him. He didn't think he had succeeded.

Dowler had never sat on the bench in his career. He had grown up in a little Wyoming town where his father was the high school coach, and he had barely come off the field in three years at Colorado, where he played quarterback, receiver, cornerback, and punter. He was as straight as a twenty-two-year-old comes, didn't drink, smoke, or even curse. His veteran roommates, Lamar McHan and Jesse Whittenton, were taking care of him, driving him to and from practice. (Dowler didn't own a car and didn't need one.) A calm, analytical coach's son, he rationalized that, as a rookie, he should be happy just to be on the team. Lombardi never singled him out for a scorching, as he did so many others.

Maybe he hasn't given up on me.

Now, starting Sunday, he would have the chance to establish himself.

Starr was back to his old self when the quarterbacks met with Lombardi on Wednesday to "game plan" for the Bears. The previous few days had been rough. On Monday, while some of his teammates slept in and then headed for Appleton, Starr stayed home and tried to straighten out his attitude, voicing his frustrations to his wife, Cherry. He couldn't believe he had fallen below Joe Francis on the depth chart.

But he eventually calmed down. It wasn't as if he had played himself down a notch; he had barely gotten off the bench all season. Lombardi had just given Francis the shot, for whatever reason. All Starr could do was continue to practice hard and prepare to play, soldier on as usual. He would take stock of his floundering career after the season if necessary. In the meantime, he was being paid to do a job.

Not that he would forget being passed over in New York. The experience had rattled him, but now that he was beyond it, he was determined to make the most of any chance he got. Enough with being perpetually disappointed, and with being viewed as the nice, unthreatening guy who didn't stir up things on or off the field. If Lombardi ever gave him a chance, Starr would grab it.

A winter-like storm blew through Green Bay, leaving eight inches of snow on the ground on November 3. Lombardi arranged for the team to practice indoors, at the Brown County Veterans Arena, where the floor was being cooled for an ice show later in the week. The players pushed banks of portable bleachers out of the way to clear the floor, and then ran through plays wearing tennis shoes.

Around town, as the fans dug out from the snowstorm, they discussed the Packers, their secular church. It was hard to know what to think. They could see Lombardi had made improvements and were hopeful about the second half of the season, but the losses to the Rams, Colts, and Giants had reminded them of prior collapses. Maybe Lombardi hadn't turned them around after all.

We've seen this before. I don't know. If we go down to Chicago and beat the Bears Sunday, maybe things have changed.

The Packers hadn't beaten the Bears in Chicago since 1952, and hadn't swept the teams' yearly home-and-home series since Don Hutson's rookie season in 1935. George Halas was loath to let it happen now. The Bears coach wanted revenge. His team had spiraled in the wrong direction after the opening loss in Green Bay; expected to contend for a division title, the Bears had lost four of their first five games to fall into last place. But they seemed to be righting themselves, having beaten the Rams on Sunday, and Halas was talking publicly about salvaging a winning season. Privately, no doubt, he was demanding that his players punish the Packers on Sunday. The Bears would be up for the game. Every ticket was long sold.

The Packers practiced outside on Thursday, and Lombardi was in an optimistic mood. McHan was throwing better, his shoulder apparently healed. Taylor was finally — finally! — ready to return to the starting lineup. The Packers had already beaten the Bears once, and Lombardi felt they should do it again. A *Chicago Tribune* sportswriter quoted him as saying his team "can . . . and will" win.

The Packers took a train to Chicago on Saturday and awoke Sunday to bright sunshine. When their bus pulled up to Soldier Field, they were greeted by the Lumberjack Band, the flannel-clad City Stadium music group, which always attended the Bears game in Chicago. Several hundred Packer fans also made the trip. Cheering, they formed a line the players walked through from the bus to the locker room.

As the game began, Lombardi watched Dowler and Taylor join the starting offense on the field. He hoped things would improve, but his hopes were quickly dashed. On first down, a gain by Hornung was negated by an offside penalty on Kramer. On second down, Hornung dropped a pitchout that hit him right in the hands. The Bears recovered and scored a touchdown in two plays. The game was eighty-seven seconds old.

The Packers started another series but kept making mistakes. They didn't appear prepared to play. McGee dropped one pass and caught another for a gain that was erased by a holding penalty. Hornung fumbled again as he charged up the middle, and the Bears recovered and rolled to another touchdown, Rick Casares scoring on a five-yard run.

Trailing 14–0, Lombardi roamed the sideline in a fury.

"You're in for Paul," he shouted at McIlhenny.

Hornung had earned a place on the bench. The Golden Boy shook his head disgustedly as the offense took the field without him. He quietly cursed Lombardi but part of him understood the move. Lombardi hated mistakes, and two fumbles in the first five minutes was more than the coach could tolerate.

On the field, the offense gathered around McHan in the huddle. This was his seventh start for the Packers, and his teammates were still trying to figure him out. They liked him well enough, and he obviously had talent, but he wasn't a commanding leader like, say, Tobin Rote. He pretty much called the plays and ran them, and while no one doubted his desire to win, he sometimes seemed preoccupied with his own situation, complaining when receivers dropped his passes, as though they did so out of spite.

His leadership would be tested now. The Packers had lost three straight games and now trailed by two touchdowns on the road.

Their season was starting to slip away from them. McHan tried to sound encouraging in the huddle.

We can do better than this. Come on. We've beaten the Bears. Let's move the ball.

Taylor gained seven behind a Bob Skoronski block. McIlhenny went for four around right end. Taylor picked up five up the middle. With the ball on the 50, McHan flipped a pass to McIlhenny in the left flat. Kramer flattened a linebacker and McIlhenny raced down the sideline to the 20 before being shoved out of bounds. Two plays later, Taylor took a handoff at the 10 and charged through a hole cleared by Gregg. Two Bears hit him at the 5, but he dragged them into the end zone. Hornung came off the bench to kick the extra point, and the Packers were back in the game, 14–7.

"That's the way to go! We're back in it!" Lombardi shouted, thinking McHan had performed well in a difficult situation.

After the defense made a stop, Carpenter returned the punt fifty-two yards. Catching the line drive kick at his 24, he burst past the first wave of coverage, which had expected a longer boot, and broke into the open field, angling from left to right as he ran. Three Bears finally tackled him at the Chicago 24.

The big crowd was quiet now, but Taylor and McIlhenny gained little on a pair of runs, and Hornung kicked a field goal that cut Chicago's lead to 14–10.

On the next Packer possession, McHan, looking for the lead, threw downfield for McGee, who was running with the Bears' J. C. Caroline. The pass was high, both men leapt for the ball, and Caroline fell to the ground with it at his 22. The Bears had the ball back. And then their offense began to roll. Casares and halfback Johnny Morris ran through big holes. At the Green Bay 36, quarterback Ed Brown lobbed a long pass toward receiver Harlon Hill on the left sideline. The ball sailed short and Whittenton was in position to grab it, but Hill wrested it away as they fell together in the end zone. The fans stood and shouted. Touchdown, Bears.

McHan tried to rally the Packers just before halftime. He threw to Dowler for a first down, then dropped back, failed to find an open receiver, and sprinted for the sideline with the ball, trying to stop the clock. Just before he reached the sideline, he jumped to elude a tackler, felt his right hamstring pop, and toppled over with a shout, clutching his leg. Bud Jorgensen, the trainer, ran to him.

A few minutes later, in the halftime locker room, Lombardi approached Starr.

Lamar can't go. You're in.

Starr nodded, pleased not to be passed over again. Having prepared for the Bears, he vowed to make the most of his chance.

We can come back and win this game, Coach.

Lombardi's rationale was simple. Francis had looked overmatched against the Giants. Starr had played fairly well against the Bears in the exhibition opener in August. Starr certainly could step in; he studied more film than anyone.

By the time the offense took the field in the third quarter, the Bears had scored again, driving eighty yards for a touchdown that gave them a 28–10 lead. Quarterback Zeke Bratkowski scrambled for forty-one yards after escaping a red-dog and otherwise picked on Bobby Freeman, who was struggling. Hands on hips, Lombardi stared at the defensive players as they came off the field. *What in the hell is going on out there?*

Starr took over in a tough spot, down eighteen points on the road. He and Dowler, who as backups had spent hours together at practice, hooked up for an eighteen-yard gain. Taylor hurled himself into the line for three on a fourth-and-one play, and then went for six around right end. After Starr completed a short pass to Taylor, the Bears' Bill George slammed the quarterback to the turf, bloodying Starr's lip.

That should take care of you, Bart Starr, you little pussy.

Jerry Kramer couldn't believe what he heard next.

Fuck you, Bill George, we're coming after you.

Kramer had never heard Starr curse. (And never did again.) They had been teammates for a year and a half, but Kramer thought of Starr as methane gas — odorless, colorless, tasteless, having little impact on his surroundings.

Kramer's eyes bulged when Starr cursed at George.

You should go over and get your lip checked, Bart.

214

The heck with that, let's go.

Kramer smiled to himself. Maybe we have ourselves a quarterback here, he thought.

The Packers rolled to a first-and-goal at the 7 and picked up six yards in two plays, putting the ball on the 1. Taylor ran behind Skoronski on third down, but massive Doug Atkins plugged the hole, and Taylor smacked into him and fell back. On fourth down, two feet from the end zone, Starr sent Taylor back into the line behind Ringo. The Bears plugged the hole, and Taylor was tackled for a loss.

Cheers echoed across the field as the Bear defense rose and trotted to the sideline. Lombardi, whose ire had been up all day, looked down with disgust. *For crying out loud, can't we score from the 1?*

A few minutes later Starr led the offense back downfield. McIlhenny swept left for twenty-three behind Kramer and Thurston. Taylor went the other way for twelve behind Gregg. On a first down at the 8, McIlhenny ran past Atkins, cut back, and was about to score but slipped and went down at the 1. Then McIlhenny tried right tackle and was knocked down. Lombardi sent in Hornung on third down to take advantage of the Golden Boy's nose for the end zone, but Hornung dropped the pitchout. Taylor fell on the fumble at the 4, but now it was fourth down. Starr rolled right and threw for McIlhenny in the end zone, but the pass skipped off McIlhenny's hands. Lombardi couldn't believe it. His offense had twice reached the 1-yard line and failed to score. That was just not acceptable.

"The best team didn't win today, I'll tell you that," he rasped to Lee Remmel of the *Press-Gazette,* who was on the sideline as the game ended.

The final gun sounded, and Lombardi walked across the field to congratulate Halas on the 28–17 win. When all the players were in the locker room, the doors were closed and Lombardi started to shout.

"You need to decide whether you want to be here with us when we start to win. I need better concentration. I need more consistency. I need fewer mistakes."

Speaking to reporters, he continued, "The defense played an adequate game, just gave up a couple of drives. And we moved the ball on offense. We played better today than we did when we beat the Bears in Green Bay. We should have had thirty-five points. But we make so many mistakes on offense. That's what is beating us."

The players showered and dressed quickly. McIlhenny, who had filled in for Hornung with almost one hundred rushing and receiving yards, was under the nozzle when he saw Lombardi standing at the entryway to the shower. The coach's shoes were getting sprayed.

"Yes, Coach?" McIlhenny asked.

"You played a hell of a football game today," Lombardi growled.

"Thank you, Coach," McIlhenny said.

Lombardi turned and departed, and McIlhenny exhaled. He had never had a coach come into the shower to compliment him.

For the first time in Packer history, the team was flying from Chicago back to Green Bay instead of taking a train. As Lombardi boarded the charter, Remmel approached him, wanting to confirm the "best team didn't win" quote before it went into print. Lombardi didn't back off. "I do think we were the better team," he said. "We should have won the ball game."

The doors closed, the plane taxied and took off, and Lombardi sat back and reflected. His revamped offense had performed adequately. Dowler had caught just two balls, but few had come his way. McGee had been shut out again. What was wrong with Max? And Hornung, good gracious, Lombardi loved him, but he had been awful today — three touches, three fumbles. And he was the cornerstone of the offense?

Lombardi wondered how long it would take for him to correct these problems and put a winning team on the field. Five years, he had originally thought, and then, after the 3-0 start, maybe three. But now he thought maybe five was right after all. Frankly, he had no idea. He sighed, feeling frustrated and tired, took off his glasses, and rubbed the bridge of his nose with his forefingers.

Four losses in a row was about all he could take.

★ **17** ★

PAUL HORNUNG KNEW what was coming when the players sat down to watch film on Tuesday. He had steeled himself for the moment with a long, happy Monday night out. What the hell, right?

But now came the hard part.

Hornung, can't you catch a simple pitchout?

Hornung, if you can't protect the ball better than that, your ass will be on the bench.

As he listened to Lombardi chide him, Hornung wondered if he might end up selling real estate in Louisville after all. He had done virtually nothing for a month after starting the season so well. His stock was plummeting. His specialty was getting the ball over the goal line, but Lombardi had mostly left him on the bench as the Packers stumbled at the 1 against the Bears. When the coach did give him a chance, he fumbled.

The Golden Boy didn't enjoy being criticized, but he was mostly angry with himself for performing so poorly. He was a man. He could admit it when he made a mistake. Lombardi had given him a great opportunity, a big role in the offense, and he was blowing it. He couldn't blame anyone else. He had dropped those balls in Chicago. He didn't know why. He had prepared for the game in his customary fashion, by having a hell of a good time the night before. Some people didn't like that about him, but it never kept him from playing his ass off the next day. He didn't need to change; the hell with that. He just needed to hold onto the ball better. He could play this game. He could get Lombardi off his ass.

He pledged to keep having a good time — and to shut the old man up.

Before the team hit the practice field on Tuesday, Lombardi called Starr into his office. *You're starting on Sunday. Lamar has a pulled hamstring.*

Starr nodded, thinking he shouldn't admit he valued playing time more after being passed over in New York. *Let's go out and win. We can do it.*

Their next game was a rematch with the Colts at County Stadium in Milwaukee. Though the opportunity to compete against the league champions excited him, Starr knew he was playing only because McHan couldn't. Lombardi's ambivalence about him was obvious. Asked by reporters about the decision to start Starr, the coach shrugged and said, "There's not much to choose between him and Francis. Perhaps Francis has a little better potential. Starr is smarter."

That was hardly a ringing endorsement. But Lombardi couldn't help himself. The coach liked Starr's work ethic and intelligence but was bothered by his mild demeanor and penchant for making mistakes. Starr had played relatively well against the Bears on Sunday, Lombardi admitted, keeping the defense guessing with his play calls, scrambling away from red-dogs, and completing several nice passes, but it was typical that the offense's failure to score from the 1-yard line marred the overall effort. Starr could grasp complex material, play well at times, and was the nicest young man, but he walked around under a dark cloud. Receivers dropped his best passes. The ball mysteriously slipped out of his hand at the worst time. Something always went wrong.

Lombardi feared Starr was just too nice. He didn't command the huddle or castigate teammates who made mistakes. He wasn't a leader like the Giants' Charlie Conerly, a grizzled ex-Marine who had fought in World War II. The decision to start him over Francis against the Colts was easy, Lombardi felt, because Starr was a better passer, more polished, and had shredded the Colts the year before in Milwaukee, passing for more than three hundred yards in that game in which the Packers blew a seventeen-point lead and, fittingly, Starr threw a late interception that cost Green Bay the game. But Lombardi didn't expect Starr to take this opportunity and elbow McHan out of the number one job.

As the Packers prepared for the game, Starr burned to play well enough to impress Lombardi. He loved the simplicity and precision of Lombardi's offense, the logical methodology, the discipline Lombardi demanded. Starr had experienced enough ineffectual coaching to know effective coaching when he saw it. The Packers were going to improve, Starr believed, and he wanted to be around to experience that. Somehow, he had to convince Lombardi he was the best option. McHan's pulled hamstring had opened the door ever so slightly.

The Packers' preparations were disrupted by another early blast of winter, this one far worse. Even though Thanksgiving was still two weeks away, temperatures dropped into the teens and snow fell on and off for two days. Drivers slipped across roads and bashed into each other, people fell walking to work, and the Packers again moved their practices indoors, this time running through plays in a large hall instead of the main arena, where the ice floor was laid down.

With a 3-4 record, they had fallen behind the surprising 49ers, whose 6-1 record put them two games ahead of second-place Baltimore. The Colts, at 4-3, had lost two straight games and were coming to Wisconsin in a desperate mood. The Packers could knock them out with an upset, and their fans were worried about it. "Can Colts Rack Pack, Get Back on Track?" read a Baltimore headline that week.

"The Colts are going to be especially tough. They surely feel they have to win this one," Lombardi told reporters. As for his own team, he said he wasn't discouraged by four straight defeats. "Actually, we played a finer game against the Bears on Sunday than we did in the three games we won," he said. "We just continue to make errors, and the same people are making them, dropping the ball and not catching passes."

The latter was an obvious reference to Hornung and Max Mc-Gee.

"Hornung is the only back we have who can run over anybody and gain where there is no hole. Taylor and McIlhenny need a crack [in the line]. But we put Paul in there and he dropped the ball," Lombardi said.

What was wrong with Hornung?

"I haven't the slightest idea," Lombardi snapped. "And if I did, I wouldn't say. But don't forget Paul has played four or five fine games for us. Just because he had a bad day doesn't mean he's all done. There's no use crucifying him for that."

Hornung was encouraged when he read Lombardi's supportive comments in the paper. And the coach similarly defended McGee: "Yes, Max has dropped some balls, but the quarterbacks haven't been throwing to him much, either. He's been open a lot and they missed him. Maybe they aren't throwing to him as much because they've lost confidence in him. But he's had some good catches and good games."

The losing streak had dulled the public's enthusiasm for the Packers in Milwaukee. A month earlier, they had brought a 3-0 record into a game against the Rams and drawn more than thirty-six thousand fans. Now, just twenty-five thousand came to County Stadium to watch them play the reigning NFL champions in wintry weather more suited to mid-January than the game's actual date, November 15.

The field had been covered during the week so it was in good shape. The Packers came out passing. Starr immediately hit McGee for a thirty-seven-yard gain, moving the ball to the Baltimore 33. It was Max's first catch in three weeks, and Starr went right back to him, spotting him open at the 10, but sailed the pass over the receiver's head. Starr then also overthrew Hornung on a screen, and the Colts' massive defensive tackle, Eugene "Big Daddy" Lipscomb, intercepted.

After Emlen Tunnell blocked a Baltimore field goal attempt, the Packer offense drove the ball again. Boyd Dowler broke open on a deep crossing route, and Starr hit him for a thirty-four-yard gain. Then Dowler ran the same route, pivoted, cut outside, and was open. Starr's pass hit him in the hands, but he dropped the likely touchdown. Dowler shuddered as he jogged back to the huddle. *I can't believe it happened again!* But Lombardi didn't pull him.

Starr threw another interception late in the first quarter, failing to see a linebacker over the middle. Lombardi paced the sideline, wondering if he needed to try another quarterback. Starr was making too many mistakes. This was the problem with him. The game was played on the field, not in front of a projector.

Starr stood next to him on the sideline, hoping he didn't get pulled, as the Colts staged an offensive clinic in the second quarter. Lenny Moore ran twenty-six yards for a touchdown. Unitas threw strikes to open receivers. Moore turned a short catch into a thirty-two-yard gain. Ameche did the same for thirty. Berry ran a square-out route, beat Hank Gremminger, and caught a touchdown pass. A few minutes later, Unitas hit Jim Mutscheller for sixteen yards, and Moore, just too fast and elusive, gained forty-three with a short pass. Unitas hit Berry for another touchdown, and the Colts led at halftime, 21–3. The Colts just had too many weapons for the Packer defense.

The Packers' locker room was tense. They knew they could do better. The defense had given up too many big plays, and the offense had misfired at key moments. Starr circled the room speaking to teammates. He felt optimistic despite his depressing first half; if the Packers just stopped beating themselves, he said, they could move on Baltimore's defense.

Come on, we get the ball, let's go out there and do something.

At the start of the third quarter, he looked around the huddle at Hornung, Taylor, Dowler, and McGee — a lineup with playmaking potential, for sure. Starr was tired of not making the most of his opportunities. Thinking back to how he felt when he was bypassed in New York, he surprised his teammates and shouted at them.

Hush up and listen! Come on! Let's do something here!

Dowler ran a crossing route and Starr hit him for a twenty-yard gain. Taylor ran left on a sweep, lost a shoe, bulled through a tackler anyway, and picked up fourteen. The huddle was upbeat; it was uplifting to see your fullback crush a tackler. Starr went back to Dowler, open along the right sideline, for fourteen. Taylor swept around right end for eighteen, sprung by Thurston's powerful clearing block. Moments later Taylor plunged over left tackle and into the end zone from the 2, cutting the margin to 21–10.

Lombardi clapped as the offense came off the field. That was a textbook drive, employing strong-shouldered runs to open up passing routes. Starr had executed the coach's wishes perfectly, and thrown some nice passes, too. Nice job by the determined young man from Alabama.

The touchdown raised spirits on the Packer bench. Down eleven with twenty-four minutes left, they felt they had a chance. Henry Jordan crashed into Ameche on a run up the middle, and the ball popped free. Dave Hanner fell on it at the Baltimore 34. The crowd cheered as the offense jogged back onto the field. *This could get interesting.*

On first down Starr looked for Dowler, who had beaten his defender, veteran Andy Nelson, and was open at the Baltimore 20. Nelson grabbed the lanky rookie's long arms, blatantly interfering to avoid a completion. The referee flagged the penalty and the Packers had a first down. Starr then handed to Taylor going off right tackle, and the fullback waited for Forrest Gregg's block and picked up eight yards. Then Taylor faked a block, slipped out of the backfield, and caught a pass from Starr in the left flat. The Colts were preoccupied with Dowler and McGee, and Taylor jogged to the end zone, scoring for the second time in seventy-eight seconds. Hornung's extra point made the score 21–17.

The fans were on their feet now, cheering the Packer defense. Ameche was stopped for a short gain. A pass to Moore gained four. On third down, Unitas retreated to pass but couldn't find an open receiver. Pressed by Jordan, he ran to his right, looking downfield, but finally just threw the ball away. The Packers had held!

After a punt, Starr and the offense started a possession at their 27, looking for the lead. Starr called for Hornung to sweep right after a fake to Taylor, who had been carrying a heavy load. The ruse worked. As the Colts ganged up on Taylor, Hornung burst through an opening, cut to his right, and broke into the clear, churning down the sideline in front of the stunned Baltimore bench. He was no sprinter, but he crossed midfield and appeared headed for the end zone until Andy Nelson caught him and tugged him down at the 10. The sixty-three-yard run was the longest of Hornung's NFL career. He rose and nodded his head. *Yes sir, that's me.*

The crowd was charged up, sending out howls, as light snow began to fall from a darkening sky; the stadium lights would need to be turned on. The Packers had come from eighteen points down against the NFL champions and were poised to take the lead. Lombardi paced the sideline, pleased to see his offense moving so well.

On the other side of the ball, Lipscomb and Gino Marchetti and the rest of the veteran Colt defense dug into the turf, accustomed to perilous situations. Starr handed to Taylor up the middle on first down. Art Donovan fended off Jim Ringo and slammed Taylor down after a one-yard gain. On second down, Starr threw too high for McGee in the end zone. On third down, Starr again looked for Dowler, but Marchetti slipped past Gregg, bore down on Starr, and trapped him at the 15.

Hornung, still breathing hard from his long run, stayed on to attempt a short field goal. The snap was perfect and Starr placed it on the turf with the laces out. Hornung swung his right leg through but didn't catch the ball flush with his toe. It sailed high but drifted to the left of the uprights. No good.

Lombardi grimaced but patted Hornung on the shoulder as the Golden Boy came off. *Hell of a run, Paul. Get the next kick.* The Packers had lost their momentum but needed to keep playing hard.

Unitas sauntered back on with his offense. The fans feared he had been held down long enough and would make the Packers pay. Sure enough, he hit Berry for thirteen and Mutscheller for twenty-nine on sharp throws over the middle. After Moore picked up four off right tackle, Unitas dropped back and looked right for Berry, covered by Dillon. Jordan and Hanner bore down on him, and Unitas drifted to his right while looking downfield. Jordan caught him with one hand and tried to sling him down, but Unitas shook off the tackle and hurled a desperate long throw for Mutscheller near the goal line. Bobby Freeman jumped for the ball but Mutscheller got his hands on it and fell into the end zone.

Unbelievable. Touchdown, Baltimore.

The cheers on the Colt sideline could be heard throughout the suddenly silent stadium as kicker Steve Myhra added the extra point to put the Colts up, 28–17.

Deflated, the fans sat down. As the Packer offense returned to the field, Starr spoke encouragingly. *Come on, we're moving the darn ball. Let's keep doing it!* He dropped back and found Dowler open over the middle. The rookie, enjoying a huge day, reeled in the pass for a twenty-six-yard gain, moving the ball to midfield. But one play later, when Starr again threw for Dowler, a Colt safety read the play and intercepted. Starr stood at midfield with his hands on his hips. *This is what always happens!*

After a punt, the Packer offense began another possession at its 25 with seven minutes left; not much time for the two scores the Packers needed. But Starr was upbeat in spite of the deficit and his mistakes. He had dented Baltimore's defense — more than dented it, actually. The Packers had generated almost four hundred yards of offense. They had moved the ball on the ground and in the air. Starr had experienced an epiphany of sorts. Some of the possibilities Lombardi had discussed during the week had crystallized right in front of him, the holes and receivers opening up just as Lombardi had said they would. Wow! Starr had been impressed with Lombardi all along, but his appreciation soared even higher. There was no doubt the man's offense could roll over defenses. That gave Starr confidence, sent an electric charge through his body. *If we run the plays right, we'll move the ball. We will!*

As the offense huddled around him, his excitement was palpable, his enthusiasm infectious. *We have time. We can do this. We're going right down the field.*

The other players' eyes met before they broke the huddle and headed to the line. They all had the same thought. Where did mild-mannered Bart go? Who was this confident new guy? Not that they disapproved of the change in their kindly teammate. They had always liked him. It was fun to see him so charged up. They felt inspired to go hit someone, go make something happen.

Starr came to the line, surveyed the defense, and audibled: One man on Dowler. He dropped back to pass and hit the rookie on the right sideline for ten yards. Then he passed to Taylor in the left flat, and the fullback bulled through a tackler and picked up eleven. Starr went back to Dowler for thirteen. Hornung gained six around left end. The offense had never looked better, accumulating chunks of yardage at a time. With the Colts expecting passes, Taylor ran twice for a first down, and then Starr dropped back, looking for McGee, who was covered. Starr eluded the onrushing Marchetti, put the ball under his arm, and scrambled for thirteen to the Baltimore 11.

His teammates pumped him up in the huddle. *Attaway, Bart. Good stuff. Good running.*

They all felt his excitement now.

After three plays gained nine yards, Starr called for Taylor to run behind Gregg on fourth-and-one at the 3. The burly tackle cleared an opening with a crushing block on Marchetti, and Taylor rolled into the end zone for his third touchdown of the day. Hornung's extra point left the Packers down 28–24, with two minutes left.

Lombardi congratulated Starr on the sideline. *Way to go there. Hell of a drive, hell of a day.* He couldn't remember the last time he had seen the Colt defense so confused. The Packers could win this thing if they could just get the ball back.

The fans stood, imploring the defense to make a stop. Phil Bengston's unit had played hard, but Unitas was never better than in the final minutes of a close game. He kept the defense guessing with a blend of passes and runs. As the Packers frantically burned up their remaining timeouts, Ameche picked up a first down with a six-yard run off left tackle, and Moore produced another first running around right end.

The fans had witnessed a superb comeback, but they watched in silence as the final seconds ticked off the clock.

Five straight losses now.

Lombardi walked to midfield and shook hands with Colts coach

Weeb Ewbank, who admitted feeling relieved. The Packers had generated 455 yards of offense, their highest single-game total since October 1956. True, the defense had allowed more (505 yards), but Unitas routinely rolled up that much, so it was no disgrace. The story of the game was Green Bay's offense — and the fact that the Packers hadn't collapsed after falling so far behind.

"It's a shame," Lombardi told the reporters. "We played well enough to win. We could have won three of these last five we've lost."

There was a pause. "So when are you going to win again?" someone finally asked.

It was the kind of question that could cause Lombardi to explode, but he answered patiently, as if he shared the frustration.

"I don't know. The way it is going, I don't now. We'll have to . . ." His voice trailed off. Then he continued: "I'll say this much. This club hasn't quit. They've stayed right in there, and it's to their credit and their credit alone."

He praised Starr, who had passed for 242 yards ("He played a fine game"); Dowler, who had caught eight balls for 147 yards ("This might be the making of him"); and Taylor, who had rushed for 79 yards, caught two passes for 30, and scored three touchdowns ("He is already playing well and will continue to get better"). Between those performances, Hornung's 63-yard run, and McGee's four catches for 65 yards, the offense had enjoyed quite a day.

"We played better today than we did in any of our wins," Lombardi said. "We just made some mistakes in the first half or we would have had two strong halves and won the ball game."

Lombardi had to give Starr credit: the young man had played a winning game, not only with his passing and running but also with his leadership. McHan would probably be ready to go next week, but how could Lombardi put Starr back on the bench after this? McHan had never run the offense so deftly.

Lombardi had to smile at how unpredictable this game was. Maybe the starting quarterback he wanted had been on his roster all along.

★ **18** ★

THE EARLY WINTER weather turned brutal as the Packers prepared for their next game, against the Washington Redskins at City Stadium. Temperatures dropped to near zero as three inches of snow fell Wednesday followed by an all-day blast Thursday. Yet the Packers had to practice outside because the Green Bay Bobcats minor-league ice hockey team was using the arena. "I've learned a lot about coaching in the weather here," Lombardi lamented. "Once November hits, you can't put in anything new. You have to go with what you've already taught them."

The players were in a grumpy mood, especially after the heater in their locker room conked out. They were cold, miserable, wrung out from months of Lombardi's criticism, and after five straight defeats, had forgotten what it felt like to win. Some of the loyalty Lombardi had developed in the locker room started to teeter. Maybe he wasn't so great after all, some players wondered. They had all experienced a moment, either in the film room or on the field, when they wanted to knock him cold. They were willing to put up with him if he turned them into a winning team, but if he didn't, well, the heck with him.

When the team separated into units to watch film of the Baltimore loss, the defense heard Lombardi through the wall, roaring at offensive players who had made mistakes.

Max! Max!!! Have you just forgotten how to catch?

No, Coach.

Fuzzy, did you notice that when you pivoted the wrong way you wrecked the play?

Yes, Coach.

As their quieter session rolled along with the professorial Phil Bengston quietly offering suggestions, the defensive players wondered if their offensive brothers would survive the season. They had played a hell of a game against the Colts and were still getting reamed out.

Of course, after Lombardi tore you down, he always came around later, flashed that grin, hit you on the shoulder, complimented you, and asked about your kids, and suddenly, instead of being angry, you just wanted to play better.

The way he plays with your attitude, damn, it's so confusing!

The players weren't dumb. They saw that some of Lombardi's plays and philosophies worked. It felt great to be in shape. The offensive line was knocking people around; Forrest Gregg had shut down Gino Marchetti on Sunday, and no one did that. The running game was formidable, especially with Jim Taylor carrying the ball. Even though they had just two more wins than Scooter McLean's 1958 Packers through eight games, they knew they were a more competitive team.

A year earlier, when they were getting pounded on Sundays, they basically gave up, and Scooter didn't command enough respect to make them work harder. They couldn't do that now. Lombardi scared them too much. They knew he was right to be pushing them, demanding that they respect themselves more. Yes, they were still coming up short on Sundays, but they were a solid team now, even a dangerous one. They would win soon enough.

They practiced crisply for the Redskins despite the weather and the losing streak. They focused on their assignments and took few missteps. Their energy level was high. "They just won't quit," Lombardi said, beaming.

But while he complimented the players publicly, he privately wondered how many would be coming with him into his second Packer season and beyond. Those decisions would be made during the off-season, but he was thinking ahead. He would keep the players who exhibited the consistency, concentration, and fire he demanded, and after five straight losses, he wondered how many fit that description.

Quietly, he asked his assistants to assess every player on the roster. Bill Austin, Red Cochran, Norb Hecker, and Bengston completed the written assignment before Sunday's game. Lombardi asked for honest opinions, and he got them. The assistants believed Lamar McHan was the team's best quarterback, but they fell short of endorsing him wholeheartedly. He was "slow mentally," one wrote, and "just a fair passer, not the type to lead us to the world title," another said. What about Starr? The assistants didn't like him, at least not as a starter, his most recent game notwithstanding. "A number two at best, but smart and serious enough to do a satisfactory job in this capacity," one wrote. Another stated flatly, "I do not believe we can win with him. Not a consistent passer or a take-charge type of player."

Hornung, who always generated strong opinions, had annoyed the assistants recently. After playing so well early in the season, he had fallen off badly. Although he was still the team's leading rusher and scorer, his long run against the Colts this past Sunday was his only memorable play in a month.

"He is a problem as far as training and social life and I don't think he is going to change. Could be a great player but lacks drive," one assistant wrote. Another felt similarly, writing, "Paul is not a team player. Has ability to do many things but is very lax. Not a good blocker. Does not make the big play when called upon to do so. I question his value as a top-flight player. I don't believe we can depend on him to do the job."

The assistants had made their assessments without consulting each other, so it was telling that they shared a negative opinion of Hornung. They felt similarly about McGee. "I don't think he tries all the time; bad for the team," one wrote. Another suggested that "Max could be a great end" but had a "poor attitude and was a bad actor off the field." They all wanted to see him traded or somehow replaced.

Taylor stirred a mixed reaction. One assistant wrote that he was "a real good one," and another called him "our best back." But one was troubled by his relatively small stature: "Size is a handicap [and] Jim is not a good blocker, but he will have to be the number one fullback until we find a bigger man as tough."

The assessments were full of strong opinions. Boyd Dowler was a "great prospect." Jerry Kramer "had great potential." Gregg was "a top tackle who could play anywhere." Henry Jordan was "very fast for a big man; no question about him." Bill Quinlan "continues to do a good job on Sundays despite having a good time all week." Dave Hanner was "a top tackle with several more good years left."

Not every review was positive. Emlen Tunnell was "at the end of the trail." Bobby Dillon was "a big disappointment, just about over the hill." And the assessments of Ray Nitschke were brutal. "He cannot think and will never be able to play for us — trade him," one assistant wrote.

Lombardi filed away the assessments, pledging to heed them, and turned his attention to the Packers' first game at City Stadium in more than a month. They had started the season by winning three straight sold-out games there — how long ago did that seem? The losing streak had quelled some enthusiasm. A thousand tickets were still available Saturday, and the crowd of 31,853 was shy of a sellout.

The Redskins, like the Packers, had a 3-5 record under a first-year head coach (Mike Nixon) and had exhibited a range of capabilities. They had upset the Colts two weeks earlier, but they had the league's worst rushing defense. Now, their diminutive Pro Bowl quarterback, Eddie LeBaron, was out with a broken rib.

The teams knew each other well from their yearly exhibition games in Winston-Salem, and they had also played a regular-season game in Washington in 1958, the Redskins rolling to a 34–0 lead before settling for a 37–21 win over Scooter's inept squad. Now the Packers were favored by five points, largely because the game was in Green Bay and LeBaron was injured.

The skies cleared as the teams warmed up Sunday, but gusting winds sent up swirls of drifted snow. Many Redskins had their hands stuffed in their pants. Winter was well under way in Green Bay on November 22.

Lombardi's game plan was straightforward. The Redskins' rush defense was soft. "Jimmy and Paul should get the ball a lot," he told Starr as the quarterbacks watched film of the Redskins during the week.

"Yes, sir," Starr replied.

Starr enjoyed that Lombardi sequestered himself with the quarterbacks and included their ideas in the offensive plan. He saw another side of the man — the levelheaded theoretician, as opposed to the growling taskmaster.

Look at the defensive end taking that hard outside rush. The forty-eight left would attack that.

Yes, sir.

Look at the cornerback giving up all that room. You know what to do with that.

Yes, sir.

With backup quarterback Ralph Guglielmi leading the offense, the Redskins drove downfield early in the first quarter behind Don Bosseler, their hard-running fullback. From a first down at the Green Bay 14, Bosseler ran straight up the middle three straight times for nine yards, crashing into Hanner and Jordan. On fourth-and-one at the 5, he went back up the middle yet again, but Hanner didn't budge and Dan Currie and Tom Bettis flew over the pile and stopped him. The wind-whipped crowd cheered the defense.

Starr and the offense trotted onto the field. *OK, let's move that ball.* Hornung swept left for five. Taylor swept right for seven. Taylor came back up the middle for five. The line cut down defenders, opening holes, and when the Redskins moved up their linebackers for support, Starr took advantage, throwing over the stacked-up front to Dowler for twenty and McGee for eleven.

The ball was in Washington territory now. Bob Skoronski and Gary Knafelc opened a hole for Hornung, who picked up sixteen. Taylor swept right for seven, and a referee tacked on fifteen for roughing when a Redskin slugged Knafelc. That moved the ball to the 12. Two plays later, Knafelc ran a curl-in route and caught Starr's low throw just over the goal line, completing a ninety-five-yard scoring drive. Hornung's conversion put the Packers up, 7–0.

The Redskins drove back into Green Bay territory but the Packer defense held and Jordan jumped up and blocked a thirty-two-yard field goal attempt, sending the ball spinning wide. Hank Gremminger scooped it up and raced twenty yards before being pushed out of bounds at midfield.

Starr kept the ball on the ground. Taylor gained eleven off left tackle and fifteen sweeping left. Starr faked to Hornung and threw to Dowler for three. Taylor carried twice more for sixteen. With the ball on the 10, Starr rolled right and threw for Knafelc, who was open in the corner of the end zone. The ball went through Knafelc's hands. Starr patted his roommate on the rump and called the same play, but faked a throw to Knafelc and threw a hard spiral toward McGee in the back of the end zone. McGee held on for the score and later joked with Starr on the sideline, "It sure got there quick." The lead was 14–0 after Hornung's conversion.

The Packers were upbeat in their locker room at halftime, encouraged to see their running game pummeling an opponent. The offense drove downfield again to start the third quarter. Hornung waited for Gregg to open a hole and sprinted through it for sixteen. Starr dumped a pass in the left flat for Taylor, who bulled for seven, dragging two tacklers. Taylor then ran up the middle, behind Jim Ringo, for a first down. Again, the Redskins fortified their front, and again, Starr took advantage, hitting open receivers everywhere — McGee for sixteen on a slant, Dowler deep over the middle for twenty-five, Knafelc for six on a curl.

At the 5, Hornung swept left, Thurston and Kramer pulled and leveled defenders, and Hornung trotted across the goal line. As the fans cheered, Hornung kicked the conversion to make the sore 21–0 with nine minutes left in the third quarter. The game was effectively over, the run-oriented Redskins not built for comebacks, especially with LeBaron out. Packer linebackers red-dogged Guglielmi, sacked him three times, and harried him into incompletions.

Starr came out of the game early in the fourth quarter after being poked in the eye. McHan came in, wondering where he stood now. He had been the starter just a few weeks earlier, but now seemingly had lost his job to Starr, who was playing error-free ball while executing Lombardi's game plans. McHan had always feared things wouldn't work out in Green Bay, and his fears finally were being realized. He hoped he would get another chance, but with the Packers winning, he kept quiet and just handed off to backs, running out the clock.

For the first time since early October, the fans, delighted with the victory, counted down the final seconds together — *six, five, four, three, two, one!* — and flung their seat cushions into the air. They couldn't complain about this game. Normally erratic and ill-fated, the Packers had dispatched the Redskins with a professional ruthlessness. As the fans left to warm up at their favorite taverns and clubs, they shook their heads, surprised but pleased that their team could play so efficiently. *Whew. They're looking pretty darn good, actually. Think they can keep it up?*

Lombardi was also delighted. Taylor had rushed for eighty-one yards, Hornung for seventy-eight. Starr had completed eleven of nineteen passes, with two going for touchdowns. The defense had recorded the Packers' first shutout since a 1949 victory over the immortal New York Bulldogs. Perfect!

As the players enjoyed the warm locker room — it had been cold out there — reporters interviewed Starr. This was, somewhat incredibly, his first personal win as an NFL starting quarterback. The Packers had gone 3-16-1 in games he had previously started going back to 1956, and Starr had split time with other quarterbacks in the three wins. This was the first win for which he was solely responsible.

He could smile about it now, but the losing had weighed on him. He shook his head in dismay and was typically humble. "That's some record, huh? Four years to get my first win," he said.

Deflecting credit, he complimented the offensive line, which had controlled the game.

"They're already good and getting better," he said. "They did a heck of a job on the runs today, don't you think? And they give you all the time you need to throw. I can count on one hand the times they have let the rush get in this season."

Lombardi was similarly effusive. "They're one of the youngest lines in the league. Other than Ringo they're almost all second-year men. They blocked very, very well today," he said. He would single out Skoronski, Kramer, and Gregg after watching the game films. Those three would get their twenty-dollar bills this week.

The players normally had Monday off, but they came in, watched film, and went through a light workout because they would play again on Thursday — Thanksgiving afternoon — in Detroit against the Lions. They had only Monday and Tuesday to prepare. Their flight left Wednesday.

The Lions had hosted a Turkey Day game since the early 1930s; the owner had seen his team lagging behind baseball's Tigers in popularity and thought a holiday game might attract fans. He was right. The game had become a staple, selling out locally and drawing national radio (and now TV) audiences in the millions. Thanksgiving was a popular date for many high school and college teams to play their traditional rivals, and the Lions' game had become the NFL's annual holiday event.

The Lions had prevailed on the league to schedule the Packers as their Thanksgiving opponent throughout the 1950s. The Lions, with Bobby Layne at quarterback, were a powerhouse, and the Packers succumbed easily, sending the Detroit fans home to their turkey feasts with smiles on their faces. But now Layne was in Pittsburgh, the Lions were in decline, and Lombardi was in Green Bay. The Packers were no longer an easy homecoming-style opponent. They had pounded Detroit in the second week of the season and were still ahead of the Lions in the division standings. At 4-5, the Packers were in fourth. Detroit had a 2-6-1 record.

At the top of the division, the Colts had pulled into a tie with fading San Francisco after pounding the 49ers, 45–14, in Baltimore. Lombardi reminded his players on Tuesday that they were only two games behind the coleaders, and while their chances of winning the division were slim, they did have a chance.

"We may not get there this year, but we're going to be in the running soon enough," he told reporters.

He avoided naming a starting quarterback, saying he would make his decision around kickoff. Starr "was getting better all the time," he said, but wanting to keep McHan's flagging spirits up, he stated that McHan had thrown four touchdown passes against Detroit earlier in the season and "has a much better arm."

Privately, Lombardi told Starr he probably would start but that McHan might also play. Starr nodded. He would follow orders.

The Packers flew into Detroit on Wednesday and found themselves in a discouraged football town. Fans and newspaper columnists, unaccustomed to losing, were giving the Lions a hard time. "Not all the turkeys are in the oven," the *Detroit Free-Press* commented. Tobin Rote, the former Packer star who had been demoted, was complaining publicly about his treatment and saying he might retire. His replacement, Earl Morrall, was on his fourth NFL team at age twenty-five.

Despite the sour headlines, almost fifty thousand fans filled Briggs Stadium on a cool, cloudy afternoon. Sports fans in Detroit went to the Lions' game on Thanksgiving regardless of how the team was faring. Lombardi stated the obvious in the locker room before sending the players out: a victory would put them at .500 with two games remaining and give them a chance for a winning season, a feat no one had thought possible.

The Packers' Bill Butler fumbled the opening kickoff and the Lions recovered on the Green Bay 19. The Packers' defensive starters grabbed their helmets and hustled out. Lombardi glared at Butler as the rookie came off the field.

The fans shouted, hoping for a fast start that would enliven the afternoon. Then Henry Jordan jumped offside, moving the Lions five yards closer to the end zone. But the Packer defense held. Fullback Nick Pietrosante plunged into the line twice, but Jordan and Quinlan knocked him back. Jordan pressured Morrall into an incompletion on third down and the Lions settled for a short field goal.

Butler gripped the ball tightly on the ensuing kickoff and zipped out to the Packer 35 before being tackled. Now the offense could get started. Starr faked a handoff to Taylor, dropped back, and spotted Dowler breaking open over the middle. In just a few weeks, the spindly rookie receiver had emerged as a primary threat. Starr loved throwing to him. This ball led Dowler perfectly and he grabbed it for a thirty-two-yard gain.

From there the offense moved into scoring territory on runs by Taylor and Hornung, and a completion to Knafelc, who was hit late, tacking on another fifteen yards. At the 6, Hornung swept to his right and faked toward the line. The Lions' Jim David was so fooled he spun like a top and almost fell. Hornung darted past him into

235

the end zone, then stayed on to kick the extra point, putting the Packers up, 7–3.

The Lions' Terry Barr returned the kickoff to his 20 and fumbled when Nitschke leveled him with a flying tackle to the chest. The Packers recovered at the Detroit 18, and the crowd groaned. "Let's take advantage!" Lombardi hollered as the offense jogged back onto the field. A tripping penalty on Skoronski moved the ball back, but Dowler sprinted over the middle and veered toward the right sideline, and Starr's pass hit him in stride at the 15. Breaking tackles, he continued to the 3 before being pushed out of bounds — a thirty-yard gain.

Starr called the same play that worked on the goal line moments earlier — Hornung sweeping right. This time the Lions' Jim David didn't fall for his fake, so Hornung put his head down and bulled through the defender, falling into the end zone in a heap with David. Hornung stood up, handed the ball to an official, took a deep breath, and booted the extra point. The Packers had a 14–3 lead after seven minutes, and Hornung had scored every Green Bay point. The Golden Boy jogged to the sideline thinking how much better things had gone since that crazy game in Chicago when he couldn't hold onto the ball. He was back in the middle of things again. That damn Lombardi had stuck with him, given him another chance. He appreciated the hell out of it.

The Lions' sloppy play continued. A receiver fumbled while running an end-around, and Bill Forester recovered, leading to a thirty-nine-yard field goal by Hornung. Then Dave Hanner barged into Morrall as the quarterback was setting up to pass. The ball bounced free and Jordan fell on it at the Detroit 49 as boos sounded.

Thinking he could knock out the Lions with another score, Starr called for a pass to McGee over the middle. McGee made a diving catch for a twenty-yard gain. "Great grab, Max," Starr said. Thinking the Lions would expect a run now, Starr called for another pass. McGee faked a sideline route and cut over the middle again. Starr's throw was slightly behind him, but McGee reached back, grabbed the ball, and reeled it in as he was being hit for a twelve-yard gain, putting the ball on the Detroit 17.

Taylor swept right, waiting for a hole to open, and Hornung, as part of the blocking convoy, dove at a linebacker and knocked the defender back. Taylor veered into the hole, but Joe Schmidt, the Lions' middle linebacker, fought off a block and knocked Taylor sideways. Stumbling, Taylor stepped right on Hornung, who remained on the ground after the play, pain shooting through his chest.

Hornung slowly rose and walked off, obviously injured, and Lombardi sent in Don McIlhenny. Starr immediately flipped him a short pass in the left flat. The Lions, focused on McGee and Dowler, left him alone, and he jogged to the end zone untouched, but Kramer was flagged for moving before the snap, erasing the score and moving the ball back to the 16. The Lions appeared to force a field goal attempt but defensive back Gary Lowe foolishly piled on Taylor after he was down, and a referee threw a flag for a personal foul, giving the Packers a first down at the 8. The defense sagged. McIlhenny ran off right tackle to the 1, and Taylor carried the ball over on second down. Hornung's extra point put the Packers up, 24–3.

The Lions were embarrassed to be so far behind, especially on Thanksgiving. When their return man fumbled the next kickoff, some fans contemplated leaving. But the Lions recovered the loose ball, and their offense, as if it knew the fans were losing patience, responded with its best drive so far. Blockers opened holes and backs charged through them. Pietrosante gained fifteen up the middle. Howard Cassady took a pitch around left end for twelve. Morrall ran a college-style option play and pitched to Pietrosante for sixteen. Cassady finished the drive with a five-yard touchdown run.

The Packers' next series ended when McGee, after making several hard catches, dropped an easy one. Then he shanked a punt, and the Lions started a possession on their 47. Pietrosante gained fifteen up the middle and eleven around left end, and a little-used receiver, Jerry Reichow, fooled Hank Gremminger on the right sideline and caught a twenty-seven-yard touchdown pass. Just like that, the Packer lead was down to 24–17.

Lombardi fumed in the halftime locker room. *We let them right*

237

back in it! What the hell is going on?! But he wondered if he had pushed the players too hard between games so close together. The defense looked tired. It had given up only one touchdown in the past six quarters before today, but clearly had lost steam in the second quarter. Lombardi spoke to Forester and Hanner about taking the lead in the huddle and making sure the letdown didn't continue.

Someone make a play. We can turn this thing back around.

Detroit's offense held the ball for the first half of the third quarter, slowly moving from its 16 to the Green Bay 25 on a blend of runs by Pietrosante and short passes by Morrall. The fans stood, excited by the comeback. The Lions were going nowhere this season, but it was nice to see life.

On first down at the 25, Bill Quinlan fended off a block and tackled Pietrosante for a two-yard loss. A backfield-in-motion penalty set the Lions back five more yards, and then Bettis correctly guessed pass, red-dogged Morrall, and tackled the retreating quarterback for an eleven-yard loss. Now the Lions were in trouble. Needing twenty-eight yards on third down, Morrall picked up twelve on a pass to Cassady, and then, strangely, the Lions went for it on fourth down rather than attempt a thirty-eight-yard field goal. Bad move. Bettis red-dogged again, and Morrall's rushed pass fluttered harmlessly to the ground.

The Lions had held the ball for more than nine minutes but come away without points.

The Packers tried to reestablish control with their running game, but with Hornung on the sidelines, the Lions focused on Taylor and he couldn't make gains. After blocking so well against the Redskins on Sunday, the Packer linemen struggled now. Green Bay gave up the ball, but the Lions went nowhere and punted back. Then Starr tried a different tactic, calling a series of passing plays. He hit Dowler on the left sideline for thirty-six, moving the ball to the Detroit 27. The Lion defense held there, though, and Hornung limped on for a thirty-two-yard field goal attempt, which sailed left, no good.

The Packers wasted an even better scoring chance a few minutes later when Forester intercepted Morrall at midfield and headed for the end zone. He was tackled at the 7, and a couple of runs moved the ball to the 1, but Taylor, showing rust, fumbled as he lunged for the goal line on third down. Lombardi jerked his head in frustration when the referees signaled that Detroit recovered.

Hold onto the damn ball, Taylor!

The Lions were running out of time, though. John Symank intercepted Morrall to end one Detroit drive, and a final Detroit series went nowhere. The Packers led at the final gun, 24–17. The Packer defense had risen up after Lombardi's halftime challenge, shutting out the Lions in the second half.

Lombardi flashed a broad smile to reporters. He didn't care that the Lions had badly outrushed his team (190 yards to 73) and controlled both lines of scrimmage for much of the game. Look at the big picture, he said. The Packers hadn't finished with a winning record since 1947 or won more than six games in a season since 1944, but now they were 5-5 with two games left, on the road against the Rams and 49ers.

"I would love to finish six and six, I will allow that," Lombardi said, "as long as you guys don't expect eight and four next year."

What happened after his team built that early lead? "I made a mistake by practicing on Monday and Tuesday," Lombardi said. "We should have taken Monday off. We were tired in the second half. Playing two games in five days had an effect."

Is that what caused the offense to shut down after it scored twenty-four points in the first twenty minutes? "Well, we lost Paul there [to a rib injury] and couldn't run the ball without him," Lombardi said. "Fortunately, Starr played a very strong game."

The game had been rough. Jim Temp showed reporters his hands, which were bloody from being scraped across the hardened turf. "I've never had so many chunks of meat taken out of me in one game in my life," Temp said. Hornung showed off the bruises on his chest from when Taylor stepped on him. He feared he had broken a rib. Bettis had twisted a knee and Thurston had sprained an ankle.

But the locker room was a happy place, the players excited to win two games in a row.

"This sure makes for a nice Thanksgiving," Starr said as the players showered and dressed for the quick charter flight home.

"Yes, the turkey is going to taste extra sweet," Knafelc said.

Hornung, looking ahead to the team's remaining games (and the trip to California, his favorite), said, "We'll be tough to beat out on the West Coast, no doubt about it; tough like we've never been tough before."

The players sensed a change in their basic condition, a transformation. They had emerged from their five-game losing streak with a harder edge they had lacked for years. They could run over you, bloody your nose, and beat you. They weren't losers anymore. Lombardi had hammered them into a tough, competitive team.

Their fans could also sense the change. Back in Green Bay, several thousand got in their cars and drove to Austin-Straubel Field to greet the team plane, adjusting holiday plans to show support.

Back in their glory days, the Packers had returned home from important road wins to find enormous, cheering crowds waiting at the train station. When they won their first NFL title in 1929 by beating the Bears in Chicago, they were greeted by ten thousand people. The custom had continued into the 1940s, with raucous station greetings serving as exclamation points to big wins — and preludes to all-night, citywide drinking binges, with the police happily looking the other way at closing time.

The tradition had faded along with the Packers in the 1950s, their airport greetings dwindling to a few diehards. But this Thanksgiving victory in Detroit kindled the old spirit. A season sweep of the Lions, who had dominated the NFL in the 1950s, reminded fans of the days when they supported a winner. Millions of TV viewers across the country had watched Lombardi's improving team. That was exciting.

Some three thousand people had gathered by early evening when the charter landed. A light snow fell in the fading light. The fans massed behind a fence and waited as the plane taxied up to the terminal. They cheered and held up signs as the players ducked out of the plane and waved. Lombardi, emerging last, thanked the fans for coming.

"We've won three more games than I expected to win," he shouted from the middle of the portable stairway, wishing he had a microphone.

The fans cheered, and Lombardi smiled as he waited for the noise to die down. Then he continued.

"With two games to go, we're still in there. We're going to go to California. Anything can happen!"

The fans roared. *Yeah, beat their asses out there!* They looked at each other with smiles, sharing the same thought: Boy, it sure was fun rooting for a good team.

★ **19** ★

OMBARDI GAVE THE players the weekend off, knowing they needed a break after playing two games in five days near the end of a long season. Most stayed around Green Bay and tended to their aches. Starr went hunting and picked up a chest cold.

The players reported back Monday morning and boarded a charter flight to California. They would practice for a week in Los Angeles before playing the Rams on Sunday, and then fly to the Bay Area, practice for another week, and play the 49ers. It was the trip the Packers always ended the season with, and to say the least, it had never gone well. They had won just one of eighteen games in California during the 1950s, their average margin of defeat almost three touchdowns.

Their on-field miseries hadn't kept the players from enjoying themselves; no matter how badly they lost on the field, they still felt they had won by trading in Wisconsin's cold and snow for California's sunny warmth — and its many clubs and restaurants.

This latest trip felt different from the beginning. Instead of staying at a soon-to-be-condemned lodge for senior citizens in Pasadena, the Packers checked into a beach resort in Santa Monica; they ate breakfast on their verandas, surrounded by lush flora and staring out at the Pacific Ocean. *Got to hand it to Lombardi: we don't travel like chumps anymore.* And they actually had something to play for. The Colts and 49ers were now tied for the Western Division lead with 7-3 records, followed by the Bears at 6-4 and the Packers at 5-5. The Packers couldn't win the division (either the Colts or 49ers would have eight wins after they played Sunday in San Francisco) but they could finish third, possibly even second if they won both games.

Mostly, beyond any such tangible considerations, they just wanted to keep winning.

The players began the trip without their coach; the first rounds of the NFL's college draft took place on Monday in Philadelphia with Lombardi, Phil Bengston, and Jack Vainisi representing the Packers. Their first two picks were offensive backs, Vanderbilt's Tom Moore and Iowa's Bob Jeter. Both had more speed than Hornung or Taylor, Lombardi said, and could develop into game breakers.

Bill Austin, Norb Hecker, and Red Cochran ran practice at UCLA on Tuesday as Lombardi and Bengston flew west, and Lombardi was back in charge Wednesday as the Packers began preparing for a Rams team that had fallen apart since its 45–6 destruction of the Packers earlier in the season. After looking invincible that day, Los Angeles hadn't won since, losing six games in a row, a startling collapse by a team that had thought it could win a championship after going 8-4 in 1958 and trading for Ollie Matson. Rams coach Sid Gillman reportedly was in danger of being fired.

The Packers enjoyed themselves during the week but slowly got ready for Sunday. It helped that Las Vegas made them five-point underdogs, obviously still doubting they had turned a corner. The bookmakers had history on their side — the Packers had lost six games in a row to the Rams going back to 1956, and hadn't won in Los Angeles since 1947 — but Lombardi told the players they could beat the Rams on Sunday as thoroughly as the Rams had whipped them earlier. It was clear from the game films that the Rams were fading, he said, their pass defense giving up big plays, their overall fire on the wane. Wally Cruice had watched them lose miserably to Baltimore the week before.

On Sunday the temperature soared near ninety degrees on the floor of Memorial Coliseum, the Rams' massive, Roman-style stadium, which had been built for the 1932 Summer Olympic Games and could hold one hundred thousand fans, more than three times City Stadium's capacity. The Rams had built a winning tradition in California since moving west from Cleveland in 1946, playing in four NFL championship games and bringing home the title in 1951. Pro football was immensely popular in Los Angeles, the game-going habit so ingrained in so many fans that, even as this miserable season ended, sixty-one thousand spectators came out to see if their Rams could win and maybe save Gillman's job.

The year before, the Packers had warmed up for their California games in silence, steeling themselves for the beatings they knew lay ahead. Now they displayed a breezy confidence before the game. They marched smartly through their calisthenics, helmets glistening in the sun as they performed jumping jacks and pushups while counting in unison, military-style. Then they broke into groups. Starr threw warm-up tosses to Knafelc. Kramer and Thurston stretched their legs. Hornung, always at home in California, ran light sprints and practiced kicks with a smile.

Gonna play big today, Paul.

Damn right.

Ray Nitschke started at middle linebacker instead of Tom Bettis, still limping on his twisted knee. Early in the first quarter Emlen Tunnell intercepted a pass at the Los Angeles 42. Starr went to work. On first down, he faked a handoff to Taylor and retreated as Max McGee ran a slant pattern across the middle. His pass was right on target for a twenty-seven-yard gain. Two plays later, pressured by a red-dog, Starr flipped to Taylor in the right flat when the fullback yelled that he was open. A linebacker sniffed out the play and came up to make a stop, but Hornung blocked him so hard that his legs flew straight up as Taylor raced past him and into the end zone. The Packers led, 7–0.

During their losing streak, the Rams had lacked the consistency to sustain long drives — they made too many mistakes. But they still had speed. Quarterback Billy Wade lobbed a ball far downfield for Del Shofner, running with Tunnell and John Symank. Shofner came down with the ball for a forty-yard gain. A few plays later Wade snuck over from the 1 for a touchdown, tying the score at 7–7.

The quick strike brought back memories of the 45–6 game, but the Ram defense had shut down the Packer offense that day, and things were different now. Lombardi had sat with Starr and carefully dissected the sagging defense during the week, proposing possible successful plays. Starr, after watching film, had his own ideas of what might work. He mentally flipped through his options, called plays, and watched them unfold just as Lombardi had drawn them on the blackboard.

Knafelc was open on a deep route over the middle for thirty-one yards. Starr hit Boyd Dowler on the right sideline for nineteen, then hit McGee on the left sideline for eleven. Taylor gained twelve on a draw.

This is incredible, Starr thought. Lombardi's offense thrived on planning, preparedness, and logical thinking, Starr's best qualities. It was simple and smart and just made sense. And the players around Starr had an array of talents and gifts, speed and toughness and guile. Starr felt like he was driving a sports car on the highway, zipping and zooming. Commanding the huddle with force, he barked out his play calls and encouraged his teammates. They wondered if someone had kidnapped their "methane gas" quarterback, the kindly, studious reserve who didn't leave a mark.

That Starr had disappeared. This one had utter faith in himself and his offense, and no doubt he could move the ball and put points on the board.

Hush up! I'm calling this. You're going to be open. Be ready!

On a first down at the Los Angeles 26, Starr called a special play that both he and Lombardi thought would work. He handed to Hornung heading right on a sweep, with Kramer and Thurston pulling in front. The Ram linebackers and defensive backs closed in to make a stop, but before they got to him, the Golden Boy slowed, drew the ball back, and arched a pass over the surprised defenders. Dowler, all alone at the 5, caught the pass in stride on his way to the end zone.

Lombardi turned to the bench with a broad smile. He also had thought this was the perfect time for that play; it was as if Starr had read his mind!

You sold that perfectly, Paul. They had no idea it was coming until you threw.

Yes, sir. Damn right.

Heh. Yeah, damn right.

Minutes later, the offense had the ball again, at its 33. Starr saw no reason to stop passing, having completed six straight attempts. He dropped back as McGee burst past a safety, and he led McGee with a soft floater that Max ran under for a thirty-one-yard gain. Then Hornung ran off right tackle behind Forrest Gregg, who leveled the Rams' Deacon Jones, leaving a wide hole. Hornung sprinted through it, swiveled his hips to elude a linebacker, and headed for the end zone. A pair of Rams corralled him at the 5 after a twenty-six-yard gain. On first down, Norm Masters opened a hole on the left side and Taylor charged through it, ran over a linebacker, and fell into the end zone. It had taken the offense 105 seconds to drive sixty-seven yards and take a 21–7 lead.

As the fans grumbled, Wade aimed a pass for Matson in the right flat on the next series. Dan Currie saw the play developing, cut in front of Matson, and grabbed the interception. He sprinted to the Los Angeles 30 before being knocked out of bounds as the grumbling turned into full-fledged booing.

As he trotted onto the Coliseum field, Starr felt invincible. He could call a run or pass; either would work. His linemen were opening big holes, his backs were making big gains, and his receivers were open.

He kneeled in the huddle and called for the halfback option again, eyes twinkling at the devilish idea. The Rams would never expect it.

Hornung took the handoff and headed right as the back of the defense closed, trying to avoid another long run. But before the linebackers and safeties realized they had been fooled again, Hornung stopped and threw for Dowler, alone again at the 5. Dowler caught the ball and trotted to the end zone.

Lombardi exulted. He hadn't been this excited all season. *Did you see that?!! Huh?! They never saw it coming!* What a brilliant call, Lombardi thought — absolutely a knockout punch. Lombardi was starting to view Starr differently. The quiet southerner could be tough and bold after all. Lombardi had underestimated him.

Hornung booted the extra point, upping the lead to 28–7. The Coliseum fans were in shock. The Rams were down twenty-one to a team they had beaten by thirty-nine earlier in the season.

Lombardi said little at halftime. This was the third game in a row in which the Packers had built a three-touchdown lead. Lombardi urged them to be decisive, finish what they had started. The Rams certainly were there for the taking, he said.

In the other locker room, the beleaguered Gillman challenged the Rams to play better. This was embarrassing, he said. The Rams responded. Tommy Wilson broke through the Packers' coverage on the second-half kickoff and almost went all the way, reaching the Green Bay 11 before Jesse Whittenton ran him down. Gillman sent in a young backup quarterback, Frank Ryan, in Wade's place, and the Rams scored in two plays to make the score 28–14.

With the crowd urging it on, the Ram defense stopped a pair of runs by Taylor and harried Starr into throwing an incompletion. McGee punted, and Jon Arnett, a big-play back who had starred at Southern Cal, caught the kick at his 29. Ron Kramer almost tackled him immediately, but Arnett jumped away, cut left into a hole in the coverage, and zipped into the open field. The fans stood and shouted, having seen this before. Arnett was gone.

The touchdown cut Green Bay's lead to 28–20. Henry Jordan leapt and deflected the extra point, but that didn't quiet the audible buzz emanating from the vast stands after the two long kick returns.

The Ram defense kept things going, forcing a punt, and the Ram offense returned to the field with the fans thinking about another big play. But the Packers produced the big play instead. Bill Forester, the steady captain, red-dogging on first down, deflected Ryan's pass, and the ball sailed to Currie. The big linebacker took off in the other direction with his second interception of the game. He was tackled at the Los Angeles 24.

The turnover quelled the Rams' momentum. On first down Starr handed to Hornung sweeping right, with Kramer and Thurston pulling in front. Hornung slowed down and the secondary stayed back, anticipating another pass to Dowler, but Hornung tucked the ball in and took off, finding room to run. A linebacker knocked him out of bounds at the 10. The Rams stopped the drive there, though, and Hornung missed a twenty-four-yard field goal attempt, sailing it wide left.

Ryan promptly drove the Ram offense back into Green Bay territory, but Nitschke leveled him on a scramble and the ball fell free, Forester falling on it for the charitable Rams' fifth turnover of the day. Kneeling in the huddle, Starr wanted to slow the game's pace. *No more trick plays or long passes. Let's just run the offense.* Taylor ran up the middle for six. Hornung swept left for seven. Don McIlhenny, replacing the tiring Hornung, gained seven off right tackle. Starr passed to Dowler for twelve. The drive rolled past midfield and into Los Angeles territory as the fourth quarter began. At the 19, Starr rolled right and looked into the end zone, but no receiver was open so he tucked the ball in and ran, picking up twelve when Masters bowled over a linebacker. On the next play Gregg opened a hole and McIlhenny charged through it and ran over a safety at the goal line. The conversion gave the Packers a 35–20 lead with thirteen minutes to play.

The score drained the Rams of the enthusiasm they had briefly mustered. They couldn't move on their next possession, and after a punt, the Packers methodically drove the ball again. Dowler gained twenty on an end-around, another trick play the Packers had practiced but not used until now. Taylor rammed up the middle for eight, six, and seven. When the drive stalled, Hornung kicked a seventeen-yard field goal for a 38–20 lead. That was a safe margin against an inexperienced quarterback.

When the final gun sounded, the Packers had their third win in a row, sixth of the season, and first at the Coliseum since Curly Lambeau's tenure. Nitschke snapped towels at people's groins in the locker room. Taylor and Jerry Kramer sat naked in front of their lockers, hurling insults at each other and all passersby. Hornung and McGee discussed the all-important matter of where they would celebrate that evening. The Packers were so exuberant, newsman Art Daley compared them to a high school team.

And no one was bubblier than Lombardi. Reporters found him in the locker room with his tie loose, his starched white dress shirt drenched with sweat, and a huge smile pasted on his face.

"This is beyond my fondest expectations," he said. "I never dreamed we would do anything like this, win six. But I'm telling you, these kids are hardnosed."

He praised Nitschke for hitting hard as Bettis's replacement, and also complimented Hornung, who had rushed for seventy-four yards, thrown two touchdown passes, caught two passes, kicked a field goal and five extra points, and cleared Taylor's path on the first touchdown with a vicious block.

"Paul is playing great football now," Lombardi said.

But Lombardi reserved his highest praise for Starr, who had directed touchdown drives of forty-two, eighty, sixty-two, thirty, and seventy-five yards. "Bart just called a wonderful game," Lombardi said.

Starr stood at his locker with a smile as broad as Lombardi's.

"I'm feeling better and better out there every week, no question about it," he said. "It probably sounds bad for me to say, but I had gotten to wondering if I could ever play like this. Now I know I can."

Starr said he sucked throat lozenges throughout the game because of the chest cold he caught when he went hunting the week before.

"I was pretty miserable, actually," he said.

But then he shook his head and continued: "This is the greatest thrill of my life, winning like this out here in the Coliseum."

As the Packers showered, Tom Miller filled them in on the key games being played elsewhere in the league. The Giants had wrapped up the Eastern Division title and a return trip to the championship game by thrashing Cleveland, 48–7. And the Colts had taken control of the Western Division by pounding fading San Francisco, 34–14. Now all the Colts had to do to win the division title was beat the Rams on Saturday here in Los Angeles. "I'm not hopeful," 49ers coach Red Hickey said.

If the Rams upset the Colts, the 49ers would be playing for a share of the division title against the Packers on Sunday. The fast-finishing Bears, now tied for second with the 49ers after winning six straight games, also would have a shot.

The Packers flew up the coast on Monday and checked into Rickey's Motel in Palo Alto, where they had stayed the year before. Lombardi liked this arrangement: the motel was comfortable and he could practice at nearby Stanford. There would be one change: instead of staying in Palo Alto all week, the team would move to San Francisco for the weekend, spending Saturday and Sunday nights at the Palace Hotel.

Practice resumed on Tuesday, and Lombardi didn't like what he saw, sensing a growing air of self-satisfaction. "This season is not over," he shouted. "You should be pleased with your improvement. But we still have a long way to go. A very long way! We are not in the championship game, and I will not be satisfied until we get there and win it. That is the goal. Let's not forget it."

Wednesday's practice was crisper.

Art Daley and Chuck Johnson were on the trip, churning out stories for their newspapers. Both focused on Starr's emergence. "His stature has zoomed," Daley wrote. The offense had been averaging fifteen points and 270 yards a game before Starr's first start against the Colts in the eighth game of the season. Since Starr took over, those averages had increased to twenty-seven points and 342 yards a game.

McHan, who had been supplanted as the number one, gave an interview to Johnson. He was understandably discouraged. He had led the team to a 3-0 start and played fairly well until injuries forced him to the sidelines, but now, even though he was healthy and itching to play, he couldn't get on the field.

"I'm happy for Bart, naturally," McHan said, "but I want back in there. I'm no good to anybody on the bench. I want to play, prove myself in this league. After all those years with the Cardinals, I wanted to show what I could do, and I was just getting to where I thought I was showing it when I got hurt. Now I can't prove anything."

Lombardi had protected McHan's fragile psyche for weeks, making sure he complimented McHan when he praised Starr; he figured he would need McHan again if Starr was injured or became ineffective. But after watching the offense run smoothly under Starr, Lombardi was less worried about what McHan thought.

"Starr is doing a wonderful job," he said. "He's a really smart boy and he is really good at recognizing defenses and taking advantage of what is there."

Another story during the week was Jim Taylor's availability for the final game. He had played the last three quarters of the Rams game with a sore hip after a defender's helmet got underneath his pads in the first quarter, and he scored two touchdowns but then could barely walk on Monday. Taylor said he would be able to play against the 49ers, but Lombardi told Lew Carpenter to be ready to go.

The Packers were six-point underdogs, a surprise considering they had won three straight games while the 49ers had lost three of four. On Saturday they moved up to the Palace, practiced briefly, and watched a telecast of the critical Colts-Rams game. The Rams just wanted their miserable season to end, but rising to the occasion, took an early lead, trailed by one point at halftime, and led, 26–24, going into the final quarter. But the Colts pulled away on a Unitas touchdown pass, an interception return, and a ninety-nine-yard field goal return, their 45–26 victory advancing them to a rematch with the Giants in the championship game. Sid Gillman resigned after the game.

The result, though not surprising, was a blow to the 49ers, whose playoff prospects had seemed so bright a few weeks earlier. They were officially out now, and a couple of players admitted they might struggle to find motivation on Sunday.

The Packers had known for weeks that they wouldn't make the postseason, but they wouldn't lack for motivation Sunday. They were having too much fun whipping teams that had toyed with them for years, including the 49ers.

On Sunday, fifty-six thousand fans nearly filled Kezar Stadium, located west of downtown San Francisco in Golden Gate Park. The date was December 13, the weather warm and windy. The Packer players listened intently to Lombardi in the locker room before kickoff. Some had started to doubt him during their losing streak, but they were with him now. *He might be a bastard at times but look at what we're doing.*

He spoke about ending the season with a winning record, an achievement no one had expected of them. *We're going to be in championship games here. But you have to establish yourself as a winning team first, and we can do that today. Let's show everyone the Green Bay Packers are winners!*

The players raced onto the field in a fighting mood.

The 49ers, to their surprise, threw a strong early punch. On the game's first possession, C. R. Roberts, a young fullback, bowled over Currie and Whittenton and ran forty-six yards for a touchdown. The Packers drove back when Starr hit McGee on a slant route, and McGee, veering back and forth, gained forty-four yards before being brought down. But the drive ended with Hornung missing a twenty-two-yard field goal, and the 49er offense quickly produced another touchdown, its ball carriers shedding tackles throughout the drive. The Packers were down, 14–0. Lombardi taunted the defense as it came off the field, his voice soaring above the cheers. *You guys can tackle better than that! That's just terrible! TERRIBLE!!*

Kneeling to call a play and start the next Packer possession, Starr smiled as he glanced up at his teammates. In previous years, the Packers would have panicked after quickly falling two touchdowns behind, especially on the road. But Starr radiated a calm assuredness. He had no doubt this deficit could be erased. He had faith in Lombardi. The Packers would crunch the 49ers into pieces before this day was over.

It's just the first quarter, guys. We have all the time in the world. Let's get going. One step at a time.

His confidence was infectious. The offensive players looked at each other, nodded, took deep breaths, and started to hammer away.

On first down, Carpenter, replacing Taylor, whose sore hip had sidelined him, gained eight yards behind Gregg. Then Starr faked a pitch to Hornung going left, dropped back, and hit Dowler over the middle for fifteen. Then he dropped back again, looked right, and threw left to McGee for fifteen.

See?! One step at a time. Let's go!

After Hornung picked up a first down on two carries, Starr hit McGee over the middle for twenty-three yards to the San Francisco 13. The next play had been set up the week before: Hornung ran right on what appeared to be a sweep, pulled up, and looked downfield, causing the defense to freeze. But he tucked the ball in, burst through an opening, bowled over a linebacker at the 5, and fell into the end zone. His conversion cut the lead to 14–7.

No doubt about it. Here we come.

Late in the first half, the Packers started a possession at their 32. Starr hit Knafelc on a square-out for fifteen. Taylor, briefly inserted, caught two short passes for fourteen yards. Carpenter raced back in and took a pitchout around left end for eleven. With the ball on the San Francisco 22, there was time for one more play before a field goal attempt. Starr went for broke, again exhibiting the innate boldness Lombardi had once thought he lacked. Knafelc blocked a linebacker and ran downfield, angling across the secondary as a safety came up to cover him. Starr zipped a pass, leading him by a stride. Knafelc caught the ball at the 4, sidestepped the defender, and crossed the goal line.

The crowd went quiet as Starr punched the air in triumph. Hornung's conversion tied the score at 14–14 as the teams jogged to their locker rooms.

Lombardi normally used the halftime break to make technical adjustments, but he issued an emotional appeal now. Like Starr, he didn't doubt that the Packers could win. It irritated him that they had dug themselves an early hole. *Dammit, we're better than they are. I know it, you know it, and you know what? They know it!! We weren't ready and they took their best shot and got up on us. Now we're hitting back. The game is there for the taking. Let's take it!*

With players shouting and pumping their fists, the mood on the Packer bench was electric as the kickoff spun high to start the second half. Bobby Freeman raced downfield and flattened the return man at the San Francisco 6, immediately backing the 49er offense into a corner. The Packer defense jogged onto the field, determined to take advantage. Forester slipped past a blocker and bore down on Y. A. Tittle, who tried to sidestep him but didn't move quickly.

Forester grabbed Tittle by the shoulder pads and slung him down in the end zone for a safety.

The Packer bench erupted. *Yaaaah! That's the way, Bubba!*

With the Packers ahead for the first time, 16–14, the offense started a possession at its 34 after the punt. Starr didn't have to say any encouraging words in the huddle; with momentum now firmly on their side, his teammates sensed a decisive burst coming. Carpenter swept left on first down and cut back sharply through a hole as Thurston flattened a linebacker. Carpenter veered into open space, shook off a safety, and picked up twenty-six yards before being knocked out of bounds. He bounded back to a huddle that practically vibrated with energy. What now? Starr called for Hornung to carry the other way and fake the option pass again. Kramer and Thurston opened a huge hole, and Hornung, after tucking the ball in, steamed into a secondary that had thought he was passing. He bowled over a cornerback, stumbled, regained his balance, and headed for the end zone, finally going down at the 2, after a thirty-eight-yard run.

One play later, the Golden Boy waited for Gregg to open a hole and easily pushed his way into the end zone behind the bulky tackle. After booting the conversion to give the Packers a 23–14 lead, Hornung came to the sideline breathing deeply, tired but immensely satisfied. He had scored two touchdowns, kicked two extra points, caught two passes, and rushed for more than sixty yards — and there were still more than twenty minutes left in the game. As he took a seat on the bench, he couldn't help thinking how drastically his fortunes had changed. The fans in Green Bay had regularly booed him during his first two seasons, but his third season was ending with a flourish. He had torn the Rams apart with his running and throwing a week earlier, and now he was doing the same to the 49ers.

The sideline was buoyant, the players sensing a chance to put away a tiring opponent. The defense took the field, and Tittle dropped back and looked downfield. When Quinlan slipped past a blocker and charged him, Tittle hurriedly lobbed a floater for Hugh McElhenny in the left flat. Symank saw the play developing, broke for the ball, and grabbed it in front of the Packer bench, at the San Francisco 35. Symank raced down the sideline until a lineman tackled him at the 18.

OK, let's finish these suckers off.

Three plays later, with the ball at the 9, Dowler ran a curl-in route, turning around as he crossed the goal line. Starr intentionally threw the ball low to keep it away from defenders, and Dowler went to one knee and grabbed it. Another touchdown! Hornung's conversion made the score 30–14. The Packers celebrated on the bench, raising fists and pounding shoulder pads. What a feeling! Their defense was making plays and their offense was ramming the ball down the 49ers' throats.

The home fans booed, voicing their disappointment over a 49er season gone awry. And then the Packer defense struck again. Whittenton ran up to Roberts and stole the ball from the young fullback as he lunged for extra yards around midfield. Some players didn't even know what had happened as Whittenton raced toward the goal line and finally was tackled at the San Francisco 31.

Starr had passed the 49ers silly, but now felt he should slow the pace. Carpenter gained three off left tackle. Hornung went for four up the middle and four around right end. On fourth-and-one at the 11 as the fourth quarter started, Carpenter charged up the middle behind Jim Ringo for a first down. Hornung ran it down to the 2 and flattened a cornerback as he crossed the goal line. His extra point was blocked, but the Packers now led, 36–14.

The players had a grand time on their sideline as the clock wound down. There was no better feeling than watching an opposing team's fans leave before the final gun. Lombardi put in subs. The starters stood on the sideline and cheered. Lombardi smiled and pounded Hornung on the back. The Golden Boy had indeed lived up to his name — three touchdowns, four extra points, eighty-three rushing yards.

Starr stayed in the game until the final gun. He had enjoyed by far his finest day as a pro, completing twenty of twenty-five pass attempts for 219 yards and two touchdowns, with no interceptions. His offense had generated twenty-seven first downs, the line opening huge holes on runs and keeping the defensive front away on pass attempts.

"Starr just completely picked us apart," Hickey said. "We couldn't get anyone in there after him, and he tore us up."

In the Packer locker room, Starr's teammates awarded him the game ball.

"He's just a brilliant boy," Lombardi said. "He needed a win to get going, and then he got one, and now he has four in a row. He was changing plays at the line all day. He takes full advantage of what we try to do."

Starr, with typical humility, deflected some of the credit. "Did you see my protection? I just stood back there until someone got open. I couldn't help but have a good day."

Standing at the next locker, Knafelc, Starr's roommate, laughed at his teammate's modesty. "I'll be his booster," he said. "He's got to be the best quarterback in the league right now, right there with Unitas. He's getting tough in the huddle, too. Sometimes he even tells us to shut up."

Starr laughed; yes, the nice-guy quarterback was no more.

A half hour after the game, many players were still wearing their uniforms and sitting on folding chairs in front of their lockers, seemingly in no hurry to shower, dress, and leave football behind, even though a night out in San Francisco loomed. In prior years they had practically counted the hours until their season ended. Now, after winning both games in California for the first time, they wanted to keep going.

"Why do we have to quit playing now? We're rolling. Boy, I tell you, wait until next year," Hank Gremminger said.

Ringo, a Packer since 1953, shook his head in disbelief. "This is the first time since I've been here that I'm hearing the guys talking about next year," he said. "What a difference one year makes."

The Packers would watch with the rest of the league when the Colts and Giants played in the championship game later in December, but after completing their first winning season since 1947, they could envision themselves playing in such an important game now. The idea was no longer ludicrous.

"We're not the Colts yet. We still need some help in places," Lombardi said an hour after the game, still perched on a locker room chair and also seemingly reluctant to leave. "But we play a real determined game. That's the wonderful thing about these boys. They have a lot of determination."

They didn't before. But yes, now they had the determination of champions, and a whole lot more.

"The other teams better watch their asses," defensive back John Symank said. "We're just starting to go."

How right he was.

★ 20 ★

ROMAN DENISSEN ORDINARILY didn't shout. An insurance man with thick black-framed glasses and an accounting degree, Green Bay's mayor was a pencil pusher elected for his competence more than his personality. But his emotions overcame him on the temporary stage at Austin-Straubel Field as he stood in front of eight thousand people, bundled into a heavy coat.

The Packers had ended the season on a roll. The city was excited about them again. The crowd's enthusiasm reminded Denissen — a lifelong Packer fan who had attended East High School when the Packers played there in the 1930s — of the team's heyday.

Look at this crowd!

He grabbed the microphone from Les Sturmer of WBAY-TV, the emcee of this "Welcome Home, Packers" event.

"I just want to congratulate the Packers!" the mayor shouted. "And particularly Coach Lombardi!"

The people roared. They had stood in a miserable, chilly rain for an extra hour, huddled under umbrellas as they waited for the Packers' charter flight from California to make its delayed arrival.

"The Packers just did a beautiful job of selling Green Bay all over the country!" Denissen continued.

The players and coaches were with him onstage, and as people applauded, Denissen beckoned to Lombardi to join him in the dim spotlight. Lombardi crossed the stage and shook hands with the mayor, who handed him a key to the city. Lombardi fingered it, smiled, and nodded to the crowd as he took the microphone.

"I know from the size of this crowd that you all must be as proud of this team as we are, the people who are connected with it," Lombardi said.

As the fans cheered, Lombardi put a hand to his eyebrows and squinted into the distance, trying to see how far the crowd stretched.

Boy, this doesn't happen in New York.

"This was a team with great determination. Even when we went down to defeat, we went down the hard way," Lombardi continued.

More cheers.

"But even when we went down to defeat, the boys never quit. They came back, and kept coming back when things got tough in the middle of the season. Now we have finished up in a strong way. And every man on the thirty-six-man roster contributed."

That elicited the loudest roar yet.

"In finishing, I would like to say I have the finest staff in the National Football League. Any accolades belong to them and not me. Thank you ever so much."

Lombardi gave the microphone back to Sturmer, who then introduced Lombardi's four assistants and gave each a chance to speak.

"How does our defense compare with the New York Giants' unit?" Sturmer asked Phil Bengston.

"We don't have to take a back seat to anybody. Our defense stacks up with the best in the league," Bengston said.

Cheers.

Asked about the offensive line, Bill Austin said, "It was a pleasure to work with the kind of boys we had this year. I hope we can do as well next year."

Red Cochran added, "It's great to be with a winner, isn't it?"

The fans loved that one. *Yesssss!*

Sturmer then introduced the players one by one. As they moved individually into the spotlight, they received a green-and-gold Packer blanket from the Association of Commerce, the businessmen's group that had put the event together. Sturmer asked the players questions and let them speak to the crowd.

"I hope everyone has a merry Christmas. And I hope I'm back for a championship next year," Emlen Tunnell said.

Yesssss!

The loudest ovations went to Bart Starr, Paul Hornung, and Boyd Dowler, the players who had carried the offense in the season's final month.

"I'm just happy about how the season turned out, especially these last three weeks," Hornung said.

Knowing that Hornung's three-year contract was up, Sturmer asked the Golden Boy if he would return in 1960.

"I sure will!" Hornung exclaimed.

Woooooooooo!

At the end, Sturmer thanked everyone for coming, and the fans and players hustled to their cars and went home to dry off and warm up.

The Packers dominated Tuesday's *Press-Gazette*. Art Daley had gathered comments about the team's surprising success from an array of politicians and celebrities, including Vice President Richard Nixon, a football aficionado who had attended the new City Stadium dedication game in 1957. Daley's story ran on the front page.

"Please express to the Green Bay Packer players and organization my congratulations on their victory Sunday and my admiration of the great comeback ability they have displayed throughout the season — often, I must reluctantly admit, at the expense of teams from my home state of California," Nixon said in a statement. "Your entire community should be very proud not only of your fine football team but also of your own spirit which has infused such vitality in the Packers. With every good wish for the holiday season — sincerely, Dick Nixon."

The paper's lead editorial, headlined "Welcome Home, Packers!" attempted to put the season in perspective:

"The Green Bay Packers have amazed themselves and their fans by completing a record of seven wins and five losses. This record is so far above the expectations of either the Packers or their fans at

260

the opening of the season as to have won them the title of 'Amazing.' This time a year ago, Packer players returned to Green Bay only if they couldn't avoid it, the coaches were writing resignations and fans were writing angry letters to the newspaper. That was a most unhappy occasion. Today Packerland is bright and cheery, with a team that represents [it] correctly as one of the solid football cities of the United States.

"At the beginning of the season [we] predicted that the Packers 'might win three or four games, perhaps more,' and that was close to the expectations of the coaching staff. But they finished two wins away from a tie for first place. They have had the advantage of hard, sound training and enthusiastic leadership, and that is the difference from a year ago. At the beginning of the season, it was made clear they were not striving for a championship now but building for the long run, which might possibly bring a championship in three or four years. Now the hopes of fans have been raised pretty high. The building may still require some time but indications are we are on the right track, and on our way to a title some time in the future. The Packers appear to have the stuff of which champions are made."

It was stunning to think how far they had come in twelve months, how much their prospects had changed.

The players scattered to their off-season homes and jobs, no longer embarrassed to say they played for the Packers. Dillon, Forrest Gregg, John Symank, Jesse Whittenton, and Bill Forester headed to Texas. Lamar McHan and Dave Hanner went to Arkansas, Jerry Kramer to Idaho, Joe Francis to Oregon. Hornung headed for Los Angeles, where he could enjoy himself without having to adhere to a curfew. Jim Taylor returned to Louisiana to spend another off-season with Alvin Roy, the strength coach. Starr went back to Alabama, his late-season successes encouraging him to prepare harder than ever for the 1960 season.

Lombardi went to New York to see family and friends, and while he was there, received word he had been selected NFL Coach of the Year by a panel of sportswriters and sportscasters assembled by the Associated Press. He was the top choice on twenty-nine of thirty-seven ballots. The runner-up, Jim Lee Howell, received four first-place votes.

"I was hoping to win five games, tops, this season. Seven was a surprise," Lombardi told reporters.

The AP, *New York Daily News, Sporting News,* Newspaper Enterprise Association, and United Press wire service all announced first-team and second-team All-Pro squads, selected by panels of sportswriters. Jim Ringo made first team on every list, Forrest Gregg in the *Sporting News.* Gregg and Hornung made the AP and UP second teams, as did Bill Forester in the *New York Daily News.* Boyd Dowler, who had caught twenty-seven passes in the last six games, was named UP Rookie of the Year.

Two games remained on the 1959 NFL schedule—the championship game between the Colts and Giants on December 27 at Memorial Stadium in Baltimore, and the Pro Bowl on January 17, 1960, in Los Angeles.

The title game was a taut thriller for three quarters as the Giants' defense gave Johnny Unitas fits and New York took a 9–7 lead. But the Colts rallied with a long touchdown drive and then intercepted three passes to set up scores. Their 31–16 victory gave them back-to-back championships, leaving no doubt who ruled pro football.

Unitas also starred in the Pro Bowl, throwing for three touchdowns in the Western Division's 38–21 victory. Five Packers played—Ringo, Hornung, Gregg, Forester, and Tunnell. Completing a breakthrough season, Hornung scored a touchdown and kicked a field goal and five extra points.

Hornung's season hadn't always gone smoothly; it had included several injuries and that infamous benching in Chicago. But in the end, he had lived up to Lombardi's expectations and become a productive halfback, turning the boos he had earned earlier in his career into sustained cheers. He had rushed for 681 yards, the league's eighth-highest individual total, caught fifteen passes, and completed five option passes. He had ended up as the league's leading scorer, his seven touchdowns, seven field goals, and thirty-one point-after conversions totaling ninety-four points.

Between Hornung, Taylor (452 rushing yards despite missing five games), Carpenter and McIlhenny (553 yards combined), and all the others, the Packers had rushed for 1,970 yards — the league's third-highest total, and more than any Packer team had gained on the ground in a season since Curly Lambeau was in charge.

Fans had scoffed when Lombardi said he would install a power offense that relied on the running game. *Yeah, right. He obviously didn't see the Packers play in 1958.* But he had done what they said he couldn't, transforming Scooter McLean's soft offense into a bone-jarring unit. The backs ran hard, the linemen blocked harder — just ask the Rams and 49ers. By the end of the season, the Packers didn't move the ball so much as shove it at opponents, knock them over with it. And this was just Lombardi's first year, supposedly a time for players to learn and adjust. Wait until they really caught on.

In January 1959 Lombardi had gone to the league meetings in Philadelphia as part of the Giant delegation and interviewed face-to-face with the Packers for the first time. Now, a year later, in January 1960, he went to the league meetings with the Packer delegation and found himself talking to the Giants about a job.

Frustrated by back-to-back losses in the championship game, Jim Lee Howell had told Giants owner Wellington Mara he was ready to step down. Had Howell arrived at that conclusion a year earlier, Mara could have chosen between the two attractive head-coaching candidates on Howell's staff, Lombardi and Tom Landry. But now Lombardi was in Green Bay, and Landry had recently announced he would be returning to his home state, Texas, to coach the new NFL expansion team in Dallas, leaving Mara without an obvious successor to Howell.

At the league meetings in Philadelphia, Mara asked Lombardi if he would consider coming back to New York to coach the Giants even though he had four years left on his five-year deal to be the Packers' head coach and general manager.

Mara believed that when he originally gave Green Bay permission to talk to Lombardi, who was under contract at the time, he had received the same permission in return, freeing him to talk to

Lombardi whenever he wanted about coming back to the Giants. Dominic Olejniczak didn't recall that coming up in any of their conversations. The head of the Packer executive committee was livid about Mara trying to lure Lombardi away; it was the definition of dirty pool, he said.

The offer startled and flattered Lombardi, and it certainly interested Marie, who had successfully put down roots in Green Bay but would rather live in New York.

But Lombardi didn't feel right about leaving.

"I haven't fulfilled my obligation to the people in Green Bay," he told Mara.

Mara asked him to think about it. Lombardi did, as he settled into his off-season routine in Green Bay, and then called Mara again.

"I would really be running out on these people if I left," Lombardi said.

Irritated, Mara talked Howell into staying on as the Giants' head coach.

Turning down a return to the Giants irrefutably marked Lombardi as a Packer. And that was fine with him. In January he moved his family into their new house on Sunset Road in Allouez. Every morning he pulled out of his driveway and drove downtown to the Packers' Washington Street offices. He graded film with his assistants, and also put on his GM's hat, talked to other teams about trades, and sent contract offers to his veterans for the 1960 season.

He was settled in Green Bay, had plenty of friends, a busy social life, a church that suited him, a regular golf game — and a healthy salary. He had complete control of the Packers, the executive committee having made good on its pledge to step back. The fans were supportive, the press largely benign. He would have to get past Unitas and the Colts in the Western Division if he wanted to win a championship, but he didn't have to deal with the Browns and Giants, two tough Eastern Division teams who showed no signs of faltering.

And most importantly, to his surprise, he had plenty of material to work with, much more than he thought when he took the job, sat down in his office, and watched those miserable 1958 game films. That had been a depressing experience, almost frightening, but it convinced him to go with his instinct, take a tough stand, and force players to measure up to higher standards on and off the field. He figured he would lose some guys with that approach, but the Packers couldn't become winners again until they regained their self-respect, he thought, so he had to find out who was willing to endure that difficult transformation. By the end of the season, the players had done so and were performing better than they probably ever imagined possible.

Sitting in his office in February 1960, as snow fell outside, Lombardi was excited about what lay ahead. His defense was already respectable and could become dominant if Lombardi found more speed for it. And the offense had just devastated opponents near the end of the season; it was going to pose a real challenge for opposing teams from now on. The line was still young and almost certain to improve. Hornung had found a home at halfback. Taylor, when healthy, had run like a star fullback. Dowler was a genuine long-ball threat. And what could you say about Starr? The young man had played like a Pro Bowl quarterback in the final weeks. Lombardi had underestimated him, plain and simple. Starr had run the offense brilliantly, thrown terrific passes, and exhibited real leadership, even telling his teammates to shut up and listen.

There was no telling what would happen now at quarterback. McHan hadn't really done anything to lose the number one job; he had played relatively well early in the season, gotten injured, and then just couldn't get back on the field. But he was a competitor and hopefully would come back determined to regain the job. Lombardi smiled; it was nice knowing he had two decent quarterbacks. That was two more than he had thought he had a year earlier.

But there was no doubt Starr would work harder than anyone in the off-season, throw more passes, study more film, and come back determined to play even better. He might be hard to deny. Lombardi couldn't stop thinking about how the season ended, with Starr resembling a savvy symphony conductor as he led the offense to those crushing wins over the Rams and 49ers. Watching those

games, Lombardi had begun to think he might have something going here — something quite good. The Packers still needed help in
places, but they had started rolling over opponents, and with Lombardi determined to keep pushing them to improve, they might just
roll right into contention for division titles and league championships — starting now.

Heh. We're going to show 'em how the Green Bay Pack-ahs do it.
We're going to knock 'em on their asses. A year later, in January 1961,
Mara again tried to lure Lombardi back to New York after Howell
retired, this time unequivocally, but by then Lombardi's position in
Green Bay had further solidified. His second season had ended with
the Packers playing in the NFL championship game. They were a
rising power, Lombardi entrenched as their leader.

He didn't take Mara's offer seriously. Big things were about to
happen in Green Bay, he thought. He was sure of it. And he was
right.

EPILOGUE

Almost a half century later, in 2008, Fuzzy Thurston, then a seventy-five-year-old Wisconsin legend, recalled the good feelings that swept through the Packer locker room toward the end of the 1959 season.

"We realized that we were going to be good," he said. "We knew what was about to happen. Maybe we didn't know that we would win as much as we did for as long as we did, but we knew we were going to be a very good team. Lombardi just wasn't going to stand for anything less. We didn't like him as a person. Damn, he was impossible. But we loved him as a coach. We hated the way he treated us, but we were glad we had him. He was going to make us special."

With their fans dreaming of a division title and ignoring Lombardi's warning not to get excited, the Packers opened the 1960 season against the Bears at City Stadium. The stands were packed and noisy, and it seemed the 1959 season had never ended as the Packers built a 14–0 lead during the first three quarters. The offense was unchanged, with Taylor and Hornung running hard behind Ringo, Kramer, Gregg, Thurston, Masters, and Skoronski, and Starr throwing to Dowler and McGee. The defense had two new starters: end Willie Davis, obtained from Cleveland in a trade (now three of Lombardi's four starting defensive linemen had come from the Browns), and cornerback John Symank, replacing Bobby Dillon, who had retired again, this time permanently.

But the Bears shocked the Packers and the crowd by scoring seventeen points in the fourth quarter to pull out the win. That night, McHan, who had been beaten out by Starr in training camp, cornered Lombardi at a restaurant and complained that the team couldn't afford to lose such games, saying he could make a difference. Impressed with McHan's fire, Lombardi started him over Starr the next week. McHan played well in a victory over Detroit and continued to shine as the Packers defeated the Colts and 49ers. McHan appeared to have taken the number one job back.

But when McHan struggled against Pittsburgh in the Packers' first road game of the season, Lombardi yanked him and Starr pulled out a tough win.

"Lamar was a real good football player but didn't handle adversity as well as Bart," Boyd Dowler recalled in 2008. "If things got bad, his head went down. If a coach fussed at him, it bothered him. He was talented but a little fragile."

Lombardi called Starr into his office the next day and said he had made a mistake by waffling between quarterbacks. "You're the starter from now on, no matter what happens," Lombardi said.

That proclamation was immediately tested when Starr struggled as the Packers lost three of their next four games, dropping their record to 5-4 with three games remaining. Then Starr and Lombardi had a confrontation that forever changed the team.

"One day in practice, a pass was deflected and intercepted, and he was all over me," Starr recalled. "After the drill I said, 'Coach, may I see you in your office when we get inside?' He said sure. When we went inside I very respectfully told him, 'If I am going to be the leader, you can't chew my ass out in front of the whole team. Do it all you want in here, between us, but not in front of the team.' Politely, I said, 'I can take your ass-chewing, that's not a problem, but please do it in here, privately, so I'm not embarrassed, especially when the mistake is not my fault. That ball was tipped out there.' He said, 'All right, I'll do that.' He never said anything to me ever again."

The Packers pulled together. They routed the Bears in Chicago, 41–13, as Jim Taylor, now an offensive centerpiece, rushed for 140 yards (on his way to gaining 1,101 for the season); and Paul Hornung scored two touchdowns and kicked two field goals and five conversions (on his way to scoring a league-leading 176 points). Then the Packers shut out the 49ers, 13–0, in a driving rain at Kezar Stadium, as the defense yielded just 81 total yards and never let the 49ers cross midfield.

With the Colts conveniently collapsing (they would end the season with four straight losses), the Packers suddenly just needed to win their last game, against the Rams in Los Angeles, to win the Western Division. The Rams scored first, but then Starr threw touchdown passes of ninety-one and fifty-seven yards to Dowler and Max McGee, and Hornung tossed a forty-yarder to McGee. The win put the Packers into the championship game just two years removed from their 1-10-1 season.

Their opponents were the Philadelphia Eagles, who also had struggled through the 1950s after a period of glory (they had won back-to-back titles in 1948 and 1949), but had risen again, winning the Eastern Division behind thirty-four-year-old quarterback Norm Van Brocklin and thirty-five-year-old Chuck Bednarik, a gritty two-way player. The game was played on Monday, December 26, at Franklin Field in Philadelphia. (The league didn't want to play on Christmas Day.) The Packers converted a pair of early turnovers into field goals, and then the Eagles went ahead when Van Brocklin threw a touchdown pass. Trailing 10–6 for much of the second half, the Packers controlled the ball and finally went ahead when Starr led a drive midway through the fourth quarter. His touchdown pass to McGee put the Packers up, 13–10. The title was within their reach.

But the Eagles had pulled off six come-from-behind wins during the season, and they came through again. Ted Dean returned the kickoff fifty-eight yards and Van Brocklin led a touchdown drive, Dean scoring on a five-yard run with 5:21 left.

Down by four points, Starr led a dramatic final drive as the clock ticked down, reaching the Philadelphia 22 with eight seconds left. Taylor caught a pass from Starr and ran to the 8 before being tackled by Bednarik, who sat on Taylor to make sure the Packers didn't have time for another play. The Eagles had won.

"Perhaps you didn't realize you could have won this game," Lombardi told the players. "But I think there's no doubt in your minds now. That's why you'll win it all next year. This will never happen again. You'll never lose another championship game."

He was right.

McHan was traded after the 1960 season to the Colts, where, Lombardi knew, he would sit on the bench and not haunt the Packers. McHan backed up Unitas for two seasons and part of a third, and then went to the 49ers, where he started nine games in 1963. His career ended after a brief stint in the Canadian Football League in 1965.

He eventually became a coach and scout, settling near New Orleans and working for the NFL's Saints. He raised a family, went into real estate, and lived happily, according to his wife, Barbara. He died of a heart attack in 1998.

Looking back, it is hard to believe Lombardi originally saw more in him than in Starr, who was later enshrined in the Pro Football Hall of Fame. But McHan was the better quarterback until the middle of the 1959 season.

"He never talked much about what happened in Green Bay," Barbara McHan said in 2009. "He made some good friends there, but he was quite a competitor so I'm sure it bothered him not to play."

"Pineapple Joe" Francis suffered a broken leg in training camp in 1960. That ended his career with the Packers. He played briefly in Canada, retired, and became a high school teacher and football coach in Hawaii.

"I thought I had a decent game when I went in for McHan that day against the Giants in Yankee Stadium [in 1959], but I didn't win and that was that, I was out of there, never played again," Francis said.

After advancing to the postseason despite losing one-third of their regular-season games in 1960, the Packers made it clear they were the best team in the Western Division in 1961. As NFL schedules expanded to fourteen games, the Packers lost their opener but then won ten of their next eleven games and easily captured a second straight division title. At one point, they won five straight games by at least twenty points.

Their defense seldom yielded. Two brilliant young pass defenders — cornerback Herb Adderley, a first-round pick, and Willie Wood, a second-year safety — made the secondary impregnable. And Ray Nitschke, in an improbable turnaround, learned to control himself on and off the field and become a dominant middle linebacker.

Offensively, there were no more growing pains. Starr efficiently executed Lombardi's plays; the fact that he had not recorded a personal win in his first twenty games as a starter was forgotten. Hornung led the league in scoring for a third straight season and was voted the league's Most Valuable Player. Taylor rushed for 1,307 yards and fifteen touchdowns, and McGee caught fifty-one passes; both made the Pro Bowl. Ron Kramer, his injured knee healed, regained the starting tight-end spot from Knafelc and grabbed thirty-five passes.

In the championship game, played at City Stadium, the Packers obliterated Mara's Giants, 37–0, in a delicious moment for Lombardi.

"He hated not moving the ball forward on a play," Jim Taylor recalled. "So we didn't go for many big strikes like other teams did. For years and years all we did was pick up one first down at a time, move the chains, not make mistakes. It was so simple, but people couldn't stop us because we were so good at it."

In 1962, Lombardi's fourth season, the Packers reached a pinnacle. Their simple power offense and tough defense overwhelmed the rest of the league. They won their first ten games, destroying the Bears 49–0 in early October and beating the Eagles by the same score later. After ending the regular season with a 13-1 record, their only loss coming on Thanksgiving in Detroit, they again defeated the Giants in the championship game, this time by a 16–7 score in icy weather at Yankee Stadium.

Taylor, who rushed for 1,472 yards and nineteen touchdowns during the season, was named the league's MVP.

"He just kept pushing us," Jerry Kramer recalled. "I was having a good time, making All-Pro, winning titles, taking care of business, but I wasn't working as hard as I could. And he just wouldn't relent. One day in practice I jumped offside, and he got his nose about eight inches from mine and said, 'Mister, the average college student can concentrate for five minutes, a high school student can last for three minutes, a child in kindergarten can go thirty seconds, and you don't even have that, so where does that leave you?' He just wouldn't let me go, refused to let me slide. And he was that way with all of us. If you weren't using any part of your talent, he wanted it. He wanted everything. It drove you crazy, and there were a lot of hurts and a lot of pain, but it was all worth it."

Tim Brown had a stellar career after Lombardi cut him. He joined the Eagles, became a top kick returner in 1961, and developed into a big-play halfback, leading the league in all-purpose yardage (rushing, receiving, and returns) in 1962 and 1963. He scored touchdowns rushing (thirty-one), receiving (twenty-six), returning kickoffs (five), and returning punts (one) in his career, and was a three-time Pro Bowl selection.

"After one game when Green Bay came to Franklin Field [in Philadelphia], Lombardi held up the Packer bus specifically to come over and speak to me," Brown recalled. "He was very gracious, said I had really made something of myself in the league, and he was pleased for me. He didn't have to do that."

Brown played ninety-six games for the Eagles, eleven for the Colts (in 1968), and one for the Packers.

"The former Packer players finally talked me into coming back for a reunion," Brown recalled. "They introduced me, and the people in the crowd went 'Ooops!'"

The team had no doubt which player Lombardi liked the most.

"He loved Hornung," Gary Knafelc said. "There was Bart, from a military background, smart, went to church, kept his closet immaculate, ask him a question and get a five-page answer. Hornung partied every night and couldn't care less what was happening, but on Sunday he played football. A little part of Lombardi would have liked to be like that. I really believed that. Lombardi was a good Catholic boy, and Paul was another good Catholic boy, but living on the edge."

Hornung's lifestyle caught up with him before the 1963 season when he was suspended by NFL commissioner Pete Rozelle for gambling on games. He missed the entire season and the Packers faltered only slightly, but it was enough to deny them a third straight title. The Bears beat them twice and finished just ahead of them in the division as George Halas coaxed a final great season out of his team at age sixty-nine.

Hornung returned in 1964, but the Packers struggled for the first time under Lombardi, falling to third place in the division with an 8-5-1 record.

Scooter McLean coached the Lions' offensive backs until the middle of the 1963 season, when he was diagnosed with cancer. He died four months later at age forty-eight.

Lombardi's final years on the Green Bay sideline were a grueling valedictory. The Packers faced challenges from the Colts, Browns, and Tom Landry's Cowboys, but they won a succession of unforgettable games. In the 1965 Western Division playoffs, they beat the Colts, 13–10, forcing overtime with a field goal the Colts swore was wide. In the 1966 NFL championship game, they beat the Cowboys, 34–27, saving the game with a last-minute goal-line stand. In the 1967 NFL championship game, they again beat the Cowboys, 21–17, in a game that became known as the Ice Bowl. Playing in Green Bay in subzero temperatures, the Packers trailed late but drove sixty-eight yards to score the winning touchdown.

They also won the first two Super Bowls, routing the champions of the AFL, the Kansas City Chiefs and Oakland Raiders, in successive years. With pro football's popularity exploding, the Packers were the sport's preeminent team, and little Green Bay was known as Titletown, USA.

Lombardi retired from the Packer sideline after winning Super

Bowl II in January 1968. The Packers didn't win another championship for twenty-nine years.

In January 1969 Lombardi joined the Washington Redskins as their head coach. He had spent a restless year as a full-time GM, watching games from the press box as the Packers went 6-7-1 with Phil Bengston as their coach—their first losing season since Scooter McLean's debacle. The dynasty was over. Lombardi missed coaching. Marie longed to return to the East Coast.

The Redskins were owned by Edward Bennett Williams, a hard-driving attorney. Still suffering from George Preston Marshall's refusal to use black players until the early 1960s, the Redskins hadn't had a winning season since 1955. Desperate to break the losing spell, the competitive Williams lured Lombardi back into coaching with a deal that included a 5 percent ownership stake in the team. Lombardi was just one year into a five-year contract to be the Packers' GM, and the executive committee, still led by Dominic Olejniczak, wasn't thrilled about letting him go, but it finally relented.

"I made a great mistake giving up coaching," Lombardi explained.

The Redskins had gone 5-9 the year before, but Lombardi turned them around in his first season, much as he did with the Packers in 1959. The formula was familiar. He drilled out-of-shape players into better physical condition, most notably quarterback Sonny Jurgensen, a notorious night owl. He brought in a veteran star (Sam Huff this time, a decade after Emlen Tunnell) to stabilize a shaky defense. He simplified the playbook, built up the running game around halfback Larry Brown, and watched his offense roll up points.

The Redskins won four of their first six games and ended up with a 7-5-2 record. They appeared ready to challenge the Cowboys in the National Football Conference's Capitol Division. But Lombardi felt ill while preparing for his second training camp in Washington, and when doctors investigated, they found intestinal cancer. Lombardi was dead within months, at age fifty-seven.

"There was no doubt in my mind that they would have been

good," Starr said. "You had an exceptional quarterback there. Sonny had more talent than I did as a passer. Combine that with a strong team around him, a stronger running game, and I am sure the Redskins would have been tough. It was so sad, what happened."

With Bill Austin, Lombardi's longtime assistant, as their head coach, the Redskins finished 6-8 in 1970. George Allen replaced Austin in 1971 and the Redskins began to realize the promise Lombardi had discovered. Starting out with many of the players Lombardi had put in place, Allen led the Redskins to seven straight winning seasons and a Super Bowl appearance in 1972.

Starr retired after the 1971 season, having played sixteen seasons for the Packers. He never threw for more than twenty-five hundred yards or sixteen touchdowns in a season, his statistics appearing increasingly meager in the coming years as pro offenses relied more and more on the pass.

When Lombardi wasn't his coach, he had a losing record as a starter. But when Lombardi was on the Packer sideline, Starr was one of the most successful quarterbacks in pro football history. He won five NFL championships and two Super Bowls, played in four Pro Bowls, and was voted MVP of the league in 1966.

"They were a perfect match, Bart and Lombardi," Knafelc said. "Lombardi was about planning and organization. Bart was meticulous and prepared. Lombardi just hated mistakes. Bart never made a big one. He was a great student of the game, really smart, and always knew the right play to run. He understood what Lombardi wanted and never tried to do more than he should. And he was as tough as they come. That was where people underestimated him. Bart took a beating and got right up."

It helped Lombardi that he joined the Packers just months after the executive committee decided to stop meddling with the team. Many other coaches around the league had to deal with owners or GMs (or both) also wielding decision-making power, but Lombardi had unchecked authority.

He also inherited some talent. Jack Vainisi, a forgotten football architect, had assembled a roster of gifted young players ready to be molded into a winning team. Eight players from the 1959 Packers — Gregg, Hornung, Starr, Taylor, Nitschke, Ringo, Jordan, and Tunnell, all but the last two drafted by Vainisi — would eventually make the Hall of Fame, as would Lombardi himself. (Sadly, Vainisi didn't live to see his team become a winner. He died of a heart attack at age thirty-three in November 1960.)

But while his timing was fortuitous and he had help, Lombardi, unmistakably, was the force that transformed the Packers from the NFL's sorriest team into its best.

"It's like we were a house, and he came in and built a new foundation," Starr said. "A house is going to fall if you don't have a solid foundation. We had been worked with before, by the other coaches, but fitness, discipline, and preparation, we did not have any of those things prior to his being there. He started putting it all in as soon as he arrived: 'This is our broad plan, our system; this is why we call this play now; this is how we function.' I'm impressed to this day how well prepared we always were. Everyone had confidence in that foundation, the way we were going to do things. When you see something work, basically from the very beginning, your confidence is buoyed, your attitude is great, and you can go out and beat the crap out of people.

"There was a day, after he had gone with the Redskins, when he came back to Green Bay to play golf with friends. Cherry and I had built a new home in De Pere, and he called and said, 'I'd love to stop by and see it.' We said, 'Gosh, we'd love to see you.' He walks in, says, 'OK, give me the cook's tour.' We showed him around and then sat down in the den. He said, 'Boy, you did a great job. You should be proud.' And Cherry said, 'Well, thank you, Coach. We owe all this to you. You're the one who made it all possible.' He choked up, got up off the sofa, walked over and gave her a hug. Then he came over and hugged me. He was tearing up, crying. Then he just walked right out of the house. We always wondered if he knew then that he had cancer."

Did the other players agree that they owed it all to Lombardi?

"Oh, absolutely," Knafelc said. "No one will dispute that. If he hadn't come in 1959 with that attitude, we never would have won. He was the right man for the right job at the right time. It was like with little kids, when they're doing bad stuff, playing with matches, someone has to step in and go, 'DAMMIT, YOU DON'T DO THAT!' He got our attention in 1959, showed us the right way, how to prepare and play hard and smart. After that first year, I was ashamed for having not played like that in my first five years. And from then on, I loved it. I would do it all again for the same money. We were crazy. We even enjoyed practice. The cold was bad, the mud was worse. One time the mud was so thick it sucked off one of my shoes. I couldn't find it! The conditions were that bad. But we didn't care. We couldn't wait to get out and practice and play. We were the Green Bay Packers, and we were on top of the world."

GREEN BAY PACKERS
1959 SEASON

DATE	SITE (ATTENDANCE)	OPPONENT	SCORE	RECORD
Sept. 27	Green Bay (32,150)	Chicago Bears	9–6 (W)	1-0
Oct. 4	Green Bay (32,150)	Detroit Lions	28–10 (W)	2-0
Oct. 11	Green Bay (32,150)	San Francisco 49ers	21–20 (W)	3-0
Oct. 18	Milwaukee (36,194)	Los Angeles Rams	45–6 (L)	3-1
Oct. 25	Baltimore (57,557)	Baltimore Colts	38–21 (L)	3-2
Nov. 1	New York (68,837)	New York Giants	20–3 (L)	3-3
Nov. 8	Chicago (46,205)	Chicago Bears	28–17 (L)	3-4
Nov. 15	Milwaukee (25,521)	Baltimore Colts	28–24 (L)	3-5
Nov. 22	Green Bay (31,853)	Washington Redskins	21–0 (W)	4-5
Nov. 26	Detroit (49,221)	Detroit Lions	24–17 (W)	5-5
Dec. 6	Los Angeles (61,044)	Los Angeles Rams	38–20 (W)	6-5
Dec. 13	San Francisco (55,997)	San Francisco 49ers	36–14 (W)	7-5

ACKNOWLEDGMENTS

Scott Waxman, my literary agent, first proposed the idea of writing a book about Vince Lombardi's inaugural season in Green Bay. Then he found a terrific home for the project. At Houghton Mifflin Harcourt, Susan Canavan was kind enough not to scream when she saw an early draft of the manuscript, and then astutely guided me as I sought to hammer it into shape. Melissa Dobson provided a clear-eyed edit, saving me in countless places and helping me sharpen the narrative.

Mary Jane Herber at the Brown County Library directed me to people who educated me about Green Bay in 1959. Paul McCardell and Andy Sussman helped with football research. The staffs of the Brown County Library in Green Bay and the Library of Congress in Washington, D.C., tended to my every need. My family put up with me hogging the computer. My thanks to all.

My special thanks to everyone who gave me (in many cases) hours of their time in interviews: Bill Austin in Las Vegas, by phone, 11/14/08; Tom Bettis in Pearland, Texas, 2/14/07; Vernon Biever in Port Washington, Wisconsin, by phone, 2/5/07; Tom Braatz in Fort Lauderdale, Florida, by phone, 1/10/07; Tim Brown in Los Angeles, by phone, 1/27/09; Pat Cochran in Green Bay, 10/19/08; Art Daley in Green Bay, 12/3/06; Bobby Dillon in Temple, Texas, 2/15/07; Boyd Dowler in Dacula, Georgia, by phone, 10/13/08; Joe Francis in Kaneohe, Hawaii, by phone, 2/5/07; Dave Hanner in Land o' Lakes, Florida, 2/2/07; Alex Hawkins in Denmark, South

Carolina, by phone, 12/20/06; Jerry Helluin in Houma, Louisiana, by phone, 1/22/07; Phil Hendrickson in Green Bay, 10/31/08; Paul Hornung in Louisville, Kentucky, by phone, 10/13/08; Gary Knafelc in Clermont, Florida, 1/30/07; Jack Koeppler in Green Bay, by phone, 1/26/07; Jerry Kramer in Boise, Idaho, by phone, 11/21/08; Ron Kramer in Detroit, by phone, 10/20/08; Bud Lea in Milwaukee, 12/6/06; Vince Lombardi, Jr., in Arizona, 12/15/08; Harry Maier in Green Bay, 10/29/08; Norm Masters in Naples, Florida, 2/1/07; Barbara McHan in Metairie, Louisiana, by phone, 1/20/09; Don McIlhenny in Dallas, 2/12/07; Tom Murphy in Green Bay, 10/30/08; Babe Parilli in Denver, by phone, 1/11/07; Peter Platten III in Longboat Key, Florida, by phone, 2/7/07; Lee Remmel in Green Bay, 12/5/06; Bob Skoronski in Boca Grande, Florida, 1/31/07; Bart Starr in Birmingham, Alabama, 2/8/07; Jim Taylor in Dallas, 2/15/07; Jim Temp in Green Bay, 12/4/06; Fuzzy Thurston in Green Bay, 10/29/08; Jesse Whittenton in Las Cruces, New Mexico, by phone, 1/25/07.

Lombardi's Packers are a well-trod subject, and the work of many journalists and authors furthered my understanding of the coach, his players, and the 1959 season. I am indebted to the authoritative beat coverage of sportswriters Art Daley and Lee Remmel in the *Green Bay Press-Gazette*, Chuck Johnson in the *Milwaukee Journal*, and Bud Lea in the *Milwaukee Sentinel*. They reported and wrote the story in real time a half century ago. Books that were especially helpful included *Golden Boy*, by Paul Hornung (New York: Simon & Schuster, 2004); *Instant Replay: The Green Bay Diary of Jerry Kramer*, edited by Dick Schaap (New York: World, 1968); *Launching the Glory Years: The 1959 Packers*, published by Jay Bengston and authored by Len Wagner (Green Bay, Wis.: Coach's Books, 2001); *Lombardi: A Dynasty Remembered*, edited by Mike Bynum (Nashville, Tenn.: Athlon, 1994); *Nitschke*, by Edward Gruver (Lanham, Md.: Taylor, 2002); *Lombardi: Winning Is the Only Thing*, edited by Jerry Kramer (New York: World, 1970); *Idols of the Game: A Sporting History of the American Century*, by Robert Lipsyte and Peter Levine (Atlanta: Turner, 1995); *When Pride Still Mattered: A Life of Vince Lombardi*, by David Maraniss (New York:

Simon & Schuster, 1999); *Mean on Sunday: The Autobiography of Ray Nitschke*, by Ray Nitschke (New York: Doubleday, 1973); *Vince: A Personal Biography of Vince Lombardi*, by Michael O'Brien (New York: Morrow, 1987); *I Remember Vince Lombardi*, by Mike Towle (Nashville, Tenn.: Cumberland House, 2001); *Bart Starr: A Perspective on Victory*, by John Wiebusch (New York: NFL Properties, 1972); *Lombardi*, by John Wiebusch (Chicago: Triumph Books, 1997); and *In Search of a Hero: The Life and Times of Tony Canadeo*, by David Zimmerman (Hales Corners, Wis.: Eagle Books, 2001).

INDEX